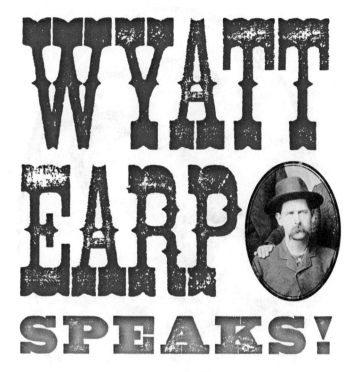

# WYATT EARP
## SPEAKS!

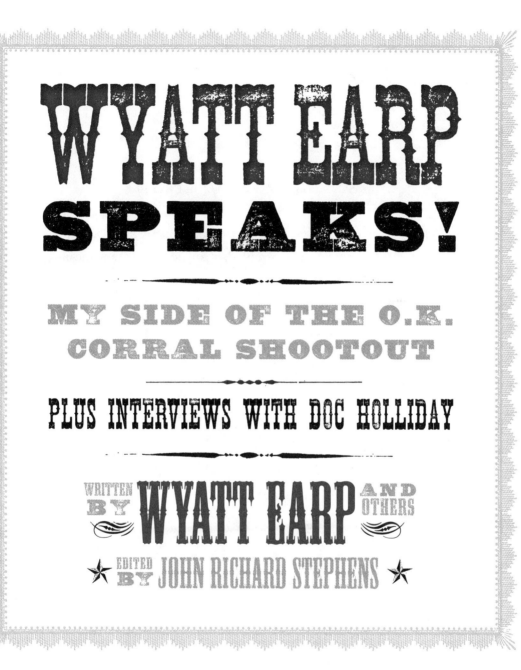

# WYATT EARP SPEAKS!

## MY SIDE OF THE O.K. CORRAL SHOOTOUT

## PLUS INTERVIEWS WITH DOC HOLLIDAY

WRITTEN BY **WYATT EARP** AND OTHERS

★ EDITED BY JOHN RICHARD STEPHENS ★

FALL RIVER PRESS

Photography credits appear on page 327.

Book design by Christine Heun

Fall River Press
122 Fifth Avenue
New York, NY 10011

ISBN: 978-1-4351-1205-6

Printed and bound in the United States of America

3 5 7 9 10 8 6 4

This book is dedicated to the memory of

# DOC HOLLIDAY

"...he was a dentist whom necessity had made a gambler; a gentleman whom disease had made a frontier vagabond; a philosopher whom life had made a caustic wit; a long, lean, ash-blond fellow nearly dead with consumption and at the same time the most skillful gambler and the nerviest, speediest, deadliest man with a six-gun I ever knew."

*Wyatt S. Earp.*

—*Wyatt Earp, as quoted by Stuart Lake*

# CONTENTS

Chances are, you know about Gunfight at the O.K. Over the years so up about what truth is now deeply a pile of distortions, embellishments, almost everything

Wyatt Earp and the

Corral is wrong.

much has been made

happened that the

buried under

faulty inferences,

and outright lies.

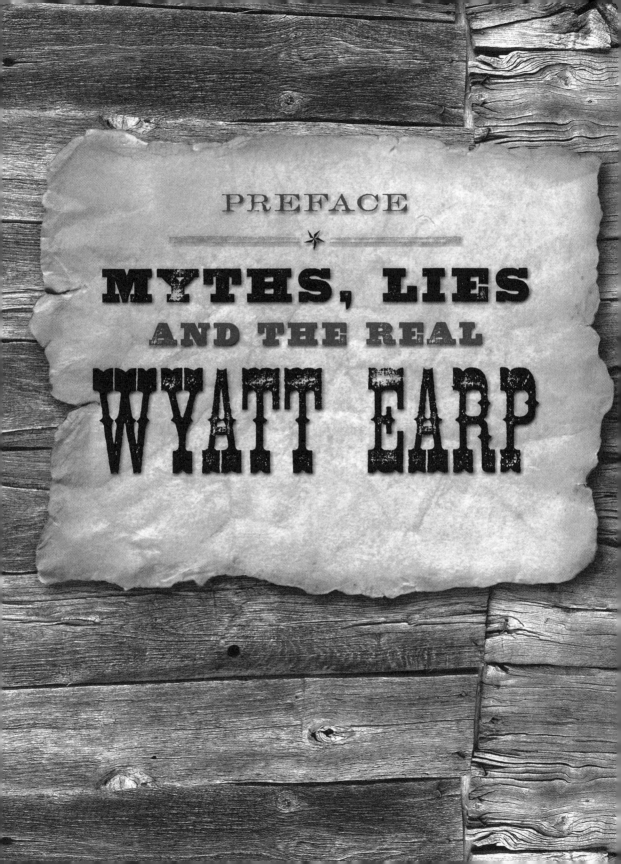

# PREFACE

✳

# MYTHS, LIES
## AND THE REAL
# WYATT EARP

HERE NEVER WAS A GUNFIGHT at the O.K. Corral. A gunfight happened, but it actually took place about a quarter of a block away from the rear entrance to the O.K. Corral. The main entrance to the O.K. Corral is on Allen Street, while the gunfight took place on Fremont Street. It began in the side yard of a house belonging to ex-Mayor William A. Harwood and spread out into the middle of Fremont Street. Of course, "the Gunfight at the O.K. Corral" sounds much better than "the Gunfight in Harwood's Yard and Fremont Street" so I guess someone decided to change it. "O.K. Corral" has more of a Western ring to it. Personally, I think "the Gunfight in Tombstone" sounds pretty good, but there's no point trying to change it now.

When it comes to the Earps and the shootout, there is a tremendous amount of erroneous information in circulation, making it awfully difficult to sort out what really happened. It began immediately after the gunfight with the outlaws' attempts to railroad the Earps into a murder trial by fabrication, perjury and spreading rumors. And it continues today with supposed Earp experts passing off fictional books as nonfiction. The falsehoods have become so prevalent that one has to go directly to original source material in order to get a handle on the truth.

> "DURING THE PAST FEW years, many wrong impressions of the early days of Tombstone and myself have been created by writers who are not informed correctly and this has caused me concern which I feel deeply."
>
> —*Wyatt in a letter to his close friend, silent-screen actor William S. Hart, on July 7, 1923*

Only recently have a few well-researched books finally begun to appear. The most notable being *Wyatt Earp: The Life Behind the Legend* (1997) by Casey Tefertiller. This is the most extensively researched and most authoritative book on Wyatt and Tombstone to date. Three other books that deserve mention are the late Richard Erwin's *The Truth About Wyatt Earp* (1993) and Bob Boze Bell's beautifully produced books—*The Illustrated Life and Times of Wyatt Earp* (1993) and *The Illustrated Life and Times of Doc Holliday* (1994).

As more primary material is made easily accessible, what actually happened in Tombstone will become clearer.[1] Hopefully this will improve the quality of the books and articles written on this subject. This book is intended to be a step in this direction.

In order to ensure this book is as accurate as possible, I've based most of my footnotes and introductions on original source material. I've also relied heavily on the tremendous knowledge of noted historian Carl Chafin, who is undoubtedly the world's leading expert on Tombstone. I'm extremely grateful for his assistance. This book would not exist without his help.

Some have accused Wyatt of seeking publicity, setting himself up as a hero, and of encouraging myths about his exploits. Frank Waters, author of *The Earp Brothers of Tombstone* (1960), even went so far as accusing him of "psychopathic exhibitionism." Carl and I disagree. Over and over we've read how he avoided reporters and publicity. When he did talk about his exploits, we believe he was just trying to counteract the lies that plagued him the rest of his life following the shootout. It's clear to us he just wanted to set the record straight.

In discussions with Carl, he and I decided it was time to give Wyatt a chance to present his side. Using available material by Wyatt and his close friends, I've tried to put this book together as I thought he would want it. I wanted this to really be Wyatt's book. I sincerely hope that if he could have read it, he would be pleased with the result.

> ☞ "I DID NOT WANT to do it in the first place, but I am in now and will have to swim out."
>
> —*Wyatt in a 1928 letter to William S. Hart, referring to his collaboration with his biographer, Stuart Lake*

# References

1. Actually, it's surprising how much material is out there on Wyatt, Doc, and Tombstone. New material surfaces all the time, and it's not that difficult to find. Besides the Arizona Historical Society collections, large amounts of primary material on Wyatt can be found in Denver, San Bernardino, San Francisco, San Diego, and probably just about any place he lived. Some of the material in this book was even found in Boston. And I'm sure there's more stuff in Alaska, California, Nevada, Texas, Idaho, Illinois, and other states just waiting for an enterprising researcher to ferret it out. Few have tried searching for information on his later life. I personally believe there are still old interviews with Wyatt out there in far-flung forgotten newspapers that no one has bothered to look for, especially since many of these old papers haven't been indexed or are poorly indexed. No doubt there's quite a bit about the lives of Wyatt and Doc that has yet to be discovered.

# BAD PRESS

IF ONE TWENTIETH PART of what is said of them [the Earps] is true, they are certainly no desireable [sic] acquisition to any community. They are a roving band; their path is strewn with blood. Strange as it may seem, when they halt in a settlement, stage robberies follow and human life ceases to be sacred."

—Arizona Star, *March 1882*

HIS [WYATT'S] BUSINESS JUST now should be that of a blackleg gambler–crooked as a dog's hind leg. If there are any honest hairs in his head they have grown since he left Arizona. He is exactly the sort of man to referee a prizefight if a steal is meditated and a job put up to make the wrong man win. Wyatt Earp has all of the nerve and dishonesty needed to turn the trick."

—*Alfred Henry Lewis*, New York Journal, *as quoted in the* San Francisco Call, *December 12, 1896*

"THERE WERE THEN TWO factions at Tombstone. Virgil and Wyatt Earp led one–the stage robbers; Johnny Behan, Ike Clanton and Jack Ringo [sic], led the other–the rustlers."

—Seattle Post Intelligencer, *July 22, 1900*

"WYATT EARP WAS A gangster."

—*Sam Aaron, a Charleston resident who died in 1940, in his memoirs.*

"WYATT WAS AN ITINERANT saloon-keeper, card shark, gunman, bigamist, church deacon, policeman, bunco artist, and a supreme confidence man. A lifelong exhibitionist ridiculed alike by members of his own family, neighbors, contemporaries, and the public press, he lived his last years in poverty, still vainly trying to find someone to publicize his life, and died two years before his fictitious biography recast him in the role of America's most famous frontier marshal."

—*Frank Waters*, The Earp Brothers of Tombstone, *1960*

"HISTORIANS SAY THAT EARP'S reputation as a lawman is hokum and that he spent most of his life as an itinerant horse thief, con-man, vagrant and gambler."

—Parade Magazine, *March, 20, 1983*

"THE SHOOTOUT, HOWEVER, IN reality was not so much a gunfight as it was the massacre of one of the outlaw factions competing with the Earps for control of Cochise County."

—Glenwood Post, *August 23, 1985*

"WHAT'S CERTAIN ABOUT WYATT Earp: fast women, stolen horses, fast feet"

—*A headline in* Rocky Mountain News, *November 1, 1987*

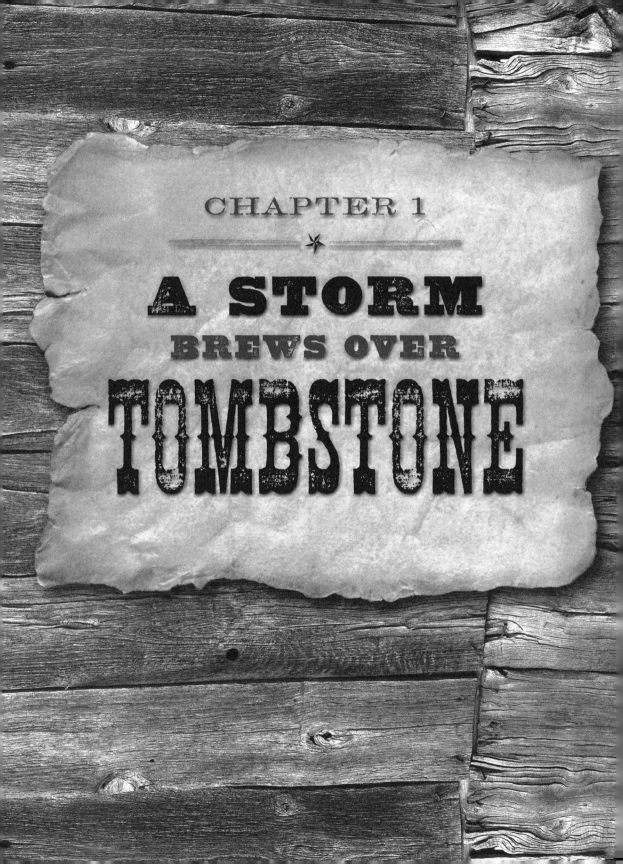

# CHAPTER 1

## A STORM
### BREWS OVER
# TOMBSTONE

THE FAMOUS GUNFIGHT took place in Tombstone on October 26, 1881. Cochise had died in 1874, and by 1875 most of the Apaches were confined on reservations, though Geronimo and his small band of Chiricahua jumped the reservation periodically over the next decade. The town of Tombstone[1] was a year old when the Earps arrived there in November of 1879. At that time its population was about 900, almost double what it was just four months previously. It doubled again in the next two months. By the time of the shootout Tombstone's population had shot up to nearly 5,000 due to the tremendous influx of money from nearby mines, which would eventually yield $40 million worth of silver.

There was considerable friction between the townspeople and country folk, partially because of lingering hostilities from the Civil War. The country people were ranchers, cowboys, rustlers, and bandits who were primarily Southerners, mostly from Texas. The townspeople, on the other hand, were largely Northerners who came to advance themselves and create an Eastern-type society where they were at the top. They wanted things nice, orderly, and quiet. The rustlers were drunken, rowdy, hell-raisers, who came off the range to party. They wanted to get drunk, find a prostitute, and shoot up the place. Thrown into this volatile mix were also the mining and gambling factions. But in many ways, the Tombstone fight was a carryover of the Civil War.

The Earps were townspeople. Wyatt, Virgil, Morgan, Warren, and James Earp[2] came to Tombstone with the four wives (Warren never married) to get ahead and establish themselves at the top of society. Wyatt, Virgil, and Morgan had all previously worked in law enforcement and they continued to do so in Tombstone. After Tombstone's city marshal, Fred White, was killed by rustler/bandit William "Curly Bill" Brocius,[3] Virgil took the position. Virgil was also a deputy U.S. marshal. Both Wyatt and Morgan worked as occasional policemen and Wyatt was planning on running for county sheriff in the next election.

The pay of policework was adequate, but it still was not uncommon for those in law enforcement to also work in the gambling establishments to supplement their income. This is what the Earps did. Wyatt primarily considered himself a saloonkeeper as he had a piece of the gambling concession at the Oriental Saloon. James,

"THE EARP BROTHERS NUMBER five—Wyatt, James, Virgil, Morgan and Warren. Jimmy, as he is familiarly called, is one of the jolliest, best natured men that ever the sun shone on. In truth he was a general favorite. Bacchus would occasionally get the better of him, but Jimmy never hunted fights, and if he accidentally found one would, as soon as sober, fix things up. Virgil was of different texture. Marshal of Tombstone for months, he kept the town as quiet as a cemetery. Poor Morgan was as brave and reckless a man as ever put foot in stirrup or pulled the trigger on a 45. Wyatt, who never drank, was as cool as the icebergs in Alaska, brave and determined as any man on earth, and General of the whole outfit. Now comes Doc Holliday, as quarrelsome a man as God ever allowed to live on earth."

—*Ridgley Tilden*, San Francisco Examiner, *May 11, 1882*

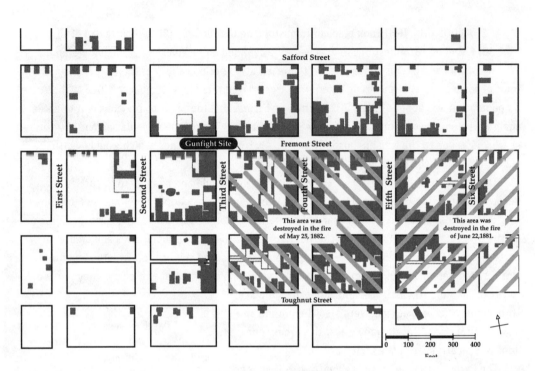

Safford Street

Fremont Street

Gunfight Site

First Street

Second Street

Third Street

Fourth Street

Fifth Street

Six Street

This area was destroyed in the fire of May 25, 1882.

This area was destroyed in the fire of June 22,1881.

Toughnut Street

0    100    200    300    400

Feet

Overview of Tombstone.

Allen Street and Fifth Street. Virgil was shot in front of where the man is sitting.

# TOMBSTONE

## OCTOBER 26, 1881

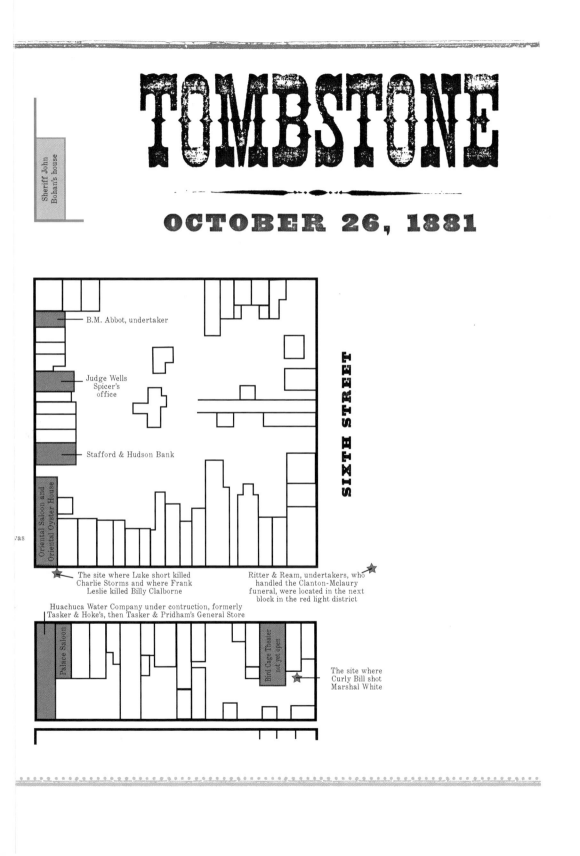

Sheriff John Bohan's house

B.M. Abbot, undertaker

Judge Wells Spicer's office

Stafford & Hudson Bank

Oriental Saloon and Oriental Oyster House

SIXTH STREET

The site where Luke short killed Charlie Storms and where Frank Leslie killed Billy Clalborne

Ritter & Ream, undertakers, who handled the Clanton-Mclaury funeral, were located in the next block in the red light district

Huachuca Water Company under contruction, formerly Tasker & Hoke's, then Tasker & Pridham's General Store

Palace Saloon

Bird Cage Theater not yet open

The site where Curly Bill shot Marshal White

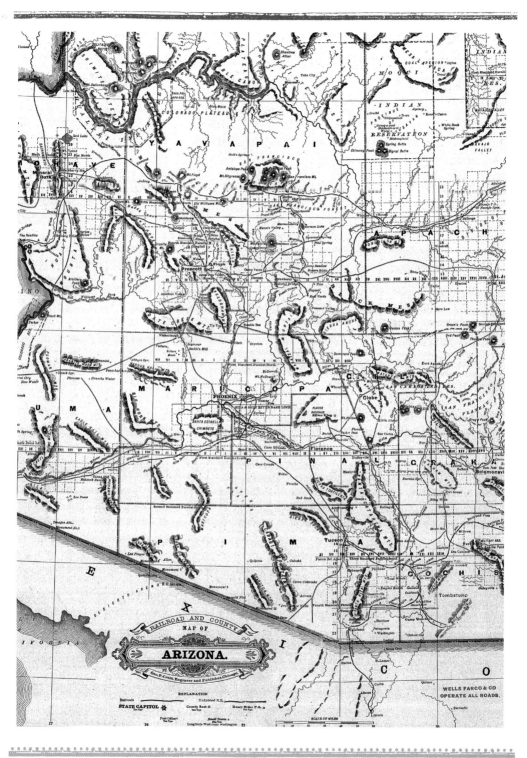

RAILROAD AND COUNTY
MAP OF
**ARIZONA.**

Geo. F. Cram, Engraver and Publisher, Chicago.

EXPLANATION

Railroads ——————
Unfinished R.R. -----------
**STATE CAPITOL** ✸
County Seat ◉
Money Order P.O. ◉

Post Office ○
Small Towns ○
Longitude West from Washington

SCALE OF MILES

WELLS FARGO & CO
OPERATE ALL ROADS.

the oldest of the Earps, was also a saloonkeeper and Warren, the black sheep of the family, was a laborer, though he did do a little policework for Virgil while he was in Tombstone. Warren was away from Tombstone at the time of the shootout. James was there, but he didn't play a part in it.[4] Morgan was riding shotgun for Wells, Fargo & Company on the stage to Benson.

And then there was John "Doc" Holliday. Doc was a former dentist, who, when he discovered he was slowly dying from tuberculosis, headed out west and turned to gambling to make a living. In those days, gambling was considered an honorable profession, and successful gamblers were highly respected. Doc was successful, but he was also temperamental, belligerent, and an alcoholic, in addition to having a quick temper. He became involved in the shootout because he was a close friend of Wyatt's, plus he'd had a few altercations with the outlaws himself.

Tombstone's gang of criminals, which they called "the cowboys," rustled cattle from Mexico and sold them in Arizona and New Mexico. Portions of this loosely knit fraternity of the outlaws were dominated by such figures as Curly Bill Brocius, John "Johnny" Ringo, Newman "Old Man" Clanton, and Joseph Isaac "Ike" Clanton. The outlaws originally numbered from one to two hundred and they committed other types of crimes besides stealing cattle and horses. Sometimes when they needed money, they would hold up a stage. There were about eight such robberies during the outlaws' heyday and Wells, Fargo & Company[5] almost stopped service to the area, which would have been disastrous for Tombstone. The local outlaws also robbed travelers, prospectors, lone ranchers, and Mexican smugglers.[6]

About a month before the shootout, the manager of a mine near Galeyville,[7] which is about 75 miles northeast of Tombstone, wrote a letter to the governor describing several of their crimes—which included robbing a saloon, murdering Mexicans, and ambushing a Mexican pack train carrying coin and bullion—and the failure of the courts to punish them. He went on to say,

> "The cow-boys frequently visit our town and often salute us with an indiscriminate discharge of fire arms, and after indulging in a few drinks at the saloons, practice shooting at the lamps, bottles, glasses etc., sometimes going to the length of shooting the cigar out of one's mouth; this of course produces a nervous feeling among visitors especially."

Even *Harper's New Monthly Magazine*[8] reported, "The trainmen at Benson were found chary [i.e. wary] of carrying the usual lanterns about the depot yard, a habit having arisen with the cow-boys of trying to snuff them out with revolvers from a distance."

After Curly Bill was released from jail for shooting Tombstone's city marshal, Fred White, he decided to celebrate in Charleston and Contention—two mining camps about ten miles west of

Tombstone—by making a minister dance in his church and by making all the people in one saloon dance for half an hour stark naked. His wild behavior continued for another four months until he was shot in the jaw by another outlaw. That really dampened his spirits.

The outlaws quickly began having run-ins with the Earps and often made threats on the Earps' lives. At one point, Wyatt's horse was stolen. When he found it several months later, it was in the possession of rustler William "Billy" Clanton. The Earps also found six mules stolen from a U.S. Army post at the ranch of dealers-in-stolen-cattle Thomas "Tom" Clark McLaury and Robert Findley "Frank" McLaury, just after the McLaurys changed the "U.S." brands on the mules. Then, about a month before the shootout, the Earps arrested Frank C. Stilwell and "Pete Spence"[9] twice for holding up stagecoachs. Both Spence and Stilwell were friends of the Clantons. Stilwell was a tough character who, according the *San Francisco Chronicle*, was "implicated in the ritual killing of an old man named Horton,[10] whose brains were beaten out with stones at the Brokow[11] Mine, south of Tombstone." One has to wonder why they called it a "ritual killing." Stilwell was released from the murder charge on technicalities. He was also a deputy of the Cochise County's sheriff, John Behan.

Sheriff Behan was an ardent supporter of the outlaws, partly because it made his job much easier if he got along with them, but the main reason was they were against the Earps.[12]

Behan didn't like the Earps—especially Wyatt. And Wyatt didn't like Behan. When Democrat Behan first put in to be appointed sheriff of the newly formed Cochise County, Republican Wyatt started to run against him for the appointment, but Behan made Wyatt a deal that if Wyatt didn't run, he would make Wyatt his deputy and allow Wyatt to run unopposed when the election came up. Wyatt agreed, but after Behan received the appointment, he made someone else deputy.[13] But this was just the start. There was also a woman—the beautiful 19-year-old Josephine Sarah "Sadie"[14] Marcus.

Sadie had run away from her home in San Francisco to join a stage troupe for an Arizona tour of *H.M.S. Pinafore*. She met Behan somewhere along the line and he followed her back to San Francisco to convince her to come to Tombstone where they would be married, though it's doubtful he actually intended to go through with a wedding. She fled home once again and moved in with Johnny and his 10-year-old son, which essentially made her his common law wife.[15]

As Stuart Lake, author of *Wyatt Earp, Frontier Marshal* (1931), wrote to his publisher on February 13, 1930, "Bat Masterson, and a score of oldtimers, have told me that she was the belle of the honkytonks, the prettiest dame in three hundred or so of her kind. Johnny Behan was a notorious 'chaser' and a free spender making lots of money. He persuaded the beautiful Sadie to leave the honkytonk and set her up as his 'girl,' after which she was known in Tombstone as Sadie Behan."

She soon discovered Behan was quite a ladies' man. She left him in July 1881 when he began running around with a married woman.[16] She apparently lived alone in town for a while and there's some evidence she may have worked for a while as a high-class call girl. It was about this time that she and Wyatt became involved.

At the time, Wyatt was "married" to his second wife, "Mattie,"[17] but their exact relationship is unclear. It's likely they were living together and just referring to themselves as "married" when it was convenient, just as Johnny Behan and Sadie had. Actually, couples living together was quite common on the frontier. Doc Holliday was also living with his girlfriend, "Big Nose Kate Fisher,"[18] who was a dance hall girl and prostitute. But regardless of whether Wyatt and Mattie had a marriage license, they were together for about eight years. After leaving Tombstone, Wyatt married Sadie[19] and they remained together until his death in 1929.

Unlike Behan, Wyatt wasn't a womanizer (though some have accused him of that in recent years). Stuart Lake very accurately wrote in the same letter to his publisher that Wyatt "steered pretty clear of entangling alliances." Wyatt's affair with Sadie was the one exception, and Behan didn't like it. It didn't look good to have his beautiful "wife" dump him and take up with his rival...and looks meant a lot to Johnny.

Behan and the Clantons set about framing Doc Holliday—and by implication the Earps—for an attempted stagecoach robbery in which two men were killed. This was in spite, or perhaps because, of the fact that the Earps captured one of the criminals, whom Behan's men later allowed to escape. A short while after this, the Earps arrested Frank Stilwell—the Clantons' friend and Behan's ex-deputy—and Pete Spence for holding up another stage near Charleston on October 8, 1881. These arrests prompted more threats against the Earps.

The night before the fight, Doc almost got into a fight with Ike. According to Wyatt, Ike had made a secret deal with him to help him catch three stagerobbing cowboys in exchange for the reward money. When Ike let this slip to Doc, Doc promptly berated him for his treachery. Virgil broke up the argument after a few minutes and a very upset Ike wandered off to spend the rest of the night drinking and playing poker. Now that the deal was no longer secret, Ike was worried about what the gang would do to him. He had to insist the whole thing was a lie and prove he was an enemy of Wyatt. The morning found a worked up Ike armed and threatening to kill some Earps and Holliday. Several people woke up Wyatt and Virgil telling them of this.

> ☞ "THERE IS ALTOGETHER TOO much good feeling between the Sherriff's office and the outlaws infesting this country."
> —Tombstone Epitaph, *August 19, 1881*

Virgil came upon Ike in an alley and as Ike swung his Winchester around, Virgil buffaloed[20] him and hauled him off to appear before the justice of the peace. When Tom McLaury threatened Wyatt outside the judge's office, Wyatt buffaloed him as well.

An hour or so later—about 3 P.M.—five of the outlaws and Sheriff Behan gathered outside Fly's Lodging House, where Doc and Big Nose Kate were staying. Outlaw hangers-on Wesley "Wes" or "West" Fuller and William "Billy" Allen were almost on the scene[21] when the Earps and Holliday showed up and it's possible others were on their way as well.

At the time of the gunfight, Wyatt was 33 years old, Virgil was 38, and Morgan and Doc were both 30. They went up against Clanton brothers, Ike (age 34) and Billy (19), and the McLaury brothers, Frank (33) and Tom (28). Ike and Tom came to Tombstone the day before the fight and the other two arrived there that morning. They were then joined by the fifth outlaw, William "Billy the Kid" Claiborne.[22]

The shootout lasted about thirty seconds, during which over thirty bullets were fired in several waves. When things settled down again, Billy Clanton and both McLaurys were dead, and Virgil and Morgan were wounded. Billy Claiborne and Ike Clanton ran away when the shooting started.

Exactly what happened is uncertain. There's still considerable controversy and conflicting evidence, but here's a brief summary of what happened as best as it can be reconstructed at the moment.[23]

Sheriff Behan was talking to the cowboys trying to get them to surrender their weapons to him, but they refused. As the Earps approached, Behan left the cowboys and approached the Earps asking them not to stop, but Virgil said he was going to disarm them and walked on by. Behan responded, "I have been down there to disarm them," which Wyatt and Virgil took to mean that he had already disarmed them.

As the Earps came up to the cowboys, they saw the rifles on Billy Clanton's and Frank McLaury's horses and the pistols on Billy and Frank's hips. Wyatt muttered, "Son of a bitch!" referring to Behan, though Frank probably thought Wyatt was referring to him. Wyatt kept a sharp eye on him as he was the best shot. As Doc brought out the shotgun that had been concealed under his coat, Vigil called out, "Throw up your hands boys, I intend to disarm you!" In response, Frank McLaury moved his hand to his gun and Wyatt pulled his from his coat pocket.

Billy Clanton's attention was no doubt focused on the Earps and didn't see Frank grab his pistol, but he did see Wyatt go for his and probably thought the Earps were about to murder them. Wyatt saw Billy Clanton jerk his gun. At the same instant Billy fired a round in his direction, he let one loose at Frank McLaury. Billy's shot missed, but Wyatt's struck Frank in the stomach, one inch to the left of his navel. The wound wasn't fatal, but it disabled the most dangerous of the bunch.

Ike Clanton, who was unarmed, jumped forward, grabbing Wyatt's arm. As they struggled, Wyatt's gun fired into the ground. Virgil was carrying Doc's cane and he moved it from his right hand to his left so he could go for his gun. Meanwhile, Tom McLaury jumped behind Billy Clanton's horse and Sheriff Behan grabbed Billy Claiborne, pushing him between Fly's Boarding House and the photograph studio out of the line of fire. Virgil was drawing his weapon when one of Frank McLaury's bullets passed through the calf of his right leg and he fell to the ground.

Wyatt pushed Ike Clanton away saying, "This fight's commenced. Go to fighting or get away!" Ike couldn't go to fighting, so he got away by running through Fly's Boarding House and off toward Allen Street. He was later arrested.

Billy Clanton was firing to no effect, but Morgan shot one that hit Billy two inches below the left nipple, piercing his lung. Billy, gasping for air, staggered up against Harwood's house and slowly slid to the ground. Morgan continued to fire several more shots and one passed through Billy's arm two inches above his right wrist. Virgil also joined in, quickly firing a round at Frank McLaury, which missed, and three shots at Billy Clanton. One of these struck Billy six inches to the right of his navel.

Frank McLaury was pulled out into Fremont Street by his frantic horse. Morgan, who turned around following Frank, was hit by one of Tom McLaury's bullets and fell to the ground. Tom had fired from behind Billy Clanton's horse. This bullet entered Morgan's back just below the left shoulder blade, passed across his back and exited about the same position below the right shoulder blade, taking off part of a vertebra on the way.

Throughout all this, Doc was standing out in Fremont Street protecting the flank, while waiting for a clear shot at Tom or Frank. When Morgan was hit, Wyatt shot at the horse Tom McLaury was hiding behind, hitting it in the withers. This caused the horse to leap out of the way, pulling Tom sideways as he tried to hold on. As Tom came in the open, Doc blasted him in the side with his shotgun, spinning him around. The twelve buckshot hit four to six below Tom's right armpit and clipped his right arm. Tom took off down the street to get away, which caused Doc to think he missed, so he threw the shotgun down in disgust and pulled his revolver from his coat pocket. Tom staggered down to the corner at Third Street and collapsed next to a telegraph pole.

☞ "TO KILL YOUR MAN seems a way of winning your spurs, as it were, and establishing yourself on a proper footing in the community."

—*William Henry Bishop*

Frank McLaury finally released the reigns of his horse and it bolted up the street. Wyatt fired off a round at Frank, who returned fire, hitting Wyatt's coattail. Frank then fired a shot at Morgan, but it went into the ground. It was obvious Frank was seriously wounded by the way he was swaying and staggering about. Finally he just sat down in the street.

While this was going on, a shot probably fired by Billy Allen from behind the corner of Fly's Lodging House caused Wyatt to call out to Morgan, "Watch it! We're getting it from the back!" Wyatt sent a shot in that direction as Morgan swung around and tripped over a mound of dirt from the newly buried waterline running down the street.

Frank McLaury, still sitting on the ground, pointed his gun at Doc and said, "I've got you now!" to which Doc responded, "Blaze away! You're a daisy if you have!" Frank's slug glanced off Doc's leather-lined pistol pocket, but Doc thought he was seriously wounded and squawked, "I'm shot right through!"

Morgan, from where he had fallen, was carefully watching Frank McLaury. He and Doc both fired at the same time at Frank. Doc's bullet cut across Frank's chest, but Morgan's passed straight through his head, entering just below his right ear.

Back in Harwood's yard, Billy Clanton was feebly snapping his empty revolver and calling for someone to give him more cartridges.

All this happened in less than thirty seconds.

Bob Boze Bell's *The Illustrated Life and Times of Doc Holliday* (2nd edition, 1995) outlines the shots fired as follows:

- Billy Clanton's six shots didn't hit anyone.
- Frank McLaury fired off four shots—the first hit Virgil in the right calf, the second hit Wyatt's coat, the third was at Morgan but hit the ground, and the fourth took a little skin off Doc's hip, giving him a temporary limp and probably a large bruise.
- The testimony was conflicting as to whether Tom McLaury had a pistol, and this was never conclusively established, but it's very likely he did.[24] Assuming he did have one, he fired two or three times, one hitting Morgan across the shoulders.
- Wyatt probably let loose with five bullets. The first struck Frank McLaury in the belly. His second went into the ground. The third hit the horse Tom McLaury was hiding behind. The fourth was at Frank McLaury. And his final shot was probably toward Billy Allen at the front of Fly's Lodging House.[25]
- Morgan probably fired five shots—four of them at Billy Clanton. The first of these hit Billy in the chest and another hit his right wrist. His fifth shot hit Frank McLaury in the head. One of his shots may have been at Billy Claiborne, since a bullet passed through Claiborne's pant's leg, just missing his knee.
- Virgil fired four times. The first missed Frank McLaury. Of three he fired at Billy Clanton, one hit his stomach.
- Doc fired a blast from the shotgun that hit Tom McLaury in the right side just below his armpit. Doc then pulled his pistol, firing two shots at Billy Clanton, both of which missed, and then one at Frank McLaury that creased his chest.

Predictably, the anti-Earp faction was upset by outcome of the shootout and claimed it was cold-blooded murder. Sheriff Behan saw this as an opportunity to get rid of the Earps. Behan and the anti-Earp faction claimed the cowboys were trying to surrender when the Earps and Doc gunned them down. They said the Earps and Doc fired five shots before the cowboys even began trying to fight back. The Earps and Doc were arrested and a hearing was held to determine whether they should be tried for murder.

The hearing, which lasted thirty days, was brought before Judge Wells Spicer, who ruled it

ie con-
commit-
, done in

this deci-
themselves.
r, Mayor
,[27] and
ation attempt
exactly eight
d and five shot-
the left arm and
that arm. Morgan

as shot in the back
The shots were fired through a window in the billiard hall's
st above Wyatt's head. The other shattered Morgan's spine
died less than an hour later.
escorting Virgil and his wife on the train to California,
well at the Tucson train station and, with three others, fol-
p with him about twenty yards in front of the engine. This
wasn't found until the next morning riddled with buckshot
tt and Doc became vigilantes and set off to deal with the
rest of the culp... This was the beginning of the Vendetta.

Previously, right after Virgil was shot, acting-Governor John Gosper[29] and U.S. Marshal Dake visited Tombstone. They authorized Wyatt to form a posse to clean up the area. Wyatt named four men as deputies—Doc, Warren Earp, Sherman "Sherm" McMaster,[30] and John "Turkey Creek Jack" Johnson.[31]

After Morgan was shot, Wyatt got this posse together again and it quickly became known in newspapers across the country as "the Earp party." From Tucson they headed back to Tombstone, and then set out looking for the rest of Morgan's murderers.

Hearing of Stilwell's death, Sheriff Behan swore in many of the outlaws as deputies to hunt for Wyatt's group. Behan's posse included rustlers Ike Clanton, Phineas "Phin" or "Fin" Clanton and Johnny Ringo. By then, the Earp party was off hunting Pete Spence. When they found Spence's camp, Spence wasn't there, but Florentino Cruz (thought to be Indian Charlie)[32] was and they promptly filled him with lead. Spence turned himself in to Behan and was put in jail for his protection.

Behan's posse gave up and turned back, but the following day, Wyatt and his men were ambushed by Curly Bill and eight outlaws as they were approaching a spring called Iron Springs for water. Wyatt promptly gave the outlaw leader both barrels from his shotgun, practically cutting Curly Bill in half. The ensuing shootout may have resulted in the death of one other outlaw and possibly the wounding of several more.

After some fruitless searching, the Earp posse then departed the territory for New Mexico to get beyond the reach of Behan and his arrest warrants. In all, Wyatt's vigilante spree lasted almost a month.

Today, when most people think of Wyatt Earp, they think of the gunfight, but that episode was just the beginning. The war between the Earps and the outlaws actually lasted for several months. The shootout put the Earps' names in newspapers throughout the country, but it was actually the Vendetta that made Wyatt famous.

The Earps risked a lot by taking on the outlaws. They were doing very well in Tombstone. They were getting ahead quickly, making lots of money, and becoming respected pillars of the community. All this was lost in their battles with the outlaws, and much more. Virgil was crippled and Morgan was dead. The Earps were also forced to rapidly liquidate their assets in Tombstone, which included mineral, water, and timber rights in the Huachuca Mountains, all or partial interest in ten mining claims,[33] ownership of the Sampling Room Saloon, partial interests in the gambling concessions at the Alhambra and Eagle Brewery Saloons,[34] plus ten lots in town that they owned.[35] Wyatt, Virgil, and Morgan were almost tried for murder. Wyatt and Warren had to flee the territory to avoid prosecution or being lynched by the outlaws and their supporters. While Wyatt became a hero to many, he had to deal with numerous lies against his reputation for the rest of his life—many of which still persist to this day.

# References

1. There were actually two Tombstones. The first one appeared in November 1878 on a nearby hill, but as the town grew, it was moved to its present location about three months later.

2. The Earps also had an older half-brother named Newton and two sisters, Virginia and Adelia. A third sister died when she was 10 and a half-sister died in infancy. Their father's ancestors were originally from England and Ireland and the name was originally spelled "Earpe."

3. Some have confused him with William "Curly Bill" Graham because they had the same nicknames. His name is variously spelled "Brocious" and "Brosciou." It's not known which is correct. Also Curly is sometimes spelled "Curley."

4. James grabbed his gun and ran to the scene, arriving just as Tom McLaury dropped.

5. At this time the company's name had a comma in it, which they have since dropped.

6. Because of high taxes on alcohol and tobacco in Mexico, some Mexicans made a lot of money by buying these goods in the U.S. and smuggling them into Mexico.

7. Galeyville was only in existence from 1880 to 1882 and had a population of about three hundred people.

8. The article in their March 1883 issue is by a reporter who was in Tombstone less than a month after the gunfight.

9. "Pete Spence" or "Spencer" was an alias. His real name was Elliot Larkin "Lark" Ferguson.

10. Sic, van Houten. His murder occurred in June of 1878.

11. Bronkow or Bronco Mine.

12. Behan was more of a politician than a lawman. After serving a sheriff for Yavapai and Cochise counties, he was elected as representative to the state assembly for Prescott and Mohave county. He was also the superintendent of the Territorial Prison at Yuma. He served in the Spanish-American War and was a government "secret agent" in China during the Boxer Rebellion. Except perhaps for his time in Prescott before he came to Tombstone, questionable activities raised questions of corruption at each stage of his career.

13. He appointed 33-year-old Harry Woods, the editor of the *Nugget*, as his undersheriff and William "Billy" or "Breck" Breakenridge as his deputy. Breakenridge later told his story through his ghostwriter, novelist William MacLeod Raine, in the book *Helldorado* (1928). Behan wasn't as closely associated with the outlaws when they made the deal or Wyatt would have never considered working under him. Wyatt had already been involved in several important arrests.

14. Wyatt and most of those who knew her called her "Sadie" for Sarah, but after Wyatt died she began going by the nickname "Josie."

15. Today, people commonly believe a couple must live together for three or seven years before they have a common law marriage. This is not true. A couple has a common law marriage just as soon as they agree to live together as if they were married. That is, as long as there's nothing that would legally prevent such a marriage, like one of them being underage or already married. The law was the same back then. And then, as now, common law marriages were treated as being less binding than licensed ones.

16. In 1886 Behan had an affair with Bert Dunbar, the wife of his former partner, John O. Dunbar. This might have been the same woman.

17. Née Celia Ann Blaylock.

18. Also known as "Kate Elder," it's thought her real name was Mary Katherine Haroney, though her last name changed to Cummings when she later married. At the time of the shootout she was just about to turn 31.

19. Record of the marriage has yet to be found, but many records were destroyed in the fire set off by the 1906 earthquake. Stuart Lake, in *Wyatt Earp, Frontier Marshal* (1931), says they were married in San Francisco. He doesn't give a year, but says it was in the five years following their return from Alaska in 1901. Others claim Sadie said they were married by a boat captain off San Diego or Baja California in 1888, but this claim doesn't ring true and has yet to be substantiated. There are also indications that they were married in Yuma County in 1888.

20. Buffalo: to hit someone over the head with the barrel of a pistol.

21. Twenty-year-old gambler Wes Fuller was in the alley right behind Fly's and Billy Allen was in front of Fly's on Allen Street. Billy Allen, along with Ike and Charles Hamilton "Ham" Light, had posted bail for stagerobbers Frank Stilwell and Pete Spence in the September 1881.

22. Billy the Kid Claiborne should not be confused with the famous William "Billy the Kid" Bonney of New Mexico, whose real name was Henry Antrim.

23. I'd like to acknowledge that several important points in my summary are from Jeff Morey's extensive and on going analysis of the gunfight.

24. According to Stuart Lake's notes, Wyatt said Wes Fuller picked up the gun and put it in his pocket. Wes's father told Wyatt he had Tom's gun.

25. Bob Boze Bell originally thought Wyatt fired at the back of Fly's, but it's now thought Wyatt was firing toward the front.

26. Thirty-year-old New Yorker John P. Clum was Tombstone's fourth mayor. He was also the postmaster and editor of the *Epitaph*.

27. Marshall was his first name, not his title.

28. Wyatt and Doc were never part of the large vigilante group in Tombstone which was called the Vigilance Committee. The pro-outlaw faction, including the *Tombstone Nugget*, referred to this group as "the stranglers." Wyatt always did everything he could to protect his prisoners from vigilantes-the most noted being Curly Bill and John "Johnny-Behind-the-Deuce" Roarke.

29. It's interesting that the June 1880 census shows Doc and Gosper living at the same place (probably a boarding house) in Prescott, Arizona.

30. Researcher Paul Cool recently discovered Sherman's family name was actually "McMaster" and not "McMasters."

31. "John Johnson" was probably an alias and it's likely his real name was John Blunt. Two other men also joined the Earp party for part of the time. They were John "Texas Jack" Vermillion and Dan "Big Tip" Tipton.

32. Cruz might have been of Mexican and Native American descent, but some historians suspect Cruz and Indian Charlie were actually two different people. If so, Cruz was most likely the guilty party.

33. They were able to sell these claims at a profit, though, like most claims in the area, none ever yielded anything of value.

34. Wyatt had already sold back their gambling concession at the Oriental in January 1882.

35. When they left town they originally intended to return, so they didn't sell some of their property. They never did return and the property was later confiscated and sold for failure to pay the taxes on it.

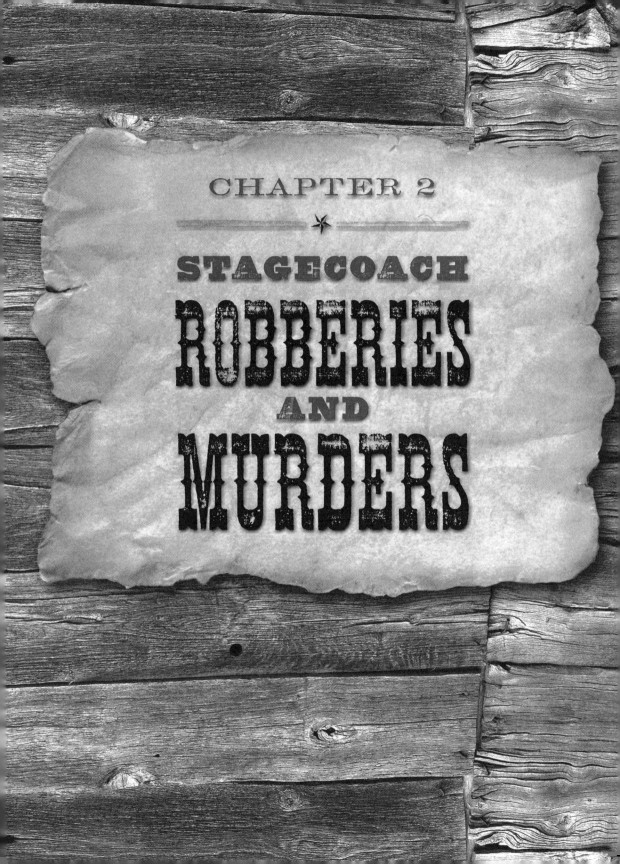

# CHAPTER 2

## STAGECOACH
# ROBBERIES
## AND
# MURDERS

THERE WERE MANY FACTORS that led to the so-called "Shootout at the O.K. Corral." Some of them are discussed in the overview. One event that affected Wyatt deeply was the attempted robbery of the Benson stage, which resulted in the murders of Eli "Bud" Philpott[1] and Peter Roerig. Philpott was the driver of the stage and Roerig was a miner who was a passenger on the stage. Philpott was a friend of Wyatt's. Wyatt had gotten to know him pretty well during his six-month stint as a shotgun messenger for Wells, Fargo & Company.

Wells, Fargo didn't own the stage line; it was just responsible for transporting large sums of money. It paid the stage company to carry their treasure box and Wells, Fargo sent along their shotgun messenger to guard it.

Tombstone was a booming mining town. In its first five years, its one hundred and fifty mines produced $25 million in gold and silver bullion.[2] As a result, many large shipments of bullion were made from Tombstone to Tucson. There were also large payroll shipments going from Tombstone out to the mines. A lot of bullion and money were moving through the desert by stagecoach and only one person was guarding it—the shotgun messenger. It was practically a robber's dream come true.

The murders took place on March 15, 1881. In addition to being Bud Philpott's friend, there were other factors that made this more personal for Wyatt. The bullets that killed Philpott were actually meant for the shotgun messenger, and just eight months previously, Wyatt had been that person. When Wyatt gave up the job to become deputy sheriff for Pima County, Morgan took over as shotgun messenger. He held the position until about two months before the murders. It was Morgan's replacement, the 6' 4" tall Robert "Bob" Paul, who was the target for all those bullets.[3]

Bob Paul was a very close friend of Wyatt's. On November 2, 1880, when Paul ran for sheriff of Pima County against Wyatt's boss, Sheriff Charles Shibell,[4] Wyatt apparently supported Paul. Shibell won by 47 votes, but Paul contested the election claiming fraud. Wyatt, who resigned as deputy sheriff shortly after the election, played a large role assisting Paul in establishing his case. Even the *Arizona Star*, which was pro-Shibell, had to admit on January 20, 1881, "There is evidently 'something very rotten in Denmark,' or in plain language there has been some big cheating somewhere, and by some persons. The evidence is very straight forward and to the point...that out of 104 votes cast at San Simon, about 100 were fraudulent." The judge declared that all of the 103 votes for Shibell cast in the San Simon precinct were invalid.[5]

Shibell appealed the judge's decision, but on April 12, 1881 the Supreme Court of the Territory confirmed the decision and Paul became Pima County sheriff. By this time Cochise County had been formed and Behan was appointed its first sheriff.

The San Simon district, where most of the fraud took place, was an outlaw stronghold. The scheduled polling place was at rustler Joe Hill's house. The election inspector was Ike Clanton, while the election judges were Johnny Ringo and cowboy H. A. Thompson. The results were certified by "Henry Johnson," whom Wyatt later discovered was cowboy James K. Johnson. Johnson had appeared as a witness for Curly Bill at his hearing for shooting Tombstone's Marshal Fred White. Ike, Ringo, and Hill were later said to have taken part in the Skeleton Canyon Robbery, where Old Man Clanton's gang captured a Mexican pack train carrying coins and bullion. Details are unclear, but estimates of the value range from about $4,000 into the millions and the number of Mexicans killed range from four to nineteen. One of the outlaws who was later killed with Old Man Clanton in retaliation for this robbery was Jim Crane, who had also been implicated in the Philpott-Roerig murders.

☞ "THE DEPREDATIONS OF THE gang of thieves denominated 'cowboys,' which has been annoying the residents of this corner of the territory for months past, regardless of all law and order, have become even more unscrupulous. It is well known that they have confederates in this town, among outwardly-respectable people, who keep them posted in regard to favorable opportunities for stealing, etc., and who buy from them the stolen stock, at reduced rates. It is high time that something were done to put a stop to this business."

—*Clara S. Brown, Tombstone correspondent to the* San Diego Union, *March 26, 1881, following Philpott's death*

While Bob Paul was waiting for the decision on the election, he was working as shotgun messenger. It was about a month and a half after the initial court ruling and about a month before the final ruling that the murders took place. It's possible that the attempted robbery was also an assassination attempt against Paul.

Paul's friendship was very helpful when Wyatt and Doc were later charged with the murder of Frank Stilwell in Pima County. Paul refused to have anything to do with Behan's posse and he may have helped ensure that Wyatt and Doc were not extradited from Colorado. Paul eventually became the U.S. Marshal for Arizona.

The anti-Earp faction claimed the real cause of "the O.K. Corral Gunfight" was that Holliday and the Earps were trying to cover up their involvement in the Philpott-Roerig murders. Texas lawyer William McLaury, the brother of Tom and Frank, wrote in a November 9, 1881 letter to his brother-in-law, David Appelgate:

> The cause of the murders was this situation: Holliday, one of the murderers, attempted to rob the express of Wells Fargo and Co., and in so doing shot and killed a stage driver and a passenger. The other parties engaged in the murder with him, the Earp brothers, were interested in the attempt on the exps. robbery, and young Clanton who was killed, a boy of eighteen years[6] old, knew the facts about the attempted robbery and had told his brother, J. I. Clanton and Thos. and Robt.[7] and they had got up facts, intending to prosecute him. The Earp brothers and

Holliday had information of it. It is now known that two other men,[8] who knew of the murder in the attempted robbery, have been killed in New Mexico, the report was by "Greasers" but at the time they were killed Holliday was out of town "said to be visiting in Georgia." There will be an indictment against Holliday and I think two of the Earps and one Williams[9] for the murder on the attempted robbery.

Ike took the accusations one step further in his testimony following the shootout. He claimed the robbery was actually staged by the Earps, Holliday, Leonard, Head, and Crane to cover up the fact that the Earps had already stolen the money that was to be carried on the stage. In court, Ike told of a conversation he said he had with Wyatt, explaining, "He said he and his brother, Morgan, had piped off to Doc Holliday and William Leonard,[10] the money that was going off on the stage, and he said he could not afford to capture them, and he would have to kill them or else leave the country, for they [were] stopping around the country so damned long that he was afraid some of them would be caught and would squeal on him."

Ike also mentioned a conversation with Morgan, saying, "I only remember that he told me that 10 or 12 days before Bud Philpott was killed, that he piped off $1400 to Doc Holliday and Bill Leonard, and that his brother Wyatt, had given away a number of dollars to Doc Holliday and Bill Leonard that was going away on the stage the night Bud Philpott was killed."

Ike explained that the O.K. Corral gunfight was an attempt to murder him, his brother, and the McLaurys to keep them from revealing the crime.[11]

There were three big problems with Ike's story. First, all the money arrived safely in Tucson. None of it was stolen as Ike claimed.[12] Secondly, Ike could have easily been killed in the gunfight if that was its purpose. He had claimed that right before the fight, Wyatt walked up to him and "stuck his pistol against my

☞ UNIDENTIFIED WELLS, FARGO & CO. executives made a rare public statement in support of Wyatt and Doc during the Vendetta to the *San Francisco Examiner* on March 23, 1882, saying that "the statement that he and his brothers were ever concerned in any of the stage robberies is pronounced by the officials of Wells, Fargo to be absolutely untrue. Doc Holliday, although a man of dissipated habits and a gambler, has never been a thief and was never in any way connected with the attempted stage robbery when Philpot [sic], the stage driver, was killed. For three-quarters of a hour after the stage passed the Wells, two and a half miles from Tombstone, he was seen at the latter place, so drunk that he was helped upon his horse, and the robbery occurred thirteen miles from Tombstone, so it was utterly impossible for him to be there. The statement that he was present on the occasion of that robbery was put forth by the cowboys and their friends to throw further discredit upon the Earp brothers and their friends."

"THE TESTIMONY OF ISAAC Clanton that this tragedy was a result of a scheme on the part of the Earps to assassinate him, and therefore bury in oblivion the confessions the Earps had made to him about piping away the shipment of coins by Wells, Fargo & Co., falls short of being a sound theory because of the great fact most prominent in the matter, to wit: that Isaac Clanton was not injured at all, and could have been killed first and easiest."

—*Judge Spicer in his decision at the Earp examination*

Ike Clayton in a photograph taken in Tombstone by C. S. Fly.

belly." He said four or five shots were then fired and he ran for cover. Obviously if Wyatt had meant to murder Ike and did have his gun in Ike's belly, he could have easily done the deed when the firing began. In reality, Wyatt wasn't aiming at Ike, he was busy firing at Frank McLaury, and he didn't shoot at Ike after that because Ike was unarmed.

The third problem is that four bandits were seen fleeing from the scene of the attempted stage robbery. A letter from Tombstone correspondent Clara S. Brown appeared in the *San Diego Union* on March 26, 1881, saying, "Parties living near the scene of the attack, hearing the shots, found 'Budd' lying dead in the road, and saw four men hurrying away on horseback." Three of the robbers were Bill Leonard, Harry Head, and Jim Crane. The fourth robber was not Holliday, but Luther "Lew" King, who confessed after he was arrested by Morgan, but insisted he had only held the other robbers' horses and didn't take part in the shooting. Behan's men later allowed King to escape from the sheriff's office. Before vanishing from the scene, King admitted the other robbers were Leonard, Head, and Crane. The anti-Earp faction never said King implicated Holliday or the Earps, just that he could have if he hadn't escaped.

Behan even got Big Nose Kate to sign a statement while she was drunk and mad at Doc saying he was involved in the Philpott-Roerig murders. Behan arrested Doc for this, but Kate later retracted her statement after she sobered up, insisting she didn't know what it was when she signed it.

The Philpott-Roerig murders feature prominently in the following article by Wyatt. This was the second in a series of three articles by Wyatt that originally appeared in the *San Francisco Examiner* on August 9, 1896—almost fifteen years after the shootout. Each of the articles

### Doc Holliday, Stage Robber

So I'm a stage robber. Well, I don't believe it. They'll have to prove this to me. If I had been there, you can bet a stack of blue chips that eighty thousand[13] never would have got away.

And I've made incriminating statements, eh? Well, it's just like me to talk a rope around my neck. I shoot up the stage, killed a couple of fellows, and blab it all over the country. No honest stage robber'll trust me after this, and serve me right.

They seem to think being armed with a rifle and a six-shooter makes the case against me look pretty black. Humph! The next time I ride out into the brush in this outlaw country, I'll wear kid gloves and carry a bunch of Sunday-school tracts.

But what's the difference? Let 'em talk their heads off. Talk's cheap. If I'm guilty and don't hanker to do a stretch in Yuma[14] or cash out at the end of a rope, I ought to run away. Or you might think they'd arrest me. They know where to find me; I'm not hiding from anybody. They're making a hulabaloo because I happened to ride out of town the day of the hold-up. I might have gone to visit an old friend. I've done such a thing before but I never thought of it as a hanging matter. Well, I'll keep my mouth shut.

A still tongue is the best policy. The Behan crowd are trying to frame me and if I told the gospel truth, they'd swear I was lying. But I'll wait for the showdown. If it ever comes, I'll spread better than a pair of deuces on the table. You can bank on that.

were featured in Sunday issues of the newspaper. Wyatt was assisted by a ghostwriter—probably the *Examiner*'s star reporter, Robert Chambers. The articles were based on several long interviews with Wyatt and the overall accuracy of the articles seems to indicate the ghostwriter followed Wyatt's narrative pretty closely, though Wyatt told Stuart Lake that the writer did take some liberties with the portions on Doc. There are also several florid passages that obviously don't sound like anything Wyatt would say, but these are of minor significance.

# WYATT EARP TELLS TALES
## OF THE
# SHOTGUN-MESSENGER SERVICE

With his gun across his knee, his treasure-box under his feet and his eyes peering into every patch of chaparral by the roadside, the shotgun messenger played an humble but important part in the economy of frontier life.

Humble, did I say? Well, yes; for there was far more of danger than of profit or honor attached to the work. And yet such a man as a big express company would be sure to single out for the safeguarding of the treasure entrusted to it must need be a man fitted to fight his way to the top in a community where the sheer scorn of death was the only safeguard of life. So, at least, it would seem. But of the many daring spirits I have known to imperil their lives in the Wells-Fargo messenger service I can recall only one who clambered to any eminence out of the hurly-burly of frontier life. And even then it was no very dizzy height that he reached. Bob Paul, as fearless a man and as fast a friend as I ever knew, graduated from a messengership to the Shrievalty[15] of Pima county, Arizona, and from that to the United States Marshalship of the Territory.[16] And now he has reft himself from the rugged road of officialism to pursue the primrose path of bourgeois contentment.

Lucky Bob Paul! In fancy I see him, his always well-nourished frame endowed with "fair round belly with fat capon lined," overseeing his smelting works in Tucson, and telling a younger generation about the killing of Bud Philpott.

Bud Philpott used to drive the stage from Tombstone to Tucson, when that was the terminus of the Southern Pacific. Later when the railroad reached as far as Benson, Bud's daily drive was only twenty-eight instead of 110 miles[17]—for which, you may be sure, Bud was duly thankful. The worst part of the road was where it skirted the San Pedro river. There the track was all sandy and cut up, which made traveling about as exhilarating as riding a rail. But that didn't perturb Bud half as much as the prospect of a hold-up. That prospect increased by an alarming arithmetical ratio when the boom struck Tombstone and the worst cut-throats on the frontier poured into the camp by hundreds.

Come to think of it, it takes some sand[18] to drive a stage through that kind of country, with thousands of dollars in the front boot and the chance of a Winchester behind every rock. Of course, the messenger had his gun and his six-shooters, and he is paid to fight. The driver is paid to drive and it takes him all his time to handle the lines without thinking of shooting. That was why I always made allowances for Bud as I sat beside him, admiring the accuracy with which he would flick a sandfly off the near leader's flank or plant a mouthful of tobacco juice in the heart of a cactus as we jolted past it, but never relaxing my lookout for an ambuscade. Indeed I often wondered that we were such good friends, considering that I as custodian of the treasure box, would infallibly draw what fire there was around Bud Philpott's massive pink ears.

That is part of the cursedness of the shotgun messenger's life—the loneliness of it. He is like a sheep dog, feared by the flock and hated by the wolves. On the stage he is a necessary evil. Passengers and driver alike regard him with aversion, without him and his pestilential box their lives would be 90 per cent safer and they know it. The bad men, the rustlers—the stage robbers actual and potential—hate him. They hate him because he is the guardian of property, because he stands between them and their desires, because they will have to kill him before they can get their hands into the coveted box. Most of all they hate him because of his shotgun—the homely weapon that makes him the peer of many armed men in a quick turmoil of powder and lead.

The Wells-Fargo shotgun is not a scientific weapon. It is not a sportsmanlike weapon. It is not a weapon wherewith to settle an affair of honor between gentlemen. But, oh! in the hands of an honest man hemmed in by skulking outlaws it is a sweet and a thrice-blessed thing. The express company made me a present of the gun with which they armed me when I entered their service, and I have it still. In the severe code of ethics maintained on the frontier such a weapon would be regarded as legitimate only in the service for which it was designed, or in defense of an innocent life encompassed by superior odds. But your true rustler throws such delicate scruples to the wind. To him a Wells-Fargo shotgun is a most precious thing, and if by hook or crook—mostly crook—he can possess himself of one he esteems himself a king among his kind. Toward the end of my story last Sunday I described the killing of Curly Bill.[19] By an inadvertency I said that he opened fire on me with a Winchester. I should have said a Wells-Fargo shotgun. Later I will tell you where Curly Bill got that gun.

The barrels of the important civilizing agent under consideration are not more than two-thirds the length of an ordinary gun barrel. That makes it easy to carry and easy to throw upon the enemy, with less danger of wasting good lead by reason of the muzzle catching in some vexatious obstruction. As the gun has to be used quickly or not at all, this shortness of barrel is no mean advantage. The weapon furthermore differs from the ordinary gun in being much heavier as to barrel, thus enabling it to carry a big charge of buckshot. No less than twenty-one buckshot are loaded into each barrel. That means a shower of forty-two leaden messengers, each fit to take a man's life or break a bone if it should reach the right spot. And as the buckshot scatters literally the odds are all in its favor. At close quarters the charge will convert a man into a most unpleasant mess, whereof Curly Bill was a conspicuous example. As for range—well, at 100 yards, I have killed a coyote with one of these guns, and what will kill a coyote will kill a stagerobber any day.

I have said that I made allowances for poor Bud Philpott. What I mean is that I forgave him for his well-defined policy of peace at any price. Whereof I will narrate an example not wholly without humor at the expense of us both. We were bowling along the road to Benson one morning when four men jumped suddenly out of the brush that skirted the road a short distance ahead of us, and took their stations, two on one side of the road and two on the other.

"My God, Wyatt, we're in for it!" gasped Bud, ducking forward instinctively and turning an appealing look on me. "What shall we do?"

"There's only one thing to be done," I said. He saw what I meant by the way I handled the gun.

"Ye ain't surely going to make a fight of it, are ye, Wyatt?" he said anxiously. "It looks kinder tough."

"Certainly I am," I said, feeling to see that my six-shooters were where I wanted 'em. "Now listen. The minute they holler 'Halt!' you fall down in the boot, but for God's sake keep hold of the lines. I'll take the two on the left first, and keep the second barrel for the pair on your side."

Now all this had passed very quickly and we were bearing down on the strangers at a steady lope. Bud groaned. "I'll do what you say," he protested, "but if I was you I'd let 'em have the stuff, and then catch 'em afterwards."

As we got within range of the four men I threw my gun on them. Even as I did so it flashed across me that they wore no masks; that their faces were wondrously pacific, and that no sign of a gun peeped out among them. Just as I realized that we had been fooled, the four threw up their hands with every appearance of terror, their distended eyes fastened on the muzzle of my gun, their lips moving in voluble appeals for mercy. Bud jammed down the brake and jerked the team onto their haunches, showering valiant curses on the men to whom he had proposed to surrender a moment before.

They were harmless Mexicans who had been searching the brush for some strayed bronchos. The impulse that led them to plant themselves by the road on the approach of the stage was sheer idiocy, and they were lucky that it did not cost them their lives. What they really had intended was to ask us if we had seen any horses back along the road.

This opera bouffe[20] situation was the nearest approach to a hold-up that came within my experience. My brother Morgan, who succeeded me, was equally fortunate. After he left the service the post was resumed by Bob Paul, whom I had succeeded at the time when he retired in order to run for Sheriff of Pima county. And it was then that Bud Philpott ran into the adventure which capped with tragedy our comedy encounter with the Mexicans.

It was in 1881.[21] The stage left Tombstone at 7 o'clock in the evening with a full load of passengers inside and out,[22] and a well-filled treasure-box in the front boot. They changed teams as usual at Drew station, fifteen miles out.[23] About three hundred yards further on the road crosses a deep ravine. Just as the horses started up the opposite side of this ravine, the coach following them by its own momentum, there came a shout of "Halt there!" from some bushes on the further bank. Before the driver could have halted even if he had wanted to, they started in with their Winchesters, and poor Bud Philpott lurched forward with a gurgle in his throat. Before Bob Paul could catch hold of him he fell down under the wheels, dragging the lines with him.

"Halt there!" shouted the robbers again.

"I don't halt for nobody," proclaimed Paul, with a swear word or two, as he emptied both barrels of his gun in the direction the shots came from. His judgment was superior to his grammar, for we learned afterwards that he had wounded one of the rustlers.[24]

Now things happened quickly on the frontier, where bullets count for more than words, and the greatest difficulty I have encountered in the task of writing these recollections is that of trying to convey an idea of the rapidity with which one event follows another.

The moment the first shots were fired and Philpott fell, the horses plunged ahead so viciously that nothing could have stopped them. In missing the messenger and killing the driver the robbers had defeated their own plans. As Bob fired he moved over to Philpott's seat to get his foot on the brake, thinking that it could not possibly improve matters to have the coach overturned while it was under fire. Imagine the horses yanking the coach out of the ravine and tearing off down the road at a breakneck gallop, with the lines trailing about their hoofs. And imagine Bob Paul with his foot on the brake hearing shots and the cries of frightened passengers behind him and wondering what was going to happen next.[25]

What did happen was this: The rustlers had made such elaborate plans for the holdup that they never dreamt of the coach getting away from them. Hence they had tied up their horses in a place where they could not be reached with the speed necessary to render pursuit practicable. With all hope of plunder vanished, and with poor Bud Philpott lying dead in the ravine, these ruffians squatted in the middle of the road and took pot shots at the rear of the coach. Several bullets hit the coach and one mortally wounded an outside passenger.[26]

Such were the coyotes who kenneled in Tombstone during the early '80's. They did this thing deliberately. It was murder for murder's saks[27]—for the mere satisfaction of emptying their Winchesters.

To return to the coach. The horses ran away for two miles, but luckily they kept the road, and when they pulled up Bob Paul recovered the lines and drove the rest of the way into Benson, with the dying passenger held upright by his companions on the rear outside seat. The man was a corpse before the journey ended.

At Benson Bob mounted a swift horse and rode back to Tombstone to notify me of the murders. I was dealing faro bank in the Oriental at the time,[28] but I did not lose a moment in setting out on the trail, although faro bank meant anything upwards of $1,000 a night, whereas manhunting meant nothing more than work and cold lead. You see, an affair like that affected me in a double capacity, for I was not only the Deputy United States Marshal for the district,[29] but I continued in the service of the express company as a "private man."

So I organized a posse which included my two brothers, Doc Holliday, Bob Paul and the renowned Bat Masterson—I may have something to say about that prince of frontiersmen at another time[30]—and lost no time in reaching the scene of the shooting. There lay Bud Philpott's body, mangled by the wheels of the coach he had driven so long. And there, among the bushes were the masks the robbers had worn.[31] In the middle of the road we found nearly forty cartridge shells,[32] showing how many shots had been fired in cold blood after the receding coach.

It was easy enough to find the place where their horses had been tied, and from there the trail into the mountains was plain enough. But the story of that chase is too long to be told here. I mentioned last Sunday that it consumed seventeen days, and those who read that narrative will remember that this holdup and that manhunt were the prologue to the bitter and bloody feud that is the central, sombre episode of my thirty years on the frontier.

And now for the story of how Curly Bill became the proud proprietor of a Wells-Fargo shotgun. Charley Bartholomew was a messenger who used to run on the coach from Tombstone to Bisbee. Once every month he was the custodian of a very tidy sum of money sent to pay off the miners. Naturally enough such a prize as that did not escape the attention of such audacious artists in crime as Frank Stilwell, Pete Spence, Pony Deal[33] and Curly Bill. In fact, the four desperadoes I have named, with one other, planned a masterly holdup which they executed with brilliancy and dash. It happened this way:[34]

The coach carrying the miners' wages had got out of Tombstone about twenty miles when the industrious quintette made their appearance on horseback, three on one side of the road and two on the other. They did not come to close quarters, but kept pace with the coach at a distance of 300 or 400 yards on either side of the road, pumping into it with their Winchesters, and aiming to kill the horses and the messenger. Of course Bartholomew's shotgun might as well have been a blowpipe at that range, and if he had a Winchester with him he did not use it to any effect.

These Indian tactics proved eminently successful in breaking down the nerve of the men on the stage, for after they had run for a mile with an occasional lump of lead knocking splinters out of the coach, Bartholomew told the driver to stop—an injunction which he obeyed very gladly, the robbers came up and made them throw up their hands. They took everything there was to be taken, which amounted to $10,000[35] and sundries. Among the sundries was Charlie Bartholomew's shotgun, with which Curly Bill afterwards tried to fill me full of buckshot, with results fatal to himself. Having marched all hands into the brush the rustlers rode off.

It was not many hours before my brother Morgan and I were on the trail.[36] Two of the men had tied gunny sacks round their horses' hoofs and ridden in the direction of Bisbee, which was twelve miles away. The trail was a difficult one at first, but after a few miles of hard riding the gunny sacks had worn out, and at that point the hoof marks became quite plain. They led directly into Bisbee, to the livery stable kept by Frank Stilwell and Pete Spence. Of course we arrested the pair of them, and they were identified readily enough. As the mails had been robbed I was able to lay a federal charge against them.[37] Stilwell and Spence were still under bonds for trial when my brother Morgan was murdered.[38] And Stilwell was the man who fired the shot. It will be recalled that Stilwell was one of a gang that waylaid me at the depot in Tucson when I was shipping Morgan's body to California, and that he was killed in the attempt. As for Pete Spence, it is only a short time ago that he was released from the penitentiary in Yuma after serving a term for killing a Mexican.[39]

Pony Deal escaped from the scene of the stage robbery into New Mexico, where he was afterward killed while stealing cattle by the gallant Major Fountain, at the head of his rangers. The story of Major Fountain's murder is so recent that I need not repeat it.[40]

There is such an appalling amount of killing in the foregoing two paragraphs that I will turn for what stage-folk call "comic relief" to a stage robber whom I had the pleasure of knowing slightly in former years. I met him first in Dodge City, Kan., and always regarded him as a meritorious and not especially interesting citizen, who was afflicted with a game knee and who spoke with a brogue. Afterward he turned up in Deadwood, when I was there.[41] There were a great many stage robberies around Deadwood at that time, and all the reports had for their central figure a lone road agent, tightly masked, who walked with a limp.

The story one shotgun messenger told me was that, when the coach had halted in response to summons from behind a tree, he plucked up courage to ask the identity of the stranger. Whereupon there came the answer, in the richest of brogues:

"It's Lame Bradley, Knight of the Road. Throw out that box."

The messenger still hesitated whereupon Lame Bradley shot a hole in his ear. The box was thrown down a moment later.

Lame Bradley robbed coach after coach around Deadwood, and then, when suspicion was directed toward him, he returned to Dodge, where he spent money very freely. Afterward he moved to the Panhandle in Texas, where he was killed and robbed by a chum. The chum, by the way, was duly captured and hanged.

Heigho! More killing! And who would ever have expected such garrulity from an old frontiersman? I actually astonish myself.

—WYATT EARP

San Francisco Sunday Examiner Magazine,

*August 9, 1896*

# References

1. Philpott's name is often mistakenly spelled with one "t," though it appears with two "t"s in census records and on his gravestone. Wyatt spelled it right. Apparently, writers took the wrong spelling from the *Epitaph*.

2. The ore mined at Tombstone produced 81 percent silver, 14 percent gold, and 5 percent lead, copper, manganese and zinc.

3. Wells, Fargo & Company records show that between 1870 and 1884 more than three hundred stages were robbed throughout the West, but that only four drivers and four passengers had been killed—two of those eight died in this robbery.

4. Twenty-nine-year-old Charles Shibell was originally from Missouri.

5. Only one of the 104 votes was cast for Paul. The *Epitaph* looked into this and reported, "The odd vote is said to have been cast by a Texas cowboy, who, when questioned as to why he was voting the republican ticket, said: 'Well, I want to show those fellows that there wasn't any intimidation at this precinct.'"

6. Nineteen years.

7. Ike Clanton, Tom McLaury and Robert Findley "Frank" McLaury.

8. Stagerobbers William "Bill" Leonard and Harry "the Kid" Head, who were known to be involved in the Philpott-Roerig murders. They were killed on June 12, 1881 by Bill and Ike Haslett. According to John Pleasant Gray, his family began building their ranch on some unsettled land, but Curly Bill claimed it was his. To avoid trouble, they paid him for it and he guaranteed the land was theirs free and clear. Then one of the Hazlett brothers told them to leave as the land was theirs. The Grays refused and told Crane about their deal with Curly Bill. He apparently sent Leonard and Head to take care of the Hazletts, but the brothers found out about it and ambushed them in Eureka (now Hachita), New Mexico. According to several newspaper reports, "Slim Jim" Crane, another of the Philpott murderers, then led a group of about twenty rustlers who shot up the brothers as they were playing cards in a Eureka saloon and killed them. Crane was one of the rustlers that died with Old Man Clanton on August 13, 1881, when they were ambushed by Mexicans in Guadalupe Canyon. Perhaps these Mexicans are the ones Will McLaury offensively refers to as "Greasers."

9. Marshall Williams ran Tombstone's Wells, Fargo office.

10. Bill Leonard was a jeweler and it's said he was an honest man until he fell in with the San Simon crowd. Several years earlier he and Doc were friends in Las Vegas, New Mexico. When Leonard moved to the Tombstone area, he joined the rustlers and set up a reduction plant in Texas Canyon, which is about 45 miles east of Tombstone. Later he and his assistant, Harry Head, moved the plant across the border into New Mexico near Cloverdale next to a piece of Old Man Clanton's property. It's possible Leonard was a morphine addict.

11. Even today, many writers still believe the Earps and Holliday were involved in stage robberies and Philpott's murder—two of the more noted being the anti-Earp historians Frank Waters and Ed Bartholomew.

    Waters was the author of *The Earp Brothers of Tombstone: The Story of Mrs. Virgil Earp*, which purports to be the story from Allie Earp's point of view. Allie was Virgil's wife. Allie Earp's grand-niece, Hildreth Halliwell—who lived with Virgil's family and then took care of James and Allie in their old age—said of Waters, "He interviewed Allie many times, for many hours, in my home. I cannot explain the anti-Earp material in his books. 'He wrote lies.' Allie was shown a draft of some of Waters' writings. She threatened to sue him if he published that 'bunch of lies.' She told this to me many times." Allie's threats of lawsuits prevented Waters from publishing this book until after her death. The original title of his manuscript was *Tombstone Travesty: The Memoirs of Mrs. Virgil Earp*.

    Bartholomew is the author of *Wyatt Earp: The Untold Story* (1963) and *Wyatt Earp: The Man and the Myth* (1964).

12. According to Wells, Fargo undercover man Fred Dodge, Marshall Williams—who ran Tombstone's Wells, Fargo office—was embezzling money to gamble with, but Dodge insisted no one was helping Williams steal the cash. There wasn't enough evidence to convict Williams, but he said Williams did make a partial restitution. The Earps' enemies wrongly linked this with the attempted stage robbery and claimed the Earps and Holliday were involved.

    It's interesting that in 1883 and 1884, after the Earps left Tombstone, several county officials were involved in issuing phony warrants for the county to pay for goods and services it never received. This theft of money from the county treasury was on a much larger scale compared t were indicted—County Treasurer John O. Dunbar and Sheriff Johnny Behan. Dunbar and Behan were the owners of the Dexter Corral, across Allen Street from the O.K. Corral. A third person involved in the corruption was Milton "Milt" Joyce, the chairman of the county board of supervisors. Joyce was very anti-Earp and at one point Doc Holliday got into a fight with him and shot him in the hand. Previously, in January of 1882, Behan had been in court for charging the county twice for the same services, but the case was thrown out on a technicality.

13. Different reports put the amount at $18,000 and $26,000.

14. The Arizona Territorial Prison at Yuma.

15. Shrievalty: the office of sheriff.

16. In 1890.

17. Sic, 75 miles. These are one-way distances.

18. Sand: courage.

19. The article Wyatt refers to here appears later in this book as the chapter titled "The O.K. Corral Shootout (Part II)." He also said it was a Winchester in an 1893 newspaper interview. Wyatt killed Curly Bill as part of the Vendetta for the murder of his brother, Morgan Earp.

20. Opera bouffe: a comic opera.

21. March 15, 1881.

22. The *Tombstone Epitaph* referred to eight passengers on the stagecoach, though it's unclear whether they included the passenger that was killed in this number.

23. This is not correct. The only gully where the attempted robbery could have occurred is just *before* Drew's Station, which was about twelve miles northwest of Tombstone. Some witnesses also said they ran through Drew's getting away from the bandits. They must have changed horses at Contention, which is about two miles south of Drew's. Drew's Station was just a single adobe building owned by Harrison Drew. It was a stage station, saloon and ranch.

24. In an account of the shooting of Leonard and Head by the Hazlett brothers, the June 23, 1881 *Arizona Weekly Star* reported, "Bill Leonard [as he lay dying after being shot by the Hazletts] said last thought [sic] that he wished someone would shoot him in the heart and put him out of his misery, as he had two big holes in his belly that he got when he tried to rob the stage at Tombstone."

25. On May 20, 1882, the *Denver Republican*—apparently getting their information from Bob Paul himself—reported:

The coach was full of passengers inside and on the outside were the driver, one passenger and Paul, who was guarding a treasure-box containing $18,000 in gold. The coach was pulling out of a gully when a band of concealed Rustlers fired from a clump of bushes only a few feet distant. The outside passenger fell back mortally wounded and the driver shot through the head, fell forward between the wheel horses, frightening them so that they dashed madly off. The Rustlers fired into the coach from the left side, upon which side Paul was sitting, but, strange to say, he was not hurt. The concealed robbers fired sixteen shots in all as the coach passed by. The driver carried the lines with him as he fell, and Paul was left helpless on the top of the coach, with a dying man beside him, and four frontier horses plowing madly forward to certain death a mile ahead, where the road crossed a chasm on an insecure, narrow and unprotected bridge. Paul knew of this place, which was approached by a sudden turn, and very difficult of passage, even by a skillful driver, but he did not lose his head. He put on the brake and tried to soothe the horses by calling to them, but without avail. The brake did not seem to make the slightest difference in the speed of the coach, and the situation began to look hopeless when the coach plunged into the last gully before reaching the fatal bridge. In the midst of the noise and whirl, Paul heard a voice calling from behind, and looking down saw an inside passenger standing on the step. The passenger was a fashionably dressed young man just from the far East

and unused to scenes of danger, but he was full of grit and cool as ice.

"Put on the brake on the next rise," he said, "and check them a little while I jump off and head them if I can."

Paul obeyed, and when the team struck a sand hill he set his teeth and broke [sic, applied the brake] with all his force. The coach slowed up almost imperceptibly, and with a half dozen bounds the young dandy had the leaders by the head, and in another instant bunched them and stopped the coach right on the edge of the chasm, into which the frightened passengers looked with a shudder.

George Parsons said the treasure box contained $26,000 in gold coins, which would have weighed about 100 pounds.

Bud Philpott was 22 years old when he died.

26. Peter Roerig.

27. Sake.

28. Faro was a popular card game that was originally spelled "Pharaoh." The Oriental Saloon was Tombstone's most popular gambling establishment. According to Stuart Lake, the author of *Wyatt Earp, Frontier Marshal* (1931), when the jealous competition hired some professional gunslingers to disrupt business at the Oriental, the three men who had the Oriental's gambling concession offered to make Wyatt the fourth partner if he would work as a dealer, guard and bouncer and take care of this problem. He and Doc promptly got rid of the thugs. That would have been in late 1880 or early 1881. At about the same time, two of Wyatt's close friends also became dealers at the Oriental. They were lawman Bat Masterson and gambler/gunfighter Luke Short.

29. Actually this was Virgil's job, though Wyatt occasionally took over for him when he was out of town. Wyatt became deputy U.S. marshal after the assassination attempt crippled Virgil in late December of 1881.

30. The third article in this series was on Masterson. It is included in this book as the chapter "Bat Masterson and the Dodge City War."

31. *The Phoenix Herald* of March 16, 1881, said the wigs and beards worn by the robbers were made of rope yarn.

32. Most other reports say there were fifteen or sixteen shells. Stuart Lake's notes indicate Wyatt told him there were fifteen.

33. "Pony Deal" or "Diehl" was an escaped Texas outlaw. His real name was Charles Ray.

34. This was on January 6, 1882, at 3 A.M.—about two and a half months after the shootout and about two and a half months before Morgan's murder. The stage was on its way to Bisbee and was near the Clanton ranch when it was held up. There were actually only three robbers and arrest warrants were issued for Pony Deal, Al Tiebot, and Charlie Haws.

35. $6,500.

**36.** Wyatt is now talking about a different robbery of the Bisbee stage. This one took place at about 10 P.M. on September 8, 1881. The robbers made off with $2,500. Stilwell was one of Behan's deputies at this time. Behan took back his badge about a week later.

**37.** Wyatt, Morgan, and Fred Dodge originally arrested Frank Stilwell and Pete Spence for the robbery, but Judge Wells Spicer released them after some of their friends provided alibis. The Earps later re-arrested them on the federal charge. Wyatt and Virgil also arrested them the following month for an October 8, 1881 stage robbery near Charleston, where the bandits made off with about $800, after returning $5 to each of the passengers. The previous October Wyatt had arrested Pete Spence for selling a couple of mules stolen in Mexico.

**38.** March 18, 1882.

**39.** He was sent there for rustling.

**40.** Albert Fountain and his 9-year-old son Henry were murdered on January 31, 1896 while traveling through the desert in White Sands near Alamogordo, New Mexico.

Their murderer or murderers were never caught, though hired gunman Jim "Deacon" Miller was credited with their deaths. At the time, Fountain was a territorial judge involved in a grand jury investigation of cattle rustling in the area.

Fountain had fought in the Civil War with the First California Infantry Volunteers and was a colonel under Benito Juarez in the Mexican War. He became president of the Texas Senate and a brigadier general of the Texas State Police. In 1870 he was shot three times by lawyer B. F. Williams. He was unarmed at the time, but staggered home to get his shotgun. He managed to wound Williams before Williams was killed by the police. Moving to New Mexico, he was elected as a state representative and became a territorial judge.

**41.** According to Stuart Lake in *Wyatt Earp, Frontier Marshal*, Wyatt and Morgan left Dodge City, Kansas, for Deadwood, South Dakota (then part of the Dakota Territory), on September 9, 1876. Wyatt returned to Dodge City on July 1, 1877.

**Deadwood in 1876.**

## Bat Masterson on Guns

☞ The first gun we had out there was the old cap and ball six-shooter. There was a little steel ramrod fastened alongside the barrel and aligned with the chambers of the cylinder. It was necessary to pour in the powder, then the ball, and then ram down the charge. Some were pretty quick at it, but naturally it was slow work at the best.

It was partly on this account that many of us carried two guns. Later when the modern cartridge came in the 'two gun man' was generally a bad man, as those who shocked the not too sensitive virtue of that country were called, but in those earlier days the two guns were a necessity. We could use two guns at once, shooting equally well with either hand. The caliber of those old guns was .36 and .44. The modern .45 Colt did not come in till about 1870, when the cavalry introduced it—just when it was needed. The first Colt .45 was of the single action type.

The double action was never used owing to the hard pull [on the trigger which cocked the gun]. The [single action] gun was cocked with the thumb for each shot, and the drawing and cocking of the weapon was a matter of such quickness that I don't suppose it occupied a fifth of a second, though I never tried to time it. If you'll just reach your hand to your side and back again as quickly as possible you'll get some idea of what I mean. To succeed in that game meant the same fineness of perception that an expert billiard player shows in directing his cue, with the difference that the billiard man can take his time.

We used to file the notch of the hammer till the trigger would pull "sweet," which is another way of saying that the blame gun would pretty near go off if you looked at it. Some of the boys used to file the notch entirely off, so that the gun would go off simply by pulling back the hammer and letting it go.

The filed notch finally became the mark of the bad man or the would be bad man, but the real gun fighters—the better class, I mean—didn't file the notches off, even though they generally did the next best thing. Many used to carry an addition to a gun in the hip holster another swung under the armpit. In this way they could draw on an adversary while he was waiting for the familiar motion toward the hip.

—*Bat Masterson's interview with the* New York Herald, *1910*

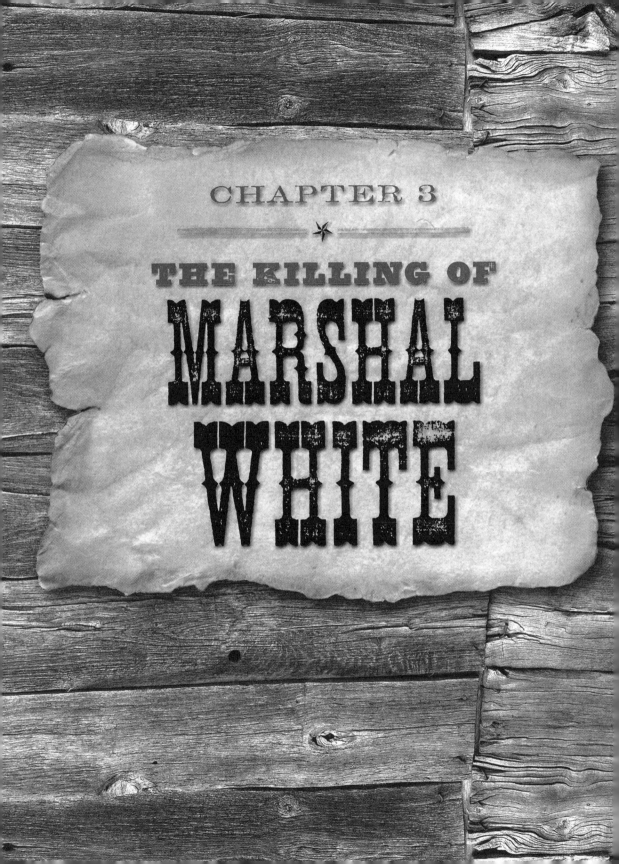

# CHAPTER 3

## THE KILLING OF

# MARSHAL WHITE

WYATT WAS DEPUTY SHERIFF when City Marshal Frederick "Fred" White was killed by Curly Bill. Tombstone was still part of Pima County at that time and Wyatt's boss, Sheriff Shibell, was headquartered 75 miles away in Tucson. This means that when it came to county police matters, Wyatt was essentially the one in charge of the Tombstone district. As a deputy U.S. marshal, Virgil was the federal authority in the area.

The shooting of Marshal White took place at about 12:30 A.M. Thursday morning on October 28, 1880. Apparently the trouble began when six to eight rustlers started shooting up the town. The *Tombstone Epitaph* said they were "firing at the moon and stars," but their bullets were also hitting houses—at least one anyway, Morgan's. As Wyatt approached the scene, the rustlers ran around a building into a vacant lot and he chased after them. Marshal White had approached the lot from the other side and caught Curly Bill. As he was taking Curly Bill's gun away, it went off. He was hit in the left groin area and the doctor later extracted the slug from where it had lodged in his left buttock. He died two days later.

Only one bullet was fired from Curly Bill's gun and that was the one that killed White. It appears the shooting was indeed accidental and Wyatt even testified in Curly Bill's favor and a gunsmith named Jacob Gruber testified that Curly Bill's gun was modified and that it could have gone off accidentally.[1] Before dying, White reportedly said it wasn't Curly Bill's fault.

Marshal White was 31 years old when he died. Wyatt was 32 at the time. It's not known how old Curly Bill was.

Since the Vigilance Committee was getting ready to lynch Curly Bill, he was taken to Tucson for his hearing under the protection of Wyatt, Virgil, Morgan, and several others.

Here is Wyatt's testimony at Curly Bill's hearing, as it appeared in the *Arizona Daily Citizen* for December 27, 1880.

# "CURLY BILL"

**His Examination concluded Before Justice Neugass[2]—Important Testimony for the Defense—The Justice's Decision.**

The examination of William Brocious alias Curly Bill, charged with murder in the killing of Marshal White, of Tombstone, was concluded this morning before Justice of the Peace Neugass. All the testimony is clear and decidedly to the point.

Wyatt Earp was called for the Territory, testified. On the 27th of last October was Deputy Sheriff; resided at Tombstone; saw defendant that night at the time Marshal

White was shot; was present at the time the fatal shot was fired; saw Mr. Johnson there at the time; my brother came up immediately after; this affair occurred in back of a building in a vacant lot between Allen and Tough Nut streets;[3] I was in Billy Owen's saloon[4] and heard three or four shots fired; upon hearing the first shot I ran out in the street and I saw the flash of a pistol up the street about a block from where I was;

several shots were fired in quick succession; ran up as quick as I could, and when I got there I met my brother, Morgan Earp, and a man by the name of Dodge;[5] I asked my brother who it was that did the shooting; he said [he] didn't know some fellows who run behind that building; I asked him for his six shooter and he sent me to Dodge;[6] after I got the pistol, I run around the building, and as I turned the corner I ran past this man Johnson, who was standing near the corner of the building; but before I got there I heard White say: "I am an officer, give me your pistol;" and just as I was almost there I saw the defendant pull his pistol out

☞ REFERRING TO WYATT, WILLIAM Hunsaker–former-Tombstoner and Dean of the Los Angeles Bar–told Wyatt's biographer Stuart Lake in 1931, "His conduct as a peace officer was above reproach. He was quiet, but absolutely fearless in the discharge of his duties. He usually went about in his shirtsleeves without a coat and with no weapon in sight. He was cool and never excited, but determined and courageous. He never stirred up trouble, but he never ran away from it or shirked responsibility. He was an ideal peace officer and a law-abiding citizen."

of his scabbard and Marshal White grabbed hold of the barrel of it; the parties were not more [than] two feet apart facing each other; both had hold of the pistol, and just then I threw my [arms] around the defendant to see if he held any other weapons, and looking over his shoulder, and White saw me and said: "Now you G-d— s— of a b——, give up that pistol;" and he gave a quick jerk and the pistol went off; White had it in his hands; and when he fell to the ground, shot, the pistol dropped and I picked it up; as he fell, he said, "I am shot." The defendant stood still from the time I first saw him until the pistol went off; when I took the defendant in charge he said, "What have I done?" "I have not done anything to be arrested for." When the pistol exploded I knocked the defendant down with my six-shooter;[7] he did not get up until I stepped over and picked up the pistol, which had fallen out of White's hands as he fell. I then walked up to the defendant, caught him by the collar and told him to get up. I did not notice that he was drunk; if he was I did not notice it. When I turned the corner he was in the act of taking the pistol out of his scabbard. I examined the pistol afterwards and found only one cartridge discharged, five remaining. The pistol was a Colt's .45 calibre.

James K. Johnson, called for the Territory, testified as follows: I live in Charleston; have lived there about four months; am a miner; know defendant. The evening of the occurrence I was with Mr. Brocius and several others. Some one proposed going up the street, and as we got in the street, some one pulled a pistol and fired. Brocius said "don't do that," but they fired several more shots, and defendant and I ran across the street. There was a terrible rush of people and Marshal White came up and demanded defendant's pistol; said he was an officer for him to give up his gun. I was standing about ten feet away, and just then Wyatt Earp past me, between me and the corner of the building, and as defendant was giving up the pistol, White jerked hold of it and said, "You d—d son of a b——h; give up that gun," and then the pistol went off; I am positive defendant did not have the pistol in his hand until White demanded it and then he pulled it from his scabbard; defendant, McCauley and myself ran behind this building to keep away from the crowd; we were afraid we would be arrested and ran behind to get out of the way;

Andrew McCauley [sic] called for Territory, sworn, testified as follows: Live in Tombstone; have lived there two years; never met defendant till the night of this shooting occurrence; I was on my way home when I stopped at Carrigan's saloon[8] and met this party and we took a drink or two together, and some one proposed going up the street, and we all started out on the street; as we were going along some of the boys pulled their pistols and fired several shots; I said to Johnson, "let's get out of this," and we ran across the street; I heard defendant make the remark, "this won't do, boys;" just before we started across the street we had just stopped behind this building when Marshal White made his appearance; I don't know which direction he came from or whether he was standing there when we arrived; anyway, he said he was an officer, and demanded defendant's pistol; I was about 10 or 15 feet away; the defendant put his hand behind him and commenced pulling the pistol, and when it got out enough so White could, he grabbed hold of it and just then Earp ran up and took hold of defendant and White said, "Now, then, you G-d—— s—of a b——, give that up, and jerked it and it went off; and I skinned out and went home.

Dr. H. M. Mathews, called for Territory, testified as follows: I am a practicing physician; reside at Tombstone; attended deceased White before he died; his death was occasioned by peritonitis, caused by the gun-shot wound; from the looks of the wound, the pistol was held at an angle of about 45 degrees.

Jacob Grubar testified: I am a gunsmith; have examined the pistol in evidence; find a defect in it in this, that the pistol can be discharged at half-cock.

Morgan Earp testified substantially to the same effect as Wyatt Earp, and the statement of defendant brocius [sic] coincided in every respect with the testimony for the Territory.

Judge Neugass, in a lengthy review of the case, discharged the prisoner from custody, the testimony showing clearly that he was not warranted in binding him over.

———— ◆◆◆ ————

Fred Dodge wrote in a letter to Stuart Lake dated October 8, 1928,[9] "White was killed at the back end of a cabin occupied by Morgan Earp and myself. When Morgan and I and several others reached Wyatt who was by the chimney of the cabin, the shooting was lively and the balls were hitting the chimney and the cabin. All of the men were squatted down on their heels. Wyatt said, 'Someone put the fire out in Fred's clothes.'...In all that fusillade of shots Wyatt's voice sounded as even and quiet as it always did."

Dodge says he then helped take Curly Bill to the lock-up, a 10-foot by 12-foot wood plank jail. Tombstone didn't have a real jail at that time and this one was made of 2-by-4s stacked horizontally and spiked together. He and Morgan remained on guard, while Wyatt, Virgil, Holliday, Turkey Creek Jack Johnson, and several others went after the other outlaws. He says they kept bringing back men until it couldn't hold any more. Dodge wrote in his journal, "The Rustlers were Shooting from an Arroya [sic, arroyo] close by the Bullets were hitting the Chimney. We all squatted down on our feet to Escape as much as possible the dainger [sic]. Curly Bill had shot Fred White at Close quarters and set fire to his clothing. Wyatt said, 'Put the fire out in Fred's clothes.' My name was Fred also and they thought it was me. The Guns clicked fast and they would have Shot Curly Bill, had I not spoken and said, 'It is Fred White, not me.'[10] Wyatt Earp had got Curly Bill at once when he killed White and was holding him there waiting for the fusilade to Cease some."

The *Epitaph* reported that five others were arrested—Edward Collins, A. Ames, R. Loyd, Frank Patterson, and James Johnson. Patterson was able to convince the judge he tried to prevent his friends from shooting up the town. Ames admitted he had done some shooting and was fined $40. The other three pled guilty to carrying concealed weapons and were each fined $10.

In Curly Bill's hearing, Judge Neugass released the outlaw primarily because of Wyatt's testimony and Marshal White's deathbed statement, he declared it to be "homicide by misadventure."

# References

1. "When the trial came up in Tucson," John Pleasant Gray wrote in his manuscript, *All Roads Led to Tombstone* (c. 1940), "Curly Bill put up a defense that his pistol would go off at half cock and that in handing over his pistol to Marshal White, at the latter's command, that it was accidentally discharged without intent on Bill's part. No doubt the truth of the matter was that Curly Bill, as was the custom among the rustler gang, had filed off the safety catch of his pistol, so that by lifting the hammer with a slight touch of the thumb it would drop back and explode the cartridge immediately. By this method the holder of the pistol could fan the six shots in rapid succession—and as being quick on the trigger was the mainstay of the gunman, to perfect himself in this was his pride."

2. Joseph Neugass.

3. Near Sixth Street where the Bird Cage Theater was later built.

4. Danner and Owen's Bank Exchange Saloon.

5. Fred Dodge, a gambler, bartender and undercover agent for Wells Fargo.

6. It's interesting that Wyatt wasn't armed and had to borrow a gun. Obviously, at this time, he felt perfectly safe in Tombstone without a gun, even though he was a peace officer.

7. Clubbing someone over the head with the barrel of a pistol was called "buffaloing." Wyatt used this technique often.

8. Thomas Corrigan's Alhambra Saloon.

9. Both of these quotations are from Fred Dodge's *Under Cover for Wells Fargo* (1969), which was edited by Stuart Lake's daughter, Carolyn Lake.

10. Fred Dodge seems to have been much more popular among these men than Fred White if they were ready to execute Curly Bill on the spot for shooting Dodge, but then wouldn't do it when they discovered White was the one who was shot.

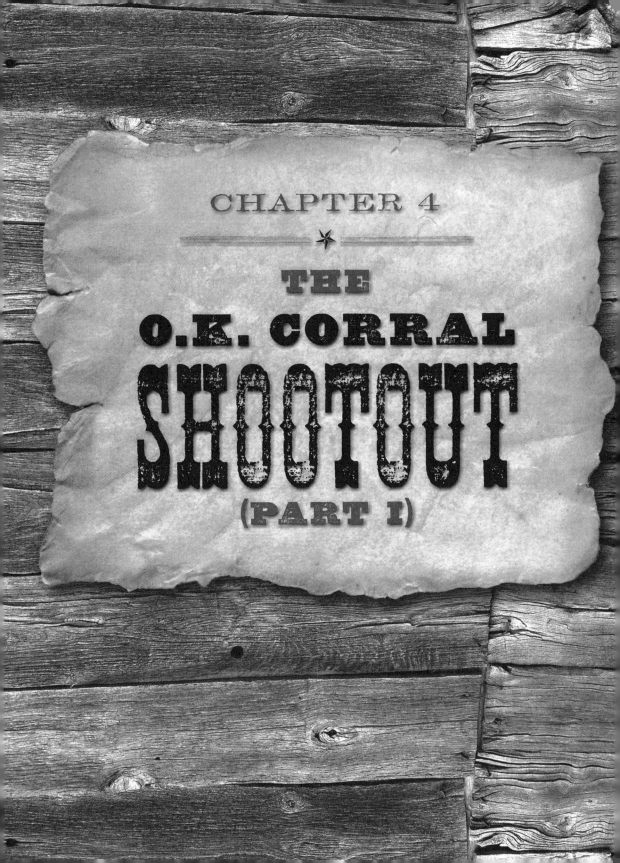

# CHAPTER 4

# THE
# O.K. CORRAL
# SHOOTOUT
# (PART 1)

IMMEDIATELY AFTER THE O.K. Corral shootout, a hearing was held to look into the causes of the shooting, what actually happened, and to determine whether the actions of the Earps and Holliday were justified. Some historians have mistakenly referred to this as "the O.K. Corral Inquest." Actually, this examination was completely separate from the coroner's inquest, which looked into the medical causes of the deaths.

The outlaws, along with their friends and supporters, claimed Billy, Frank, and Tom were murdered in cold blood and wanted the Earps and Holliday to swing for their deaths. Because of this, the Earp examination was much more extensive than it normally would have been. It ran for an entire month and much of the testimony was printed verbatim in at least two of Tombstone's newspapers.

The coroner's inquest was held on October 28th—two days after the shootout—and concluded that Billy, Frank, and Tom were indeed killed by Wyatt, Virgil, Morgan, and Doc. The following day, Ike Clanton filed murder charges with Justice Wells Spicer. Then on October 31st, Spicer began the preliminary hearing that would decide whether the Earps and Holliday should be bound over for a murder trial before a grand jury in the district court. The prosecutor only needed to show "probable cause" for there to be a trial.

Lyttleton Price officially headed the prosecution team, though it was Ben Goodrich who carried much of the case. Goodrich was a Texas attorney hired by the Clantons and their friends. Virgil later said the outlaws spent about $10,000 in attorney fees to prosecute the Earps and Holliday.

William "Will" McLaury—a lawyer from Fort Worth, Texas, and the brother of Tom and Frank—arrived in Tombstone on November 4th. Joining the prosecution, he soon convinced Judge Spicer to have Wyatt and Doc re-arrested and held without bail. Previously, Wyatt and Doc were arrested and released after they each posted $10,000 bonds. Harry Woods[1] arrested them again on November 7th and they were taken to the makeshift two-room clap-board jail, where they were held for sixteen days. Heavily-armed friends of the Earps took turns guarding the prisoners around the clock to protect them from harm. Virgil and Morgan were not arrested because they were still suffering from the wounds they received in the gunfight.

Initially, the hearing was held behind closed doors, but the newspapers raised such a stink the Judge Spicer was forced to open it to the public. In all, thirty witnesses testified at the hearing and various documents were entered as evidence.

Witnesses for the prosecution testified the Clantons and McLaurys were simple ranchers who were on their way out of town when they were confronted by the murderous Earps. They claimed two of the four cowboys were unarmed and three of the four had their hands in the air when Morgan and Doc started gunning them down. They also said the Earp party fired six shots before Billy Clanton and Frank McLaury began returning fire.

By the time the prosecution closed its case, the future looked pretty bleak for the Earps. Public opinion had shifted against them and it looked like they would be tried for murder. Will McLaury was pretty confident and wrote to his law partner, "...I think we can hang them."

The prosecution's case quickly unraveled when testimony from defense witnesses cast serious doubt over the testimony of all the prosecution's witnesses—even Sheriff Behan's. Ironically, it was largely because the testimony of the prosecution's star witness, Ike Clanton, was so full of holes that the case was swung in the Earp's favor.

The testimony finally came to a close on the 29th of November and a couple days later Judge Spicer released his decision exonerating the Earps and Holliday of any wrongdoing, but the whole thing left the public confused and divided on the controversy. Most people fell on one side of the fence or the other depending on who their friends were and which newspaper they read. In the public's mind, the Earp examination was far from conclusive.

☞ "TOM FITCH OF CALIFORNIA, who defended him [Doc Holliday in the Earp examination[2]], told me that the witnesses for the prosecution were the best witnesses for the defense."

—*E. D. Cowen, former reporter for* the Denver Tribune, *1898*[3]

Just over halfway through the examination, on November 16th, it was Wyatt's turn to testify. Thomas Fitch represented Wyatt, while Thomas J. Drum was Doc's attorney. Fitch, who was a friend of Mark Twain, was an excellent attorney who knew that under Arizona Territory law, if Wyatt read from a written statement, he couldn't be cross-examined.

There are three versions of Wyatt's statement. The original handwritten court documents are now lost, destroyed, or stolen. They were apparently last seen in 1937 by anti-Earp historian Frank Waters—the author of *The Earp Brothers of Tombstone* (1960). This leaves just a version of the court documents that has been reworked and the two versions that were printed in two of Tombstone's newspapers the day after Wyatt testified. Of these, the *Daily Nugget*'s transcripts of the hearings are the most accurate. This newspaper was actually pro-Behan and anti-Earp, while the *Epitaph*—which was edited by Tombstone's mayor, John Clum—was on the

☞ JUDGE WELLS SPICER, IN his final decision in the Earp examination, said, "Considering all the testimony together, I am of the opinion that the weight of evidence sustains and corroborates the testimony of Wyatt Earp."

Earp's side. What makes the *Daily Nugget*'s version better is they had journalist Richard Rule, who was also a professional court reporter, take down the testimony in shorthand. Thus they were able publish transcripts that were more accurate and complete than those in the *Epitaph*. The *Epitaph*'s version contains many discrepancies and has sections missing.[4]

The version based on the original court documents is a transcript that was made as part of a W.P.A. program during the depression. This was done by a part-time journalist named

Pat Hayhurst, who makes it very clear in footnotes he added to his transcript that he was very anti-Earp.[5] Some historians report that he altered testimony in his transcript. It's also said there are two or three different Hayhurst transcripts, which makes things even more confusing. A comparison of the version I have of Hayhurst's transcript and the *Daily Nugget*'s version shows very few discrepancies and most of them are minor. It's likely these alterations primarily resulted from misreading the handwriting in the original records or that he left out the parts he couldn't read. Still, it is possible his anti-Earp bias did influence other portions of his transcript. Since Wyatt's testimony was read from a written statement, this part of Hayhurst's version might contain fewer alterations than the rest. Only a detailed comparison of the Hayhurst manuscripts with testimony as it appeared in the *Nugget* and the *Epitaph* will tell for sure.

The version presented here is the *Daily Nugget*'s.[6] I have also included all the significant differences in the Hayhurst manuscript and the *Epitaph*'s version in footnotes, though I didn't bother listing the many gaps in the *Epitaph* version. In Hayhurst's version, many of the sentences appear to have been reworded by the court recorder or Hayhurst to make them more grammatically correct. I've only mentioned it where it alters the meaning.

# THE EARPS' EXAMINATION

## Fifteenth Day.

Testimony for the Defense—Statement by Wyatt Earp.

The prosecution rested on the afternoon of the 15th and on the morning of the 16th the defense put Wyatt Earp on the stand. Under the laws of this Territory the accused can make any statement he pleases in justification or mitigation of the crime charged. Under this right, witness took the stand and commenced his statement by reading a carefully prepared manuscript. Prosecution objected to witness reading from a manuscript, and contended that the law contemplated an oral statement and read it before the court. Court ruled that the statute was very broad, and under it he felt that the accused could make any statement he pleased whether previously prepared or not.

Witness then principally read from a manuscript the following statement:

My name is Wyatt S. Earp; 32 years old the 19th of last March;[7] born at Monmouth, Warren County, Ill., reside in Tombstone, Cochise County, Arizona, and have resided here since December 1st, 1879,[8] and am at present a saloon-keeper; also, have been Deputy Sheriff and detective.[9]

The difficulty which resulted in the death of Wm. Clanton and Frank and Tom McLowry,[10] originated last spring.

[*Here prosecution objected to defendant reading a prepared statement. Overruled and excepted to.*][11]

A little over a year ago[12] I followed Frank and Tom McLowry and two other parties[13] who had stolen six government mules from Camp Rucker—myself Virg. and Morgan Earp and Marshall Williams, Captain Hurst[14] and four soldiers—we traced those mules to McLowry's ranch.

[*Here prosecution moved to strike out above as irrelevant and having nothing to[15] with the case; overruled and excepted to.*]

LEFT: Frank McLaury in 1879 before coming to Tombstone. RIGHT: Tom McLaury in 1879.

While at Charleston I met a man by the name of Dave Estis.[16]

He told me I would find the mules at McLowry's ranch. He had seen them there the day before; he said they were branding the mules with D S,[17] changing the U to a D. We tracked the mules right up to the ranch; also found the branding iron D S, and after quite a while the mules were found with the same brand. After we arrived there at McLowry's ranch, there was a man by the name of Frank Patterson, who made some kind of a compromise with Captain Hurst. Captain Hurst came to us boys and told us he had made this compromise; by so doing, he would get his mules back.

## WE INSISTED

on following them up. Hurst prevailed on us to go back to Tombstone, and so we came back. Hurst told us two or three weeks afterward that they would not give up the mules to him after we went, saying that they only wanted to get us away, that they could stand the soldiers off. Captain Hurst cautioned me and my brothers, Virgil and Morgan, to look out for those men, that they had made some hard threats against our lives. About one month after that—after those mules had been taken—I met Frank and Tom McLowry in Charleston; they tried to pick a fuss out of me down there and told me if I ever followed them up again as close as I did before they would kill me. Shortly after the time Bud Philpot[18] was killed by the men who tried to rob the Benson stage,[19] as a detective I helped trace the matter up, and I was satisfied that three men named Leonard, Head and Crane[20] were in that robbery. I knew that Leonard, Head and Crane were friends and associates of the Clantons and McLowrys, and often stopped at their ranch;[21] it was generally understood among officers and those who have informa- tion about criminals, that Ike Clanton was sort of chief amongst the cowboys; that the Clantons and McLowrys were cattle thieves and generally in the secrets of the stage robbers,[22] and that the Clanton and McLowry ranches were meeting places and places of shelter for the gang; I had an ambition to be Sheriff of this county at the next elec- tion, and I thought it would be a great help to me with the people and business men if I could capture the men who killed Philpot; there were rewards offered of about $1200 each for the capture of the robbers; altogether there was about $3600[23] for their capture.

## I THOUGHT

this might tempt Ike Clanton and Frank McLowry to give away Leonard, Head and Crane, so I went to Ike Clanton, Frank McLowry, and Joe Hill[24] when they came to town; I had an interview with them in the back yard of the Oriental Saloon; I told them what I wanted; I told them I wanted the glory of capturing Leonard, Head and Crane, and if I could do so it would help me make the race for Sheriff at the next election; I

told them if they would put me on the track of
Leonard, Head and Crane and tell me where those
men were hid, I would give them all the reward
and would never let anyone know where I got the
information; Ike Clanton said he would like to
see them captured; he said that Leonard claimed
a ranch that he claimed, and that if he could get
him out of the way he would have no opposition
in regard to the ranch.[25] Clanton said Leonard,

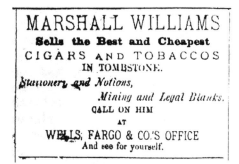

Head and Crane would make a fight, that they would never be taken alive; that I must
find out if the reward would be paid for the capture of the robbers dead or alive. I then
went to Marshall Williams, the agent of Wells, Fargo in this town, and at my request he
telegraphed to the Agent or superintendent of Wells, Fargo in San Francisco to find out
if the reward would be paid for the robbers dead or alive. He received, in June, 1881, a
telegram which he showed me promising the reward would be paid dead or alive. The
next day I met Ike Clanton and Joe Hill on Allen Street in front of a little cigar store next
to the Alhambra; I told them the dispatch had come; I went to Marshall Williams and
told him I wanted to see the dispatch for a few minutes. He went to look for it and

COULD NOT FIND IT

just then; he went over to the telegraph office and got a copy and came and gave it to me.
I went and showed it to Ike Clanton and Joe Hill and returned it to Marshall Williams,
and afterwards told Frank McLowry of its contents. It was then agreed between us that
they should have all the $3,600 reward, outside of necessary expenses for horse hire in
going after them, and that Joe Hill should gowhere[26] Leonard, Head and Crane were hid
over near Eureka,[27] in New Mexico, and lure them in near Frank and Tom McLowry's
ranch, near Soldier Holes, 30 miles from here, and I would be on hand with a posse and
capture them.[28] I asked Joe Hill, Ike Clanton and Frank McLowry what tale they would
tell them to get them over here. They said they had agreed upon a plan to tell them that

This is the earliest known advertisement for the O.K. Corral. It appeared in *Arizona Quarterly* in July 1880.

there would be a paymaster going from Tombstone to Bisbee shortly to pay off the miners, and that they wanted them to come in and take them; Ike Clanton then sent Joe Hill to bring them in; before starting Joe Hill took off his watch and chain and between two and three hundred dollars in money, and gave it to Virgil Earp to keep for him until he got back; he was gone about ten days, and returned with the word that he got there one day too late, that Leonard and Harry Head had been killed the day before he got there by horse thieves; I learned afterward that the thieves had been killed subsequently by members of the Clanton and McLowry gang; after that, Ike Clanton and Frank McLowry claimed that I had given them away to Marshall Williams and Doc Holliday, and when they came in town, they shunned me, Morgan, Virgil Earp, Doc Holliday, and we began to hear their threats against us; I am

### A FRIEND OF DOC HOLLIDAY,

because when I was City Marshal[29] of Dodge City, Kansas, he came to my rescue and saved my life when I was surrounded by desperadoes; about a month or more ago,[30] Morgan Earp and myself assisted to arrest Stilwell and Spencer[31] on the charge of robbing the Bisbee stage;[32] the McLowrys and Clantons have always been friends of Stilwell and Spencer, and they laid the whole blame of their arrest on us, though, the fact is we only went as a Sheriff's posse; after we got in town with Spencer and Stilwell Ike Clanton and Frank McLowry came in; Frank McLowry took Morgan Earp into the street in front of the Alhambra, where John Ringgold,[33] Ike Clanton, and the two Hicks boys were also standing by, when Frank McLowry commenced to abuse Morgan Earp for going after Spencer and Stilwell; Frank McLowry said he would never speak to Spencer again for being arrested by us; he said to Morgan: "If you ever come after me you will never take me;" Morgan replied if he ever had occasion to go after him he would arrest him. Frank McLowry then said to

Morgan: "I have threatened you boys' lives, and a few days ago had taken it back, but since this arrest it now 'goes.'" Morgan made no reply and walked off; before this and after this Marshall Williams, Farmer Daly, Ed Byrnes, Old Man Winter,[34] Charley Smith and three or four others had told us at different times of threats to kill us made by Ike Clanton, Frank McLowry, Tom McLowry, Joe Hill, and John Ringgold; I knew all those men were desperate and dangerous men; that they were connected with outlaws, cattle thieves, robbers and murderers; I knew of the McLowrys stealing six government mules and also cattle, and when the owners went after them—finding his stock on the McLowry boy's ranch—that he was drove off, and told that if he ever said anything about it they kill him, and he kept his mouth shut until several days ago

FOR FEAR OF BEING KILLED.

I heard of John Ringold[35] shooting a man down in cold blood near Camp Thomas;[36] I was satisfied that Frank and Tom McLowry killed and robbed Mexicans in Skeleton Canyon three or four months ago, and I naturally kept my eyes open, for I did not intend that any of the gang should get the "drop" on me if I could help it; Ike Clanton met me at Vogan's old saloon[37] five or six weeks ago and told me that I had told Holliday about this transaction concerning the "giving away" of Head, Leonard, and Crane; I told him that I had never told Holliday anything; I told him that when Holliday came up from Tucson I would prove it; Ike Clanton said that Holliday had told him so; when Holliday came back I asked him and he said so;[38] on the 25th of October—the night—Holliday met Ike Clanton in the Alhambra lunch room[39] and asked him about it; Clanton denied it; they

☞ "WHILE MORG AND I were sitting in the rear part [of the Can Can Lunch and Eating Counter in the Alhambra], Ike Clanton come in and set at the Lunch Counter. It could be seen that he had been Drinking Sufficiently to loosen his tongue and make him talkitive [sic]. Soon after, Doc Holliday come in and Seeing Ike, he went over to him and Said, "I hear you are going to kill me, now is your time to go to work." Ike Clanton said that he did not have any Gun. Doc called him a liar. Doc's vocabulary of profanity and obscene language was monumental and he worked in proficiently in talking to Ike. Morg was going to take me to my room, I was sitting in a Chair and Morg was sitting on the Edge of a Table when these men Come in. Morg remarked, 'This won't do,' and stepped over to Doc Holliday and took him by the Arm and led him away to the door where he met Wyatt and Virgil Earp and they took Doc Away."

—*Fred Dodge in his journal, Under Cover for Wells Fargo, 1969* quarreled for three or four minutes; Holliday told Clanton that he was a damned[40] liar if he said so; I was sitting eating lunch at the lunch counter, Morgan Earp was standing at the Alhambra bar talking with the bartender, I called him over to where I was sitting, knowing that he was an officer, and told him that Holliday and Clanton were quarreling in the lunch room, and for him to go in and stop it; he climbed over the lunch counter from the Alhambra bar, went into the room, took Holliday by the arm and led him into the street; Ike Clanton in a few moments followed them out; I got through eating and walked out; as I opened the door of the bar, I could hear that they were still quarreling outside;[41] Virgil Earp came up, I think out of the Occidental, and told them (Holliday and Clanton) that if they did not stop their quarreling he would have to arrest them.

## THEY ALL SEPARATED

at that time, Morgan Earp going down the street, home; Virgil Earp going in the Occidental saloon, Holliday up the street to the Oriental Saloon, and Ike going across the street to the Grand Hotel. I walked in the Eagle Brewery where I had a faro game which I had not closed. I stayed in there a few minutes and walked out on the street and there met Ike Clanton. He asked me if I would take a walk with him, he wanted to have a talk with me. I told him I would if he did not go too far, as I was waiting for my game in the brewery to close, as I had to take care of the money. We walked about half way down the side of the brewery building on Fifth street and stopped. He told me when Holliday approached him in the lunch room, that he was not fixed just right. He said that in the morning he would have man for man, and that this fighting talk had been going on for a long time, and he guessed it was about time to fetch it to a close. I told him I would not fight no one if I could get away from it, because there was no money in it. He walked off and left me saying, "I will be ready for you in the morning." I walked over to the Oriental, he came in, followed me in rather, and took a drink, having his six-shooter on and playing fight[42] and saying, "you must not think I won't be after you all in the morning."[43] He said he would like to make a fight with Holliday now. I told him Holliday did not want to fight, but only to satisfy him that this talk had not been made. About that time the man who was dealing my game closed it, and brought the money to me. I locked it up in the safe and started home.

## I MET HOLLIDAY

on the street between the Oriental and Alhambra. Myself and Holliday walked down Allen street, he going to his room, and I, to my house to bed. I got up the next day, October 26th, about noon. Before I got up, Ned Boyle[44] came to me and told me that he met Ike Clanton on Allen street near the telegraph office, and that Ike was on it,[45] that he said that as soon as those d——d Earps make their appearance on the street to-day the ball will open; that Ike said "We are here to make a fight and we are looking for the s—s of b——s!" I laid in bed some little time after that; got up and went down to the Oriental saloon. Harry Jones[46] came to me after I got up and said, "What does all this mean?" I asked him what he meant. He says, "Ike Clanton is hunting you Earp boys with a Winchester rifle and six-shooter.[47] I said, "I will go down and find him and see what he wants." I went out, and at the corner of Fifth and Allen, I met Virgil Earp, the marshal. He told me how he heard that Ike Clanton was hunting us. I went down Allen street, and Virgil went down Fifth and then Fremont[48] street. Virgil found Ike Clanton on Fourth, near Fremont, in an alley way. He[49] walked up to him and said, "I heard you were hunting for some of us." I was coming down Fourth Street at the time. Ike Clanton then threw his Winchester around toward Virgil; Virgil grabbed it and hit Clanton with his six-shooter and knocked him down. Clanton had his rifle and his six-shooter in his pants. By that time I came up. Virgil and Morgan Earp took his rifle and six-shooter and took them to the Grand Hotel after examination and took[50] Ike Clanton before Justice Wallace. Before the examination Morgan Earp had Ike Clanton in charge as Virgil Earp was out. A short time after I went to Wallace's Court and sat down on a bench. Ike Clanton looked over to me and said, "I will get even with all of you for this. If I had a six-shooter now I would make a fight with all of you." Morgan Earp then said to him, "If you want to make a fight right bad I'll give you this," at the same time offering Ike Clanton his own (Ike's) six-shooter. Ike Clanton started to get up and take it, and Campbell, the Deputy Sheriff, pushed him back in his seat, saying he would not allow any fuss. I never had Ike Clanton's arms at any time, as he stated. I would like to describe the positions we occupied in the court room at that time.

## IKE CLANTON SAT

on a bench like this, with his face fronting to the north wall of the building like that; I, myself sat down on a bench that sat up against and along the north wall, in front of Ike Clanton; Morgan Earp stood up on the floor[51] against the wall, with his back against and to the right of where I sat two or three feet; Morgan Earp had Ike Clanton's Winchester in his left[52] hand, with one end on the floor and Ike Clanton's six-shooter in his right hand; he had them all the time; Virgil Earp was not in the court-room any of this time; we were in Judge Wallace's office; Virgil came there after I had walked out; he was out, he told me, looking for Judge Wallace; I was tired of being threatened by Ike Clanton and his gang; I believed from what they said to me and others and from their movements that they intended to assassinate me the first chance they had, and I thought that if I had to fight for my life with them I had better make them face me in an open fight, so I said to Ike Clanton, who was then sitting about eight feet away from me, You d—n dirty cow[53] thief, you have been threatening our lives, and I know it, I think I would be justified in shooting you down any place I would meet you, but if you are anxious to make a fight I will go anywhere on earth to make a fight with you, even over[54] the San Simon, among your own crowd; he replied, all right, I will see you after I get through here, I only want four feet of ground to fight; I walked out, and just then, outside of the court-room and near the Justice's office, I met Tom McLowry; he came up to me and said to me, "if you want to make a fight I will make a fight with you anywhere;" I supposed at the time that he had heard what had just transpired between Ike Clanton and myself; I knew of his having threatened me, and I felt just as I did about Ike Clanton that if

☞ "Bob Hatch came and beckoned to me, as though he wanted to speak to me, and said, 'For God's sake, hurry down there to the gun shop, for they are all down there, and Wyatt is alone!' He said, 'They are liable to kill him before you get there!'"

*—Virgil in his testimony at the Earp examination, November 22, 1881*

The interior of the Oriental.

the fight had to come I had better have it come when I had an even show to defend myself, so I said to him, : 'all[55] right, make a fight right here," and at the same time slapped him in the face with my left hand and drew my pistol with my right; he had a pistol in plain sight, on his right hip, in his pants, but made no move to draw it; I said to him

## JERK YOUR GUN

and use it; he made no reply[56] I hit him on the head with my six-shooter and walked away down to Hafford's corner, went into Hafford's and got a cigar and came out and stood by the door. Pretty soon after I saw Tom and Frank McLowry and William Clanton. They passed me[57] and went down 4th street to the gunsmith shop;[58] I followed down to see what they were going to do; when I got there Frank McLowry's horse was standing on the sidewalk with his head in the door of the gunsmith shop; I took the horse by the bit, as I was deputy city marshal, and commenced to back him off the sidewalk; Tom and Frank McLowry and Billy Clanton came to the door; Billy Clanton laid his hand on his six-shooter; Frank McLowry took hold of the horse's bridle. I said, "You will have to get this horse off the sidewalk." Frank McLowry backed him off on the street. Ike Clanton came up about that time and they all walked into the gunsmith shop. I saw them in the shop changing cartridges into their belts. They came out of the shop and walked along 4th street to the corner of Allen; I followed them as far as the corner of 4th and Allen streets, and then they went down Allen Street and over to Dunbar's corral.[59] Virg Earp was then City Marshal; Morgan Earp was a special policeman for six weeks or two months, wore a badge and drew pay; I had been sworn in Virgil's place to act for him while Virgil was gone to Tucson to Spencer and Stillwell's trial; Virgil had been back several days but I was still acting; I knew it was Virgil's duty to disarm those men; expected he would have trouble in doing so and I followed up to give assistance if necessary, especially as they had been threatening us, as I have already stated. About ten minutes afterwards, and while Virgil, Morgan, Doc

☞ "IN VIEW OF THE past history of the country and the generally believed existence at this time of desperate, reckless and lawless men in our midst, banded together for mutual support and living by felonious and predatory pursuits, regarding neither life nor property in their career, and at the same time for men to parade the street armed with repeating rifles and six-shooters and demand that the chief of police and his assistants should be disarmed is a proposition both monstrous and startling! This was said by one of the deceased [Frank McLaury] only a few minutes before the arrival of the Earps."

—*Judge Wells Spicer in his final decision in the Earp examination, November 30, 1881*

Holliday and myself were standing on the corner of Allen and 4th streets, several persons said there is minutes afterwards, and while Virgil, Morgan, Doc Holliday and myself were standing on the corner of Allen and 4th streets, several persons said there is

GOING TO BE TROUBLE

with those fellows, and one man named Coleman said to Virgil they mean trouble. They have just gone from Dunbar's Corral to the O.K. Corral all armed. I think you had better go and disarm them. Virgil turned around to Doc Holliday, Morgan Earp and myself, and told us to come and assist him in disarming them. Morgan Earp said to me, they have horses, had we not better get some horses ourselves so that if they make a running fight we can catch them, I said no. If they try to make a running fight we can kill their horses and then capture them. We four then started through Fourth to Fremont streets. When we turned the corner of Fourth and Fremont, we could see them standing near or about the vacant space between Fly's Photograph Gallery and the next building west.[60] I first saw Frank McLowry, Tom McLowry, Billy Clanton and Sheriff Behan standing there. We went down the left hand side[61] of Fremont street, when we got within about 150 feet of them.[62] I saw Ike Clanton and Billy Claiborne[63] and another party.[64] We had walked a few steps from there when I saw Behan leave the party and come toward us. Every few steps he would look back as if he apprehended danger. I heard Behan say to Virgil, "Earp,[65] for God's sake don't go down there for you will get murdered." Virgil replied, "I am going to disarm them;" he being in the lead.

When I and Morgan came up to Behan, he said, "I have disarmed them." When he said this, I took my pistol which I had in my hand under my coat, and put it in my overcoat pocket. Behan then passed up the street,[66] and we walked on down. We came up on them close; Frank McLowry, Tom McLowry, and Billy Clanton standing in a row against the east side of the building on the opposite side of the vacant space west of Fly's photograph gallery. Ike Clanton and Billy Claiborne and a man I don't know were standing in the vacant space about halfway between the photograph gallery and the next building west. I saw that Billy Clanton and Frank and Tom McLowry had their hands by their sides, Frank McLowry and Billy Clanton's six-shooters were in plain sight. Virgil said, "Throw up your hands, I have come to disarm you."[67] Billy Clanton and Tom[68] McLowry commenced to draw their pistols. At the same time, Tom McLowry threw his hand to his right hip, throwing his coat open like that (showing) and jumped behind

## THE GUNFIGHT AT HARWOOD'S LUMBERYARD

☞ WILLIAM HARWOOD, IN WHOSE yard the gunfight began, was Tombstone's second mayor, but the first to be elected to the office. He was elected in December 1879, but he soon had a falling out with Richard Gird, a former assayer who had become very wealthy as part owner of Tombstone's largest mines. Gird arranged a special election to get rid of Harwood, and after being mayor for only six weeks, Harwood was replaced in January 1880 by Alder Randall.

Harwood was in the lumber business as an agent for Morse & Company. Normally he had his side yard full of wood, but the town was growing so rapidly, lumber was in high demand and his wood often went just as fast as he could get it. The day of the gunfight, Harwood was sold out of lumber.

☞ ONE WITNESS TO THE shootout, who didn't testify at the hearings, was Mrs. J. C. Collier. She was interviewed by the *Kansas City Star* and the article was reprinted in the *Epitaph* on December 30, 1881. In it she said, "My sister and I drove into the town with the children. All the way in the children kept talking about the cow-boys, and asking what we'd do if we saw any of them. As we drove around the corner, near the post-office, we saw five cow-boys standing in the middle of the road. We stopped at the post-office and my sister went in–while I sat in the wagon with the children. We were not fifty yards from the cow-boys. Presently the chief of police, Virgil Earp, came around the corner accompanied by his brothers, Wyatt and Morgan, and another man. They were all armed to the teeth. The Sheriff met them and said; 'For God's sake boys don't go down there or there'll be war.' The chief of police told him he must go, that it was his duty to disarm the cow-boys who had been making threats against the officers. They approached the cow-boys and told them to hold up their hands. The cow-boys opened fire on them and you never saw such shooting that followed. Three of the five cow-boys were killed, and two officers seriously wounded. One of the cow-boys [probably Frank] after he had been shot three time [sic] raised himself on his elbow and shot one of the officers [probably Doc] and fell back dead. Another [Tom McLaury] used his horse as barricade and shot under his neck. You see the chief [Ike] had been disarmed that morning by the police and handled pretty roughly, and they were bent on revenge."

a horse.[69] I had my pistol in my overcoat pocket, where I had put it when Behan told us he had disarmed the other parties. When I saw Billy Clanton and Frank McLowry draw their pistols, I drew my pistol. Billy Clanton leveled his pistol at me, but I did not aim at him. I knew that Frank McLowry had the reputation of being a good shot and a dangerous man and I aimed at Frank McLowry. The first two shots were fired by Billy Clanton and myself, he shooting at me and I shooting at Frank McLowry. I do not know which shot was fired first. We fired almost together. The fight then became general. After about four shots were fired, Ike Clanton ran up and grabbed my left arm. I could see no weapon in his hand, and thought at the time he had none, and so I said to him, "The fight had commenced;

## GO TO FIGHTING,[70]

or get away." At the same time I pushing[71] him off with my left hand. He started and ran down the side of the building and disappeared between the lodging house and photograph gallery;[72] my first shot struck Frank McLowry in the belly he staggered off on the sidewalk, but fired one shot at me; when we told them to throw up their hands Claiborne held up his left hand and then broke and ran, I never seen him afterwards until late in the afternoon; I never drew my pistol or made a motion to shoot until after Billy Clanton and Frank McLowry drew their pistols; if Tom McLowry was unarmed, I did not know it, I believe he was armed and fired two shots at our party before Holliday, who had the shotgun, fired and killed him; if he was unarmed there was nothing in the circumstances, or in what had been communicated to me, or in his acts or threats, that would have led me even to suspect his being unarmed; I never fired at Ike Clanton, even after the shooting commenced, because I thought he was unarmed; I believed then, and believe now, from the acts I have stated and the threats I have related, and the other threats communicated to me by different persons as having been

Tom McLowry, Frank McLowry, and Billy Clanton's corpses were placed on display in a hardware store window.

## The Funeral

☞ The funeral was described by Clara S. Brown, Tombstone correspondent to the *San Diego Union*:

> "A stranger viewing the funeral cortege, which was the largest ever seen
> in Tombstone, would have thought that some person esteemed by the entire
> camp was being conveyed to his final resting place. The Tombstone band
> headed the long line of carriages, footmen and horsemen. The two McLowry
> brothers were interred in the same grave. No one could witness this sight
> without realizing the solemnity of the occasion, and desiring proper regard
> to be observed for the dead; but such a public manifestation of sympathy
> from so large a portion of the residents of the camp seemed reprehensible
> when it is remembered that the deceased were nothing more or less than
> thieves. It is but a few weeks since all these were found to be implicated in
> the stealing of cattle and horses from some ranches on the San Pedro, which
> they ran off to the Sulphur Spring valley; and this was not by any means
> their first depredation of the kind. The divided state of society in Tombstone
> is illustrated by this funeral. While there are many people of the highest
> order sojourning here, whose business is honorable, and whose voices are
> always heard on the side of law and order, there yet remains a large element
> of unscrupulous personages, some outwardly regardless of restraining influ-
> ences, and others (more than one would suspect) secretly in sympathy with
> the 'cowboys,' acting in collusion with them. Even the officers of the law have
> not escaped the stigma of shielding these outlaws, some of them being be-
> lieved to have accepted bribes to insure their silence." (November 3, 1881)

made by Tom McLowry, Frank McLowry and Ike Clanton, that these men last named had formed a conspiracy to murder my brothers, Morgan and Virgil, Doc Holliday and myself; I believe I would have been legally and morally justified in shooting any of them on sight, but I did not do so; nor attempt to do so.

I sought no advantage when I went, as Deputy Marshal, to help disarm them and arrest them: I went as a part of my duty and under the directions of my brothers, the marshals;[73] I did not intend to fight unless it became necessary in self-defense and in the performance of official duty; when Billy Clanton and Frank McLowry drew their pistols, I knew it was

## A FIGHT FOR LIFE

and I drew and fired in defense of my own life and the lives of my brothers and Doc Holliday; I have been in Tombstone since Dec. 1, 1879;[74] came here directly from Dodge City, Kansas, where against the protest of business men and officials I resigned the office of City Marshal which I had held from 1876;[75] came to Dodge City from Witchitaw,[76] Kansas; was on the police force in Witchitaw from 1874 until the time I came to Dodge City. The testimony[77] of Isaac Clanton that I ever said to him that I had anything to do with any stage robbery or giving informa-tion of money[78] going on the stage or any improper communication whatever with any criminal enter-prise is a tissue of lies[79] from beginning to end.

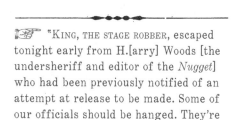

Sheriff Behan made me an offer in his office on Allen street in the back room of a cigar store where he had his office, that if I would withdraw and not try to get appointed Sheriff of Cochise county, that we[80] would hire a clerk and divide the profits. I did so and he never said another word[81] afterwards in regard to it, but claimed in his state-ment and gave his reason for not complying with his contract which is false in every particular. Myself and Doc Holliday happened to go to Charleston the night that Behan went down to subpoena Clanton;[82] we went there for the purpose to get a horse that I had stolen from me a few days after I came to Tombstone; had heard several times that the Clantons had him; when I got there that night was told by a friend of mine that the man that carried the dispatch from Charleston to Clanto 's[83] ranch had rode my horse. At this time I did not know where Clanton's ranch was.

## A SHORT TIME AFTERWARDS

I was in the Hauchucas locating some water rights and I had started home to Tombstone, had got within ten[84] or fifteen miles of Charleston and met a man by the name of McMasters;[85] he told me that if I would hurry up that I would find my horse in Charleston. I drove into Charleston; and seen my horse going through the streets toward the corral; I put up for the night in another corral; I went to Burnett's[86] office to get out papers for the recovery of the horse; he was not at home, having gone down to Sonora to some coal fields that had been discovered. I telegraphed to Tombstone to James Earp to have papers made out and sent to me; he went to Justice Wallace and Mr. Street and made the papers out and sent them to Charleston by my youngest brother, Warren Earp;[87] while I was waiting for the papers Billy Clanton found out I was in town and went and tried to take the horse out of the corral. I told him that he could not take him out, that it was my horse. After the papers came, he gave the horse up without any service of papers, and asked me if I had any more horses to lose. I told him I would keep them in the stable after this and give him no chance to steal them. I give here as part of this statement a document sent me from Dodge City since my arrest in this town, which I wish attached to this statement and marked "Exhibit A."[88]

[*Witness here produces a paper, and prosecution objects to its being used or attached as an exhibit to this statement, as it is not a statement of the defendant, but a statement of other people, and a statement made long after the alleged commission of this crime. Objection overruled and paper filed.*]

[*Counsel for defense object to any objection being interpolated in the statutory statement of a party charged with crime.*][89]

And another document sent to me from Witchita County since this arrest, which I wish attached to this statement, and marked "Exhibit B."[90]

In relation to the conversations that I had with Ike Clanton, Frank McLowry, and Joe Hill. They were four or five different times and they were all held in the back yard of the Oriental saloon. I told Ike Clanton in one of the conversations that there were some parties here in town that were trying to give Doc Holliday the worst of it by their talk;[91] that there was some suspicion that he knew something about the attempted robbery and killing of Bud Philpot, and if I could catch Leonard, Head, and Crane, I could prove to the citizens that he knew nothing of it.[92] In following the trail of Leonard, Head, and Crane, we struck it at the scene of the attempted robbery and never lost the trail and hardly a foot track from the time we started from Drew's ranch, on the San Pedro, until we got to Helm's ranch in the Dragoons. After following about eighty miles down the San Pedro River and capturing one of the men that was supposed to be in with them—a man by the name of King; we then across the Catalina Mountains, within fifteen miles of Tucson, following their trail around the foot of the mountains, after they had crossed over and followed the trail to Tres Alamos,[93] and thence[94] to Helm's ranch; we then started out from there and got on their trail.[95] They had stolen fifteen or twenty head of stock, so as to cover their trail; Virgil Earp, Morgan Earp, R. H. Paul,[96] Breakenridge, Deputy Sheriff, Johnny Behan, Sheriff, and one or two others still followed the trail up into New Mexico; their trail[97] never led south from Helm's ranch, as Ike Clanton has stated; we used every effort we could to capture those men;[98] I was out ten days; Virgil and Morgan Earp were out sixteen days and we did all we could to catch those men;[99] I safely say if it had not been for myself and Morgan Earp, they would not have got King, as he started to run when we rode up to his hiding place and was making for a big patch of brush on the river and would have got into it, if it had not been for us.[100]

Court here adjourned until 9 o'clock (Thursday) to-day.[101]

# References

[1] Behan's undersheriff and editor of the *Nugget*.

[2] Actually, Fitch was Wyatt's attorney.

[3] E. D. Cowen wrote this in an article for the *Chicago Chronicle* that was reprinted in the *Rocky Mountain News* on October 23, 1898.

[4] That is, the version as it appears in the book *Tombstone's Epitaph* edited by Douglas D. Martin (1951).

[5] His actual name is alternately given as Howell Pat Hayhurst and Howell L. Hayhurst, but he was generally known as Pat.

[6] The original is in the hands of Carl Chafin, who furnished my copy.

[7] Actually, Wyatt was 33. He was born on March 19, 1848.

[8] As far as I know, this date has not been confirmed elsewhere. It is known that Wyatt, Virgil, James and their families arrived in Tombstone sometime between November 29th and December 1st.

[9] The Hayhurst transcript breaks this paragraph up and adds questions, as follows:

Q. What is you name and age?
A. My name is Wyatt Earp—32 years old last March the 19th.
Q. Where were you born?
A. In Monmouth, Warren County, Illinois.
Q. Where do you reside and how long have you resided there?
A. I reside in Tombstone, Cochise County Arizona. Since December 1st, 1879.
Q. What is your business and profession?
A. Saloon keeper at present. Also have been deputy sheriff and also a detective.
Q. Give any explanation you may think proper of the

circumstances appearing in the testimony against you and state any facts which you think will tend to your exculpation.

10. Sic throughout this statement. Hayhurst spells this "McLoury" throughout his version. At this time the spelling of names varied and a person, if he could even spell his name, might spell it several different ways. The newspapers were particularly bad at getting names right. I have seen Earp spelled "Earpp," "Erp," "Erpe," "Earb," "Urp" and "Arp." In this case, "McLaury" is probably the correct spelling since that's the way William McLaury spelled his name in his letters.

11. In Hayhurst, this bracketed statement is inserted after the next sentence and says, "(Objection made by the counsel for the prosecution against the defendant Wyatt Earp in making his statement, of using a manuscript from which to make such statement, and object to the said defendant being allowed to make statement without limit as to its relevancy. Objection overruled by the court)."

12. On either the 15th or the 25th of July 1880.

13. Lt. Hurst in the *Epitaph* claimed the thieves were rustlers Pony Deal, Sherman "Sherm" McMaster, and A. T. Hasbrough, with Frank Patterson and Frank McLaury helping to hide the mules. Others say it was Pony Deal, Sherm McMaster, Curly Bill Brocius, and Zwing Hunt. Sherm McMaster later became Wyatt's friend and rode with him during the Vendetta.

14. Marshall Williams ran Tombstone's Wells, Fargo office. J. H. Hurst was actually a lieutenant, not a captain.

15. The word "do" is missing here in the original.

16. Hayhurst has "Estes."

17. A notice in the *Epitaph* by Lt. Hurst said the brand was "D 8," but Virgil said in a *San Francisco Examiner* interview the following year that it was "D S."

18. Philpott.

19. March 15, 1881.

20. Hayhurst has "Billy Leonard, Harry Head, and James Crane."

21. Hayhurst correctly has this as "ranches."

22. Hayhurst has "and generally in on the secret of the stage robbery."

23. The *Epitaph* wrongly had "$3000."

24. The *Epitaph* doesn't have Joe Hill here. Hayhurst spells it "Jo Hill" here and in a few other places, but he also has it as "Joe."

25. After the robbery, Ike moved his cattle onto Leonard's ranch near Cloverdale, New Mexico, thinking Leonard would flee the area. When Leonard returned, he told Ike to either buy the ranch or move his cattle. Ike didn't want to do either.

26. Sic.

27. Hayhurst mistakenly has "Yreka." Eureka was renamed Hachita in 1882 and is one hundred miles east of

Tombstone in Southwestern New Mexico, but within the outlaws' stomping grounds.

28. One of the reasons Wyatt went into so much detail about his deal with Ike is because Ike, in his testimony, said that Wyatt tried to make a deal with him to lure the robbers to a place where the Earps could murder them so as to guarantee they wouldn't reveal the Earps' and Holliday's involvement in the Philpott-Roerig murders and the attempted holdup. This was a key point in the prosecution's case. They claimed it was the reason why the Earps and Holliday wanted to murder the Clantons and McLaurys even though they were trying to surrender (so they claimed).

At the hearing, Ike testified that he would have nothing to do with Wyatt's deal to help kill Leonard, Head and Crane in exchange for the reward money. Ike apparently forgot that at the coroner's inquest he testified that he *did* make a deal with the Earps, saying, "They don't like me. We had a transaction—I mean myself and the Earps—but it had nothing to do with the killing of these men," meaning Billy Clanton and the McLaurys. So he wasn't quite so convincing when he later testified there was no transaction and it was the cause of the shootout. Ike also slipped in his testimony at the hearing when he said, "I was not going to have anything to do with helping to capture Bill Leonard, Crane and Harry Head." Ike immediately said he made a mistake and meant to say "kill" instead of "capture."

29. Wyatt was deputy city marshal and assistant city marshal.

30. Hayhurst adds "(October 1881)."

31. Frank Stilwell and Pete Spence or Spencer. Both were friends of the Clantons and Stilwell had been one of Behan's deputies until September 14, 1881—almost a week after the robbery of the Bisbee stage. Wyatt swore out federal warrants on them and took them to Tucson for trial so Behan couldn't help them.

32. On September 8, 1881.

33. It should be "John Ringo" throughout this statement.

34. The Hayhurst version says, "Ed Byrries, Old Man Urrides." The *Epitaph* has "Ed Barnes" and doesn't have Old Man Winter or Charley Smith. Ed Byrnes was reputed to be the leader of the Top and Bottom gang of gambler conmen.

35. Here they spelled the name with only one "g."

36. There is no evidence that this actually happened.

37. Vogan & Flynn's Saloon was on the south side of Allen, midway between Fifth and Sixth. After the May 25, 1882 fire that burned down four blocks that were the western half of the business district. They moved down where the Tivoli Saloon had been and where the Johnny-Behind-the-Deuce affair occurred in January of 1881, across from the newly constructed Crystal Palace. It was then renamed Vogan's Bowling Alley and Saloon. The *Epitaph* has "the Alhambra" instead of "Vogan's old saloon," while Hayhurst mistakenly has "Vogan's, (Vogan's Bowling Alley), old saloon."

Tombstone was not quite as rustic as it's usually presented. Besides a bowling alley, it also had a gym, a swimming pool, a roller rink, baseball and football teams, a library, ice cream parlors, an oyster bar, and gourmet restaurants. About the only thing it didn't have was the elderly. It was a very new town.

Tombstone was very different from a gold mining camp where individual prospectors panned for gold. Extracting silver was a large scale operation that required deep mines, large mills and big money. Most of the miners worked for companies run by wealthy businessmen. A stream of East Coast investors passed through town and a nationwide recession prompted an influx of a class of well-educated professionals. To entertain these people there were dances, socials, costume balls, and even Shakespearean plays. Tombstone was a very complex town.

38. Hayhurst leaves out, "when Holliday…he said so;." The *Epitaph* says, "When Holliday came back I asked him if he said so. I told him that Ike Clanton had said so."

39. The *Epitaph* says "saloon" instead of "lunch room."

40. Here the *Daily Nugget* spells out "damned," while later it has "d—d."

41. In the *Epitaph* version, portions of this and the next paragraph are missing. At about this point it says, "I then went to Holliday who was pretty tight and took him away. Then I came back alone and met Ike Clanton. He called me out to one side and said his gun was on the other side of the street at the hotel. I told him to leave it there. He said he would make a fight with Holliday any time he wanted to. I told him Holliday did not want to fight, but only to satisfy him that this talk had not been made. I then walked away and went to the Oriental, and in a few minutes Ike Clanton came over with his six-shooter on. He said he was not fixed right…" The narrative then continues from this point in the next paragraph.

42. Hayhurst has this as "in plain sight."

43. The *Epitaph* then just says, "Myself and Holliday walked away, and we went to our rooms."

44. A bartender at the Oriental.

45. Hayhurst and the *Epitaph* have "armed."

46. One of Wyatt's lawyers.

47. The closing quotation mark is missing in the original.

48. Hayhurst wrongly spells this "Freemont" throughout.

49. Hayhurst mistakenly has "in the mouth of an alleyway. I." It was Virgil who did this. Because Hayhurst thought it was Wyatt, it appears he moved the location to the mouth of the alley because Wyatt said he was on Fourth Street.

50. Hayhurst has, "I took."

51. Instead of "on the floor," Hayhurst has "on his feet with his back."

52. Hayhurst leaves out "left."

53. The *Epitaph* says "cur."

54. In the original, the word "to" is missing here.

55. Sic.

56. The period here is missing.

57. Hayhurst says, "Pretty soon after I saw Tom McLoury, Frank McLoury and William Clanton passed me."

58. G. F. Spangenberg, Pioneer Gun and Locksmith Shop.

59. The Dexter Corral, owned by County Treasurer John O. Dunbar and Sheriff Behan, was directly across from the O.K. Corral on Allen Street.

60. It has long been known to historians that the gunfight did not take place in the O.K. Corral, but recently some people have tried to put the gunfight back in the corral by claiming John Montgomery—co-owner of the corral with Edward Benson—had leased the lot between Fly's and Harwood's as a second rear entrance to the corral. There are a couple of problems with this. First, there wasn't a lot between Fly's and Harwood's. Harwood's house was on lot 2 of block 17 and Fly's was on lot 3. The fifteen-foot space between the two buildings was actually Harwood's side yard. Harwood was a lumber dealer and normally had his lumber here. The known rear entrance to the corral was down on lot 6.

A second, more significant problem is that if the yard was part of the corral, Virgil could not have gone down there to disarm the outlaws. The law said a person could only wear guns while entering or leaving town. It also said they could wear guns while in a corral. Virgil, in his testimony, said, "J. L. Fonke…said, 'The cowboys are making threats against you.'…I told him I would not bother them as long as they were in the corral; if they showed up on the street, I would disarm them. 'Why,' he said, 'they are all down on Fremont street there now.' Then I called on Wyatt and Morgan Earp, and Doc Holliday to go with me and help disarm them." The cowboys weren't breaking the law until they left the O.K. Corral and went down the street to Harwood's yard to wait for Doc to show up.

61. The south side.

62. Hayhurst has this as, "When I got within about 150 feet of them I saw Ike Clanton…."

63. William "Billy the Kid" Claiborne. Hayhurst has "Billy Clanton" here.

64. Possibly Wes Fuller.

65. Hayhurst and the *Epitaph* don't include this as part of the quote.

66. Behan followed them into Harwood's yard. When the shooting started he jumped into the space between Fly's Lodging House and the photograph gallery, taking Billy Claiborne with him.

67. Here Hayhurst and the *Epitaph* add, "Billy Clanton and Frank McLowry laid their hands on their six-shooters. Virgil said, 'Hold, I don't mean that! I have come to disarm you!'"

68. Both Hayhurst and the *Epitaph* correctly have "Frank."

69. Hayhurst says "his horse" indicating it was Tom's, when actually it was Billy Clanton's horse.

70. The *Epitaph* has "shooting."

71. Sic.

72. Wyatt is mistaken. His attention was probably focused elsewhere. Ike ran into Fly's by the front door.

73. Hayhurst and the *Epitaph* both correctly have "my brother, the marshal."

74. Wyatt, Virgil, James Earp, their wives, and James's 16-year-old step-daughter arrived in Tombstone sometime between November 29th and December 1st.

75. It's unclear exactly which positions Wyatt held in Dodge City and when he held them. Titles were used more loosely back then, and even as a deputy, he would have been called "Marshal Earp." So far there's no evidence to confirm that Wyatt was ever city marshal there, except perhaps the statement by Dodge City residents, but even that's unclear because he couldn't have held the position during the entire time period stated. Currently we know that Wyatt became deputy city marshal on May 18, 1876. But in June, Wyatt and Bat Masterson were deputy county sheriffs. Then in October, the *Dodge City Times* lists him as assistant city marshal. The marshal in 1876 was 300-pound Lawrence "Larry" Deger, who held the post largely for political reasons. As assistant marshal, Wyatt would have been Dodge's top officer in all but title only. Wyatt would have been appointed by the mayor, but he may have been able to choose his own deputies. Wyatt left Dodge and spent the winter of 1876–1877 in Deadwood, Dakota Territory.

So far there's no evidence he served when he returned to Dodge in 1877. On May 8, 1878, he returned from wintering in Texas and was appointed assistant city marshal. In 1879 we know he served in some position for several months before he resigned in the first week of September to go to Tombstone.

While it's possible he was city marshal at some point, we do know that others held that position most of the time.

76. Wichita, throughout this statement.

77. Hayhurst has "boasting."

78. Instead of "money," Hayhurst has "Morg," which doesn't really make sense.

79. Hayhurst originally had "falsehoods," but he crossed it out and replaced it with "lies."

80. Hayhurst has "he."

81. Hayhurst has "word to word about it afterwards, but claimed."

82. The *Epitaph* has "Ike Clanton."

83. The "n" is missing in the original.

84. Hayhurst says twelve.

85. Sherman McMaster—one of the rustlers who stole the mules from the Army and who later accompanied Wyatt on the Vendetta. At this time he was one of Wyatt's informants.

86. The *Epitaph* has "Barnett's."

87. Hayhurst and the *Epitaph* add, "that night."

88. The statement marked "Defense Exhibit 'A'" said:

**To All Whom It May Concern, Greetings:**
We, the undersigned citizens of Dodge City, Ford County, Kansas, and vicinity do by these presents certify that we are personally acquainted with Wyatt Earp, late of this city; that he came here in the year 1876; that during the years of 1877, 1878, and 1879, he was Marshal of our city; that he left our place in the fall of 1879; that during his whole stay here he occupied a place of high social position and was regarded and looked upon as a high-minded, honorable citizen; that as Marshal of our city he was ever vigilant in the discharge of his duties, and while kind and courteous to all, he was brave, unflinching, and on all occasions proved himself the right man in the right place.

Hearing that he is now under arrest, charged with complicity in the killing of those men termed 'Cow Boys,' from our knowledge of him we do not believe that he would wantonly take the life of his fellow man, and that if he was implicated, he only took life in the discharge of his sacred trust to the people; and earnestly appeal to the citizens of Tombstone, Arizona, to use all means to secure him a fair and impartial trial, fully confident that when tried he will be fully vindicated and exonerated of any crime.

89. Hayhurst adds, "…, for the reason that the law contemplates such statement shall not be interrupted by the court, the counsel for the prosecution, not the counsel for the defense, or for the farther [sic] reason that it is perfect evidence of character lacking only the absurd? [sic] formality. Objection of counsel for prosecution overruled and the paper ordered to be filed as part of this statement."

90. Hayhurst adds, "(Same objection by prosecution and same ruling by the court.)"

The statement marked "Defense Exhibit 'B'" read:

We, the undersigned citizens of Wichita in the County and State aforesaid are well acquainted with Mr. Wyatt S. Earp and that we were intimately acquainted with him while he was on the Police force of this city, in the years A.D. 1874, 1875 and part of the year 1876. We further certify that the said Wyatt S. Earp was a good and efficient officer, and was well known for his honesty, and integrity, that his character while here was of the best, and that no fault was ever found with him as an officer, or as a man.

Geo. E. Harris, Mayor in 1875
M. Zimmerly, Councilman in 1875
C.M. Garrison, Councilman in 1875
R.C. Ogdell, ex-City Marshal
J.M. True, ex-City Treasurer
Fred Sclattner, City Clerk
James Cairns, City Marshal

Sworn and subscribed to and before me this fourth day of November A.D. 1881.

CHARLES HATTON, NOTARY PUBLIC

I hereby certify that I knew personally Wyatt S. Earp during his residence in the city of Wichita. That I served four years as city attorney of said city and have known personally all of the officers of said city for the past ten years. I take great pleasure in saying that Wyatt S. Earp was one of the most efficient officers that Wichita ever had and I can safely testify that Mr. Earp is in every sense reliable and a trustworthy gentleman.

[signed] Chas. Hatton

91. They were accusing Holliday of being the one who shot Philpott.

92. The *Epitaph* has, "I told him one reason why I wanted to catch them was to prove to the citizens of Tombstone that Doc Holliday had nothing to do with it."

93. Hayhurst leaves out "after they had crossed over and followed the trail" and after Tres Alamos has "on the San Pedro." The *Epitaph* just leaves out, "and followed the trail."

94. Hayhurst adds "to the Dragoons."

95. Hayhurst has, "They then started out from Helm's ranch. Got on their trail."

96. Robert H. Paul. This is the Bob Paul who was shotgun messenger when Bud Philpott was murdered. The *Epitaph* incorrectly has "H. R."

97. Hayhurst has "trails."

98. Hayhurst adds "or robbers."

99. And Sheriff Behan apparently did what he could to hinder them. In a May 28, 1882, interview with the *San Francisco Examiner*, Virgil said:

> At the time Bud Philpot [sic], the driver, was killed there were four cowboys, Billy Leonard, Jimmy Crane, Harry Head and a man named King were the robbers. That night Bob Paul telegraphed to me that the stage had been robbed and the driver and one passenger killed, and wanted me to meet him at Drew's, where the robbery was made. I got Wyatt and Morgan and Bat Masterson, ex-Sheriff at Fort [sic, Ford] county, Kansas, to go with me. The night was so dark we could not follow the trail and had to lie there until daylight, when Sheriff Behan came down. Twenty-five or thirty men offered their services to pursue, and he told them all he wanted was the Earp boys and Bob Paul. We agreed to go and to stay in pursuit as long as he thought it best to follow them. We struck the trail, followed their footprints for three days and caught King. He told who the rest of the party was. Behan went back to Tombstone with, and we followed the rest for six days longer before we could get to a place to telegraph for advice. We telegraphed to

Behan for fresh horses, as ours were played out with their nine days work, and Behan met us where we expected to get the horses, but he did not bring them. That night Bob Paul's horse laid down and died. Wyatt's and Masterson's horses were so used up they were left at the ranch and the boys had to foot it in eighteen miles to Tombstone. During this time [Jim] Hume, Wells, Fargo & Co.'s detective had came [sic] to work up the case. Wyatt told him that there were about seventy-five cowboys in town, who would try to release King. Hume got Wyatt to go with him to the Sheriff's office to notify them, and they asked as a favor of the Under Sheriff [Harry Woods] to put King in irons. He promised to do so, and fifteen minutes afterward King escaped, going on a horse that was tied back of the Sheriff's office. After Behan met us we followed the trail for nine days more, the last five days going without a mouthful to eat, and the last two days being without water. The horses were played out, and we had to give up the chase and return. Behan brought in a bill against the county for $790.84. We supposed it was to pay expenses for the whole party, but he rendered it as a private account. I went before the Supervisors and they said Behan must vouch for us. This he refused to do, saying he had not deputized us. Everybody but myself and brothers were paid, and we did not get a cent until Wells-Fargo found it out and paid us for our time. From that time our troubles commenced, and the cowboys plotted to kill us. They met at Charleston and took an oath over blood drawn from the arm of John Ring[o], the leader, that they would kill us.

Virgil fails to mention that when King was arrested, Wyatt told Behan specifically not to let the prisoner talk to either of the brothers who owned the ranch where he was captured. When Wyatt returned he found King talking to both of the brothers. King eventually confessed where Leonard, Head and Crane were hiding, but by then one of the brothers had already ridden off, no doubt to warn them.

100. Behan insisted on taking custody of Luther King and his men allowed King to escape from the sheriff's office. The anti-Earp faction later claimed the Earps were behind King's escape.

Oddly, Hayhurst's transcript added here, "In relation to Holliday," but then crossed it out.

101. Instead of this sentence, Hayhurst concludes with:
(sig.) Wyatt S. Earp.

Usual sworn statement by Wells Spicer, J. P., November 17, 1881.

Wyatt's statement was actually made on November 16th.

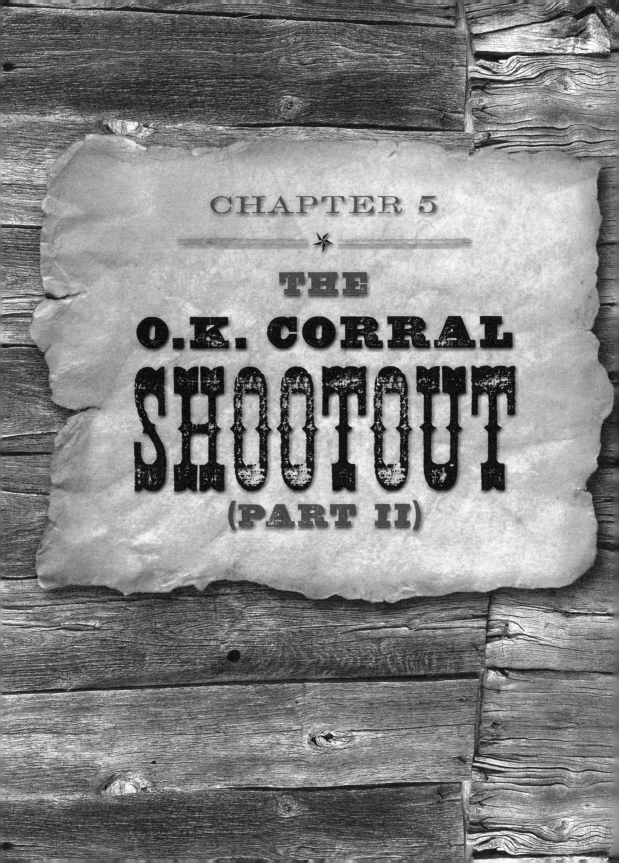

# CHAPTER 5

## THE
## O.K. CORRAL
## SHOOTOUT
### (PART II)

THIS IS THE FIRST of Wyatt's *San Francisco Examiner* articles. It originally appeared on Sunday, August 2, 1896. Compared to the Wyatt's previous account, this one is considerably more dramatic. Of course, that's because his previous account is a legal document and he had to be much more cautious about what he said; after all, there was a chance his enemies would be successful in getting him tried for murder. This account, on the other hand, is much more entertaining, though it's obviously been embellished by the *Examiner*'s ghostwriter, since some of it—especially the beginning—sure doesn't sound like Wyatt.

## HOW WYATT EARP ROUTED A GANG OF ARIZONA OUTLAWS

It may be that the trail of blood will seem to lie too thickly over the pages that I write. If I had it in me to invent a tale I would fain lighten the crimson stain so that it would glow no deeper than a demure pink. But half a lifetime on the frontier attunes a man's hand to the six-shooter rather than the pen, and it is lucky that I am asked for facts, for more than facts I could not give.

Half a lifetime of such turbulent days and nights as will never again be seen in this, or, I believe, in any land, might be expected to tangle a man's brain with memories none to easy to sift apart. But for the corner-stone of this episodic narrative I cannot make a better choice than the bloody feud in Tombstone, Ariz., which cost me a brave brother and cost more than one worthless life among the murderous dogs who pursued me and mine only less bitterly than I pursued them.

And so I marshal my characters. My stalwart brothers, Virgil and Morgan, shall stand on the right of the stage with my dear old comrade, Doc Holliday; on the left shall be arrayed Ike Clanton, Sheriff Behan, Curley Bill and the rest. Fill in the stage with miners, gamblers, rustlers, stage robbers, murderers and cowboys, and the melodrama is ready to begin. Nor shall a heroine be wanting, for Big Nose Kate was shaped for the part by nature and circumstances. Poor Kate! Frontier whiskey must have laid her low long since.[1] And that gives me an opportunity to introduce the reader to both Doc Holliday and Kate by telling of an episode in their checkered lives two years before the action of my melodrama begins.

It happened in '77, when I was City Marshal of Dodge City, Kan.[2] I had followed the trail of some cattle thieves across the border into Texas, and during a short stay in Fort Griffin I first met Doc Holliday and the woman who was known variously as Big Nose Kate, Kate Fisher and, on occasions of ceremony, Mrs. Doc Holliday. Holliday asked me a good many questions about Dodge City and seemed inclined to go there, but before he had made up his mind about it my business called me over to Fort Clarke.[3] It was while I was on my way back to Fort Griffin that my new friend and his Kate found it necessary to pull their stakes hurriedly. Whereof the plain, unvarnished facts were these:

Doc Holliday was spending the evening in a poker game, which was his custom whenever faro bank did not present superior claims on his attention. On his right sat Ed Bailey, who needs no description because he is soon to drop out of this narrative. The trouble began, as it was related to me afterward, by Ed Bailey monkeying with the deadwood, or what people who live in cities call discards. Doc Holliday admonished him once or twice to "play poker"—which is your seasoned gambler's method of cautioning a friend to stop cheating—but the misguided Bailey persisted in his furtive attentions to the deadwood. Finally, having detected him again, Holliday pulled down a pot without showing his hand, which he had a perfect right to do. Thereupon Bailey started to throw his gun around on Holliday, as might have been expected. But before he could pull the trigger, Doc Holliday had jerked a knife out of his breast-pocket and with one sideways sweep had caught Bailey just below the brisket.

Well, that broke up the game, and pretty soon Doc Holliday was sitting cheerfully in the front room of the hotel, guarded by the City Marshal and a couple of policeman, while a hundred miners and gamblers clamored for his blood. You see, he had not lived in Fort Griffin very long, while Ed Bailey was well liked. It wasn't long before Big Nose Kate, who had a room downtown, heard about the trouble and went up to take a look at her Dock[4] through a back window. What she saw and heard led her to think that his life wasn't worth ten minutes purchase, and I don't believe it was. There was a shed at the back of the lot, and a horse was stabled in it. She was a kind-hearted girl, was Kate, for she went to the trouble of leading the horse into the alley and tethering it there before she set fire to the shed. She also got a six-shooter from a friend down the street, which, with the one she always carried, made two.

It all happened just as she had planned it. The shed blazed up and she hammered at the door, yelling, "Fire!" Everybody rushed out, except the Marshal, and the constables and their prisoner. Kate walked in as bold as a lion, threw one of her six-shooters on the Marshal and handed the other to Doc Holliday.

"Come on, Doc," she said with a laugh.

He didn't need any second invitation and the two of them backed out of the hotel, keeping the officers covered. All that night they hid among the willows down by the creek, and early next morning a friend of Kate's brought them two horses and some of Doc Holliday's clothes from his room. Kate dressed up in a pair of pants, a pair of boots, a shirt and a hat, and the pair of them got away safely and rode the 400 miles to Dodge City, where they were installed in great style when I got back home.[5]

Which reminds me that during my absence the man whom I had left behind as a deputy[6] had been killed by some cowboys who were engaged in the fascinating recreation known as "shootin' up the town." This incident is merely mentioned as a further sign of the time, and a further excuse for the blood which cannot but trickle through the web of my remembrance.

Such, then, was the beginning of my acquaintance with Doc Holliday, the mad, merry scamp with heart of gold and nerves of steel, who, in the dark years that followed stood at my elbow in many a battle to the death. He was a dentist, but he preferred to be a gambler. He was a Virginian,[7] but he preferred to be a frontiersman and a vagabond. He was a philosopher, but he preferred to be a wag. He was long, lean, an ash-blond, and the quickest man with a six-shooter I ever knew. It wasn't long after I returned to Dodge City that his quickness saved my life. He saw a man draw on me behind my back. "Look out, Wyatt!" he shouted, but while the words were coming out his mouth he had jerked his pistol out of his pocket and shot the other fellow before the latter could fire.

On such incidents as that are built the friendships of the frontier.

In 1879 Dodge City was beginning to lose much of the snap which had given it a charm to men of restless blood,[8] and I decided to move to Tombstone, which was just building up a reputation. Doc Holliday thought he would move with me. Big-Nose Kate had left him long before—they were always a quarrelsome couple—and settled in Las Vegas, N. M. He looked her up en route, and, the old tenderness reasserted itself, she resolved to throw in her lot with his in Arizona.[9] As for me, I was tired of the trials of a peace officer's life and wanted no more of it. But as luck would have it I stopped at Prescott to see my brother Virgil, and while there I met C. P. Dake,[10] the United States Marshal of the Territory. Dake had heard of me before, and he begged me so hard to take the deputyship in Tombstone that I finally consented.[11] It was thus that the real troubles of a lifetime began.

The boom had not struck Tombstone then, but it did a few months later, when the mills for treating the ore were completed and tales about the fabulous richness of the silver mines were bruited abroad.[12] Before long the town had a population of 10,000 to 12,000,[13] of whom about 300 were cattle-thieves, stage robbers, murderers, and outlaws.[14]

For the first eight months I worked as a shotgun messenger for Wells, Fargo & Co., and beyond the occasional excitement of an abortive hold-up and a few excursions after cattle-thieves and homicides in my official capacity, everything was quiet as a grave. Then the proprietors of "The Oriental," the biggest gambling-house in town, offered to take me in to partnership. One of them—his name was Rickabaugh and he was a San Francisco man—was unpopular, and a coterie of the tough gamblers was trying to run the firm out of town. The proprietors of the Oriental had an idea that their troubles would cease if they had the Deputy United States Marshal for a partner,[15] and so it proved, for a time at least. So I turned over my position with Wells, Fargo & Co. to my brother Morgan, who held it for six months, after which I gave him a job in "The Oriental." My brother Virgil had also joined me, and when the town was incorporated he was appointed Chief of Police.[16]

About this time was laid the foundation of the vendetta which became the talk of the frontier and resulted in no end of bloodshed.

A band of rustlers held up the coach and killed the driver and one of the passengers.[17] Virgil and I, with another man, followed them into the mountains for seventeen days, but our horses gave out and they got away from us. When we got back to town I went to Ike Clanton, who was sort of a leader among the rustlers, and offered to give him all the $6,000[18] reward offered by Wells, Fargo & Company if he would lead me to where I could arrest the murderers. After thinking about it deeply he agreed to send a partner of his, named Joe Hill, to lead them from where they were hiding to some place within twenty-five miles of Tombstone, where I could get them. But in case I killed his partners he wanted to be sure that the reward would be paid alive or dead. In order to assure him, I got Wells-Fargo's agent, Marshall Williams, to telegraph to San Francisco about it, and a reply came in the affirmative. So Clanton sent Hill off to decoy the men I wanted. That was to take several days, and in the meantime Marshal[19] Williams got drunk, and, suspecting that I was using Ike Clanton for some purpose, tried to pump him about it. Clanton was terrified at the thought of any third person knowing of our bargain and accused me of having told Williams. I denied it, and then he accused me of having told Doc Holliday. Fear and whiskey robbed Clanton of his discretion and he let out his secret to Holliday, who had known nothing about it. Doc Holliday, who was the soul of honor, berated him vigorously for his treachery, and the conversation was heard by several people.

☞ "[IKE] CLANTON AND [TOM] McLaury came to us and said they heard we had revealed the contract to catch Leonard, and said they could not live in the country an hour if Leonard's friends learned that they had plotted against him. This was on the night of October 25th. They got drunk, and on the morning of the 26th [the day of the gunfight] they were still drinking."

—*Virgil Earp, in an interview with the San Francisco Examiner, May 28, 1882; The Earps, on the other hand, were well-rested and sober*

That was enough for Clanton. He knew that his only alternative was to kill us or be killed by his own people. Early next morning[20] Virgil and I were told that he was out with a Winchester and a six-shooter looking for us. So we went out looking for him, taking different routes. Virgil was going down Fourth street when Clanton came out of a hallway, looking in the opposite direction. "I want you, Ike," said Virgil, walking up behind him. Clanton threw his gun around and tried to take a shot, but

Virgil knocked it away, pulled his own and arrested his man. Ike was fined $25 for disturbing the peace.

Ike Clanton's next move was to telegraph to Charleston, ten miles away, for Billy Clanton, Tom McLowery, Frank McLowery,[21] and Bill Clayton[22]—hard men, every one. They came galloping into town, loaded up with ammunition and swearing to kill us off in short order. Thirty or forty citizens offered us their help, but we said we could manage the job alone. "What had we better do?" asked Virgil. "Go arrest 'em," said I.

The four newcomers and Ike Clanton stationed themselves on a fifteen-foot lot between two buildings in Fremont street and sent us word that if we did not come down there and fight they would waylay and kill us.[23] So we started down after them—Doc Holliday, Virgil, Morgan and I. As we came to the lot they moved back and got their backs against one of the buildings. "I'm going to arrest you, boys," said Virgil. For answer their six-shooters began to spit. Frank McLowery fired at me and Billy Clanton at Morgan.[24] Both missed. I had a gun in my overcoat pocket and I jerked it out at Frank McLowery hitting him in the stomach. At the same time Morgan shot Billy Clanton in the breast. So far we had got the best of it, but just then Tom McLowery, who got behind his horse, fired under the animal's neck and bored a hole right through Morgan sideways. The bullet entered one shoulder and came out at the other.

"I've got it, Wyatt!" said Morgan.

"Then get behind me and keep quiet," I said—but he didn't.

By this time bullets were flying so fast that I could not keep track of them. Frank McLowery had given a yell when I shot him, and made for the street, with his hand over his stomach. Ike Clanton and Billy Clayton were shooting fast,[25] and so was Virgil, and the two latter made a break for the street. I fired a shot which hit Tom McLowery's horse and made it break away, and Doc Holliday took the opportunity to pump a charge of buckshot out of a Wells Fargo shotgun into Tom McLowery, who promptly fell dead. In the excitement of the moment Doc Holliday didn't know what he had done and flung away the shotgun in disgust, pulling his six-shooter instead.

Then I witnessed a strange spectacle. Frank McLowery and Billy Clanton were sitting in the middle of the street, both badly wounded, but emptying their six-shooters like lightning. One of them shot Virgil through the leg and he shot Billy Clanton. Then Frank McLowery started to his feet and staggered across the street, though he was full of bullets. On the way he came face to face with Doc Holliday. "I've got ye now, Doc," he said. "Well, you're a good one if you have," said Holliday with a laugh. With that they both aimed. But before you can understand what happened next I must carry the narrative back half a minute:

After the first exchange in the lot Ike Clanton had got into one of the buildings from the rear[26] and when I reached the street he was shooting out of one of the front windows.[27] Seeing him aim at Morgan I shouted: "Look out, Morg, you're getting it in the back!"

Morgan wheeled round and in doing so fell on his side.[28] While in that position he caught sight of Doc Holliday and Frank McLowery aiming at each other. With a quick drop he shot McLowery in the head. At the same instant, McLowery's pistol flashed and Doc Holliday was shot in the hip.

That ended the fight. Ike Clanton and Billy Clanton[29] ran off and made haste to give themselves up to the sheriff, for the citizens were out a hundred strong to back us up.

I have described this battle with as much particularity as possible, partly because there are not many city dwellers who have more than a vague idea of what such a fight really means, and partly because I was rather curious to see how it would look in cold type. It may or may not surprise some readers to learn that from the first to the last shot fired, not more than a minute elapsed.[30]

Of the exciting events which followed, I can give no more than a brief account. The principal factor in all that happened was Sheriff Johnny Behan, my political rival and personal enemy. Doc Holliday and I were arrested on a charge of murder.[31] My two brothers were exempt from his proceeding because they were both disabled. We were acquitted at the preliminary hearing and

☞ A COUPLE OF STRANGE events took place on the day of the shootout. Right after his argument with Doc and just a few hours before the gunfight, Ike joined a poker game with Virgil, Tom McLaury, John Behan and an unknown player. Obviously they didn't let their differences get in the way of a good game of cards. Then when Billy Clanton and Frank McLaury arrived in town, Doc walked over to Billy and shook his hand. Doc had a strange sense of humor.

☞ "COMPLAINT UPON OATH HAVING this day been made by I. I. Clanton [sic, J. I. Clanton], that Wyatt Earp, Morgan Earp, Virgil Earp, and J. H. Holliday, did on the 26th day of October, in the year A.D. 1881, wilfully [sic], feloniously, premeditatedly and of their malice aforthought [sic] kill and murder in the City of Tombstone, County of Cochise and Territory of Arizona, William Clanton, Thomas McLowery [sic] and Frank McLowery by the said Wyatt Earp, Morgan Earp, Virgil Earp, and J. H. Holliday, shooting with Guns and Pistols then and there loaded with gunpowder and leaden bullets and shot off by them and each of them to, at and against the bodies of the said William Clanton, Thomas McLowery and Frank McLowery which said leaden bullets shot out of the guns and pistols aforsaid [sic] by the said Wyatt Earp, Morgan Earp, Virgil Earp and J. H. Holliday, to, at and against the bodies of the said William Clanton, Thomas McLowery and Frank McLowery of which said wounds so inflicted as aforsaid they and each of them then and there died."

*—The arrest warrant from the complaint Ike Clanton filed in Contention, February 9, 1882*

rearrested on another warrant charging the same offense.[32] This time the hearing was held at Contention, nine miles from Tombstone, and we would have been assassinated on the road had not a posse of the best citizens insisted on accompanying the Sheriff as a guard. The hearing was never completed, because Holliday and I were released on a writ of habeas corpus. In the meantime the Grand Jury persistently refused to indict us.

But the determination to assassinate us never relaxed. Three months later,[33] Virgil was returning home to the hotel, and when he was half way across the street five double-barreled shotguns were discharged at him from an ambuscade.[34] One shot shattered his left arm and another passed through his body.[35] I arrested several of the assassins, but twenty or thirty rustlers swore to an alibi and they were acquitted.[36] Three months later, before Virgil had recovered from his wounds, Morgan was shot dead through the glass door of a saloon, while he was playing a game of pool. I sent his body home to Colton, Cal., and shipped off Virgil—a physical wreck—on the same train from Tucson.[37] But even at the depot I was forced to fight Ike Clanton and four or five of his friends who had followed us to do murder. One of them, named Frank Stilwell, who was believed to be Morgan's murderer, was killed by my gun going off when he grasped it.[38] When I returned to Tombstone, Sheriff Behan came to arrest me, but I refused to surrender and he weakened.

For a long time thereafter I occupied the anomalous position of being a fugitive from the county authorities, and performing the duties of Deputy United States Marshal, with the sanction and moral support of my chief. With Doc Holliday and one or two faithful comrades, I went into camp among the hills and withstood more than one attack from outlaws who had been implicated in the death of one brother and the disablement of another—attacks which resulted fatally to some of my enemies and left me without a scratch.

Two years later on April 13, 1884, Texas lawyer Will McLaury wrote to his father, "My experience out there [in Tombstone] has been very unfortunate as to my health and badly injured me as to money matters–and none of the results have been satisfactory. The only result is the death of Morgan and the crippling of Virgil Earp and death of McMasters[39]..." It sounds as though Will may have been responsible for hiring the assassins to kill Wyatt, Virgil and Morgan.

One such encounter I will describe because it illustrates as well as anything what could some of the exigencies of a frontier vendetta.

We had ridden twenty-five miles over the mountains with the intention of camping at a certain spring.[40] As we got near the place I had a presentiment that something was wrong, and unlimbered my shotgun. Sure enough, nine cowboys sprang from the bank where the spring was and began firing at us. I jumped off my horse to return the fire, thinking my men would do the same, but they retreated. One of the cowboys, who was trying to pump some lead into me with a Winchester,[41] was a fellow named Curly Bill, a stage-robber whom I had been after for eight months, and for whom I had a warrant in my pocket. I fired both barrels of my gun into him, blowing him all to pieces.[42] With that the others jumped into a clump of willows and kept on firing, so I retreated, keeping behind my horse. He was a high-strung beast, and the firing frightened him so that whenever I tried to get my Winchester from the saddle he would rear up and keep it out of my reach. When I had backed out about a hundred yards I started to mount. Now, it was a hot day, and I had loosened my cartridge belt two or three holes. When I tried to get astride I found that it had fallen down over my thighs, keeping my legs together. While I was perched up thus, trying to pull my belt higher with one hand, the horn of the saddle was shot off. However, I got away all right, and just then my men rallied. But I did not care to go back at the rustlers, so we sought out another water hole for camp. The skirt of my overcoat was shot to pieces on both sides, but not a bullet touched me.[43]

Sheriff Behan trailed us with a big posse composed of rustlers, but it was only a bluff, for when I left word for him where he could find us and waited for him to come, he failed to appear.

My best friends advised me to leave the Territory, so I crossed into Colorado. While I was there, they tried to get a requisition for me, but the Governor refused to sign it.[44]

It's an old story now. I have been in Arizona in recent years—as near Tombstone as Tucson, in fact—but no one sought to molest me. The outlaws who were my worst enemies are mostly killed off or in the penitentiary. Poor Doc Holliday died of consumption three years ago in Colorado.[45] My brother Virgil is running a stock ranch in Texas. A large section of his upper arm is entirely without bone, and yet he can use his fingers.

On reading it over it seems to me that there is not only too much blood, but too much of myself in my story. However, a man gets in the habit of thinking about himself when he spends half a lifetime on the frontier.

—WYATT S. EARP.

# References

1. Big Nose Kate died in Prescott, Arizona, in 1940.

2. There's no proof Wyatt was a policeman in 1877.

3. Fort Clark.

4. Sic.

5. So far, no contemporary account of Doc stabbing Ed Bailey has been found to confirm this story.

6. Ed Masterson, Bat's older brother. Ed was assistant city marshal in 1877 and became the marshal the following year. When Ed was killed, Charlie Bassett became marshal and Wyatt became the assistant marshal.

7. He was born in Griffin, Georgia. The only record of his birth is his birthdate in the family bible.

8. Reformers were elected who said they wanted to do away with gambling, alcohol and prostitution.

9. Doc and Kate did not move to Tombstone until about September 1880.

10. Crawley P. Dake.

11. Statements like this are often quoted as examples of Wyatt exaggerating his importance. Though others will disagree, this seems out of character to me. Perhaps he was just trying to simplify a complicated situation. Wyatt did become deputy U.S. marshal. He took over the position after Virgil was ambushed and crippled on December 28, 1881. He also served briefly as deputy U.S. marshal in Tonopah, Nevada in 1902. It seems more likely that the *Examiner's* ghostwriter purposely or mistakenly substituted Wyatt's appointment for Virgil's.

12. Actually the mills were completed and began shipping ore in June 1879, a few months before Wyatt arrived, but the boom started about the time he arrived.

13. Tombstone reached a peak population of about 6,000 in the winter of 1882–1883.

14. Most of the outlaws initially lived in San Simon Valley. Then they moved to Galeyville and Charleston.

15. Wyatt wasn't deputy U.S. marshal at this time.

16. Ben Sippy was elected city marshal in January 1881 and resigned in June of 1881 at the insistence of the business community, who wanted the stronger Virgil Earp. Virgil served from June until October 29, 1881.

17. The Philpott-Roerig murders on March 15, 1881.

18. $3,600.

19. Marshall.

20. October 26, 1881.

21. Sic throughout this article.

22. Billy Claiborne. Tom McLaury was already in town. He had arrived the previous day with Ike. Ike may have telegraphed, but if so, it was probably to his brother Phin. Charleston is west of Tombstone, while Billy Clanton and Frank McLaury were east of town at Chandler's Milk Ranch. They were not responding to Ike's call, but just happened to arrive in town at this unfortunate moment.

23. They didn't actually send a message to the Earps, but several people did relay the threats to them.

24. The rustlers falsely accused Doc and Morgan of firing the first shots and some still claim this today. A detailed analysis of the fight shows this is extremely unlikely. At any rate, most of the rustlers claims are contradictory and easily disproven. Suffice it to say, if Doc did fire first, he would have had to have fired with his pistol first, then put his pistol away and switched to the shotgun he was carrying, and then go back to his pistol again. Hardly likely in the heat of such a fast paced battle. No, he fired the shotgun first, then cast it aside and pulled his revolver.

25. Ike didn't have a gun, so he couldn't have been shooting, and there's no evidence Billy Claiborne fired any shots.

26. Ike entered Fly's Lodging House from the front door on Fremont Street.

27. Ike did not shoot out of Fly's. He ran straight on through and out the backdoor. What Wyatt heard or saw was probably Billy Allen firing from the east side of Fly's around the corner from the front door.

28. Morgan tripped over a recently filled water line running down Fremont Street.

29. Billy Claiborne.

30. It was actually about half a minute.

31. They were arrested under a warrant sworn out by Billy the Kid Claiborne, who was at that time under indictment for murder in Charleston.

32. Ike refiled the charges in Contention on February 9, 1882. On the 14th, the Earps and Holliday appeared before Probate Judge J. H. Lucas—who was an eyewitness to the gunfight and had testified at the previous hearing. He issued a writ of habeas corpus barring further prosecution because the case had already been found to be without merit in the hearing and the grand jury refused to indict. He explained there couldn't be a second hearing unless new evidence was presented.

33. Two months later on December 28, 1881.

34. The period is missing here.
    Five shots were fired from three shotguns at a distance of about sixty feet. The next day the *Epitaph* said three men were seen fleeing the scene. Other witnesses said they saw five men running away, naming Frank Stilwell, Johnny Ringo, Ike Clanton, Hank Swilling and someone unknown. Wyatt wrote in a letter to Stuart Lake, "Virgil saw Stilwell go into the vacant building just as he was coming out of the Oriental….We found Ike Clanton's hat, that he dropped in getting away from the rear end of the building." Wyatt later said Virgil didn't tell anyone about seeing Stilwell at the time because he wanted to get him

himself. Stuart Lake wrote in notes apparently from one of his interviews with Wyatt that Swilling and Florentino Cruz were also involved, adding, "Wyatt started to round them up, hot on trail they came in to Tombstone and gave selves up. False alibis & acquitted. Later Florentino Cruz told of this just before Wyatt shot him."

35. In the May 27, 1882 *San Francisco Examiner* interview with Virgil, the interviewer said Virgil was wearing "a blue diagonal coat and vest, both the latter with bullet holes in them, bearing testimony of a recent fight when he was shot in the back, the bullet coming out at the front of the vest." One slug entered his back just to the left of his spine. His left arm was also hit by a shotgun blast that required six inches of bone be removed from his arm. Both Wyatt and George Parsons said Virgil could still use his arm and hand to some extent. By 1891 this arm had shortened by four inches.

36. Unless an outlaw was caught in the act, it was practically impossible to get a conviction in court because they would always produce a parade of witnesses to swear they were somewhere else at the time of the crime. There were no forensics or fingerprinting back then to help place the criminal at the scene of the crime. Even though Ike's hat was found at the scene of crime, this was just circumstantial evidence. Judge Stillwell released Ike and his brother Phin after some of their friends provided alibis. Wyatt said Stillwell privately told him, "Wyatt, you'll never clean up this crowd this way; next time you'd better leave your prisoners out in the brush where alibis don't count." And that's exactly what Wyatt began doing. He also realized that waiting for the outlaws to attack just made him a sitting duck and that he was better off striking first, or—as Earp biographer Casey Tefertiller put it—"to become the victor before he became the victim."

37. Actually, James accompanied Morgan's body to Colton on March 19, 1882. Morgan was shot on Saturday night the 18th. His body was shipped on Sunday—Wyatt's 34th birthday. Virgil, Allie and Wyatt were on Monday's train. Mattie and Bessie, the wives of Wyatt and James, didn't leave Tombstone until the following Friday the 24th. Morgan's wife, Lou, was already in California.

38. Stuart Lake's notes indicate Wyatt told him Hank Swilling and another man were also there. Virgil said Billy Miller and another man were there. It was still light out and Wyatt spotted Stilwell near the train, looking for a chance to murder another Earp. Stilwell and possibly the others headed up the track, either because he had been seen or to find a spot from which he could shoot at the train as it passed by. If Stilwell had others with him at this point, then they split up and Wyatt, Doc,

Sherm McMaster, and one other—probably Turkey Creek Jack—went after Stilwell.

39. McMaster wasn't killed during the Vendetta and did make it to Colorado with the Earps. So far I haven't found any record of when he died or the circumstances surrounding his death.

40. The *Epitaph* said this was Burleigh Springs, about eight miles south of Tombstone and around four miles east of Charleston, but this was probably disinformation to confuse Behan's posse. It actually took place at Iron Springs, which is 25 miles west of Tombstone. Many authors say this is the same as Mescal Springs, but there is apparently at least one map that shows them as two separate springs several miles apart.

Wyatt needed some money to keep his posse going, so he met with Charlie Smith and had him take a note to mine operator E. B. Gage requesting a $1,000 loan. Smith was to deliver the money to Wyatt at Iron Springs, but he was detained by one of Behan's deputies, so the task fell to Austrian immigrant Tony Kraker and "Whistling Dick" Wright.

Meanwhile, as the Earp party approached Iron Springs, Warren was left behind on the trail to wait for the messenger with the loan. Wyatt and the others continued to the spring and rode right into Curly Bill's ambush.

After the fight was over, Kraker and Wright rode into a camp at Iron Springs expecting to find Wyatt, but instead they found what remained of Curly Bill's men. The cowboys, unaware Kraker and Wright were carrying Wyatt's money, told them what happened and the two messengers returned to Tombstone without delivering their package.

41. Wells Fargo shotgun.

42. Stuart Lake's notes show that Wyatt told him he was sorry he fired both barrels, for if he had saved one, he could have gotten the rest before they made it to cover.

43. Fred Dodge, in a letter to Stuart Lake dated October 8, 1928, wrote, "Johnny Barnes, who was in the fight and was badly wounded, and was one of the Curly Bill party, told me that they opened up on the Earp party just as Wyatt Earp swung off his horse to the ground and they thought they had hit Wyatt but it was the horn of his saddle that was struck. That Wyatt Earp throwed [sic] down on Curley Bill right across his horse and killed him. That the Earp party made it so hot that all of the Curley Bill party that could, got away."

44. Actually, they tried to extradite Doc. This is covered in detail later in the book.

45. Holliday died on November 8, 1887, in the Hotel Glenwood in Glenwood Springs, Colorado. Doc was 36.

A view of the old O.K. Corral, where legend had it that Tom and Frank McLowery and Billy Clanton were shot, though the gunfight actually took place down the street in and around Harwood's Lumberyard.

# CHAPTER 6

## THE

## RESIGNATION

THREE MONTHS AFTER the gunfight and two months before Morgan's death, the Earps were getting tired of being the focus of controversy. They were doing well in Tombstone and didn't want to leave. For Wyatt, that would have seemed like running away.

The town was also tired of the controversy. With Sheriff Behan, the county officials, the outlaws, and their friends and supporters continually twisting facts, spreading lies and rumors, stirring up trouble, and doing everything in their power to make the Earps look bad, most people didn't know what to believe.

Even though the Earp examination was over and the Earps exonerated, tensions were still mounting. Virgil and Mayor Clum had been ambushed, the stage robberies continued, there was the death list, and rumors of a possible raid on the town.[1]

Tensions with Mexico were also high and there was a threat of war because of rustler depredations along the border. The Mexican government had taken steps to protect the border, so the outlaws were forced to focus more on stealing and robbing within Cochise County.

Most people in Tombstone didn't pay much attention to these and other factors causing the rise in crime, to them it seemed like it was all caused by the Earp-outlaw conflict. Many people also began to feel Wyatt's actions were motivated by revenge and personal interest over enforcement of the law and the good of the community. As a result, the election returns in early January 1882 were strongly in favor of the Democrat anti-Earp faction.[2]

In late January, U.S. Marshal Dake came to town under pressure from the state and federal governments to do something about the crime wave. He soon had three posses sweeping the countryside for outlaws.

Virgil hadn't been able to perform his duties since the assassination attempt and would still be bedridden for another month and a half, so Marshal Dake called a meeting to select someone to take Virgil's place. Both Wyatt and Virgil had badges at this point.[3] The new mayor, John Carr,[4] called a meeting to recommend a candidate for the position and they soon decided on a troublemaker and friend of the outlaws, Ben Maynard. When the citizens jokingly backed this up, Wyatt decided he'd had enough. He could deal with Behan's political maneuvering, but he wasn't about to risk his hide for a county that didn't want him. So on February 1, 1882, Wyatt decided to submit his resignation at the same time as Virgil. The following day, it was reprinted in both the *Epitaph* and the *Daily Nugget*.

It is reprinted here as it appeared in the *Nugget*.[5] The *Epitaph* printed it under the headline, "DRAW YOUR OWN INFERENCE/ Resignation of Virgil W. Earp and Wyatt S. Earp as Deputy

> ☞ "WHEN CATTLE ARE NOT handy the cowboys rob stages and engage in similar enterprises to raise money. As soon as they are in funds they ride into town, drink, gamble and fight. They spend their money as free as water in the saloons, dancehouses or faro banks, and this is one reason they have so many friends in town."
>
> —*Virgil Earp in an interview with the San Francisco Examiner, May 27, 1882*

Marshals." Since Virgil was still very close to death, it's possible this was written by Wyatt.[6] If not, he must have had a hand in it.

# RESIGNATION TENDERED

## A Joint Card from Wyatt and Virgil Earp.

The following card explains itself.

TOMBSTONE, February 1, 1882.

MAJOR C. P. DAKE, United States Marshal, Grand Hotel, Tombstone— DEAR SIR: In exercising our official functions as Deputy United States Marshals, in this Territory, we have endeavored always, unflinchingly to perform the duties intrusted[7] to us. These duties have been exacting and perilous in their character, having to be performed in a community where turbulence and violence could at almost any moment be organized to thwart and resist the enforcement[8] the processes of the courts issued to bring criminals to justice.

And while we have a deep sense of obligation to many of the citizens for their hearty cooperation in aiding us to suppress lawlessness, and their faith in our honesty of purpose, we realize that, notwithstanding our best efforts and judgment in everything which we have been required to perform, there has arisen so much harsh criticism in relation to our operations, and such a persistent effort having been made to misrepresent and misinterpret our acts, we are led to the conclusion that, in order to convince the public that it is our sincere purpose to promote the public welfare, independent of any

☞ "IN VIEW OF THE past history of the country and the generally believed existence at this time of desperate, reckless and lawless men in our midst, banded together for mutual support and living by felonious and predatory pursuits, regarding neither life nor property in their career, and at the same time for men to parade the street armed with repeating rifles and six-shooters and demand that the chief of police and his assistants should be disarmed is a proposition both monstrous and startling! This was said by one of the deceased [Frank McLaury] only a few minutes before the arrival of the Earps."

—*Casey Tefertiller*, Wyatt Earp: The Life Behind the Legend, *1997* personal emolument[9] or advantages to ourselves, it is our duty to place our resignations as Deputy United States Marshals in your hands, which we now do, thanking you for your continued courtesy and confidence in our integrity, and shall remain subject to your orders in the performance of any duties which may be assigned to us only until our successors are appointed.

Very Respectfully Yours,
VIRGIL W. EARP.
WYATT S. EARP.

While the *Nugget* published this without comment, the *Epitaph* added, "The document is a manly and generous one, and should meet with impartial criticism from the public. The position of deputy marshal on the frontier is no sinecure.[10] An officer who honestly tries to do his duty encounters many perils that the public know not of, and raises within the breasts of criminals that desire for their death that comes from fear of the gallows and imprisonment. It would be much out of place for a public journal, under the attendant circumstances, to endeavor to create public opinion upon these resignations, as to prejudge a case at court. It is sufficient that the matter is before the United States Marshal, who has had ample opportunity to investigate the condition of affairs, and who will give the subject that deliberate and careful consideration that comes of experience in official life."

The same day he submitted this resignation, Wyatt sent a message to Ike Clanton. According to the *Nugget*, Wyatt "wished to interview with him with a view of reconciling their differences and obliterating the animosity that now exists between them. Mr. Clanton most emphatically declined to hold any communication whatever with Earp."

The county's recommendation of Ben Maynard for Virgil's position was just that—a recommendation, and Marshal Dake chose to ignore it. He turned down Wyatt's resignation and appointed John Henry Jackson as the additional deputy U.S. marshal.

# References

1. On December 30, 1881, the *Epitaph* reprinted an article from the *Kansas City Star* which quoted Mrs. J. C. Collier as saying, "The Earps own the Oriental saloon and gambling rooms [sic, Wyatt just had part of the gambling concession], in which every night from 400 to 500 people congregate. The night before we left the cow-boys had organized a raid on this saloon. Fifteen or twenty cow-boys were heavily armed in the saloon. Just on the edge of town were thirty more and others were scattered around town ready to jump into the fight at the signal. A fire broke out and so rustled them that they gave it up for that time. You see we became intimately acquainted with a gentleman who boarded at the same hotel that we did, and who was in sympathy with the cow-boys, and acquainted with all their plans. He told us about this raid being in contemplation, and said that this was the second time they had been prepared to make a raid, and were thwarted by a fire breaking out and calling all the people out on the streets. He said: 'You are going away, and I don't mind telling you this.'"

   Then on March 30, 1882, George Parsons wrote in his journal, "Calky times, very. Fourteen murders and assassinations in ten days. More than one a day. A hanging bee anticipated tonight, but not carried out. Cowboy raid on town expected tonight. Things quiet thus far....A regular epidemic of murder is upon us."

2. In the previous election it was the Republicans who had ousted the Democrats from power.

3. Dake had a third deputy U.S. marshal in the area. That was Leslie Blackburn.

4. Initially Mayor Carr supported Wyatt and his posse, issuing the following statement:

   PROCLAMATION

   To the citizens of the city of Tombstone: I am informed by his Honor, William H. Stilwell [sic, Stillwell], Judge of the District Court of the First Judicial District, Cochise county, that Wyatt S. Earp, who left the city yesterday with a posse, was intrusted [sic] with warrants for the arrest of divers[e] persons charged with criminal offenses. I request the public within this city to abstain from any interference with the execution of said warrants.

   Dated January 24, 1882
   JOHN CARR, Mayor.

   But Mayor Carr was elected on the anti-Earp ticket and he was quickly brought into line. A few days later was quoted in the *Nugget* as suggesting the posse was just a cover to use several thousand dollars.

5. A facsimile reproduction of this article was kindly provided for inclusion in this book by Carl Chafin, editor of *The Private Journal of George Whitwell Parsons: The Tombstone Years 1879–1887*, Volumes I and II, Cochise Classics, Tombstone, 1997.

6. Some think this is too well written to be by Wyatt and suggest it might have been written by *Epitaph* editor John Clum, but his letters indicate he was capable of writing this resignation. Stuart Lake wrote in a letter to Burton Rascoe dated January 9, 1941, "Wyatt had an excellent background, was much better educated and read than most men of his time and place."

   When Wyatt resigned as deputy sheriff on November 9, 1880, his letter to Sheriff Shibell was much shorter, though not without humor. It said, "Sir, I have the honor herewith to resign the Office of Deputy Sheriff of Pima County. Respectfully &c., Wyatt S. Earp."

7. Sic.

8. The word "of" was left out here, but it appears in the *Epitaph*'s version.

9. Emolument: profit or compensation.

10. Sinecure: a position requiring little or no work.

Wyatt Earp, most likely in the mid-1870s, when he was a lawman in Wichita.

# CHAPTER 7

## THE DEATH OF CURLY BILL

A N INTERESTING ACCOUNT of the Vendetta and the Iron Springs shootout was printed eleven years after these events in the *Denver Republican* on May 14, 1893.[1] Here Wyatt provides some details that cannot be found elsewhere. But first they review the Earp-outlaw conflict.

# HE IS A DUDE NOW

## Wyatt Earp Formerly of Tombstone Spends a Day or Two Here.

---

He wears Tailor Made Clothes and Russet Shoes,
but There Was a Time When He Did Not—
Of Some of His Experiences While Engaged in Filling
a Private Graveyard He Tells a Coterie of Friends.

---

Wyatt Earp, a man whose trigger finger had considerable to do in making the border history of the West, was in Denver for several days last week. He is tall and athletic. His eyes are blue and fringed with light lashes and set beneath blonde eyebrows. His hair, which was once as yellow as gold, is beginning to be stranded with white.[2] A heavy, tawny mustache shades his firm mouth and sweeps—below his square, strong chin. He wore, while here, a neat gray tailor-made suit, immaculate linen and fashionable neck-wear. With a derby hat and a pair of tan shoes he was a figure to catch a lady's eye and to make the companions of his old, wild days at Tombstone and Dodge, who died with their boots on and their jeans pants tucked down them, turn in their graves.

But the country has changed materially since Tombstone was a booming mining camp and Dodge was the toughest town on the cattle trail from Texas. It is consequently no more than natural that Wyatt Earp's attire should have changed too as well as his associations and manner of life.

## FAST PASSING AWAY.

The men who shared his early dangers are mostly under the sod. Wild Bill is dead and gone, Ben Thompson too, Clay Allison, Doc Holliday and the rest who were making names and records for themselves, while Wyatt Earp was making his. Most of his enemies are dead, too. He attributes that fact to a steady eye and a sure gun which had the knack of going off at the right time.

He was once marshal of Dodge City for four years[3] and Bat Masterson served under him as deputy.[4] He and Masterson had many a hard passage at arms in those days with outlaws and desperadoes and murderous cowboys. But it was at Tombstone, Arizona, that Earp came into a national notoriety. He went there in 1881,[5] soon after leaving Dodge. The town was then in its palmiest period. It had sprung up like a mushroom with the discovery of precious mineral in the neighboring mountains. All the gamblers and toughs of the West had focused there. Its character was typical of the frontier. Every other house on the main streets was a saloon. Miners paid for their produce in gold dust as in the days of '49.[6] The lumbering mule stages which connected the town with the outskirts of civilization were robbed at nearly every trip.[7] The clinking of ivory chips upon the layouts made continual music night and day. The crack of revolvers added frequent staccato passages by way of variation.

James Cooksey Earp in 1881 at about the age of 40.

## THE EARP TRIUMVIRATE.

Earp was appointed a United States marshal soon after his arrival there.[8] His brother, Virgil Earp, was already town marshal.[9] Morgan Earp, another brother lived there.

Virgil Earp in 1887 at
about the age of 44.

Morgan Earp in 1881 at
about the age of 30.

This fraternal triumvirate did a great deal to make the name of Tombstone quite an appropriate one.

A band of thieves and cattle rustlers infested that country then. They were led by a develishly[10] bloodthirsty and desperate cutthroat named Curly Bill. He had got about him a crew of congenial thieves as reckless and murderous as he.[11] They were outlaws as reckless and murderous as he. They were outlaws even in that lawless country. They had their haunts in the fastnesses[12] of the mountains, whence they swooped down upon the fat beeves[13] of the ranges and ran them off to the markets of Tucson and Prescott. They came into Tombstone and other towns to squander their booty in wild carousels and licentiousness and no one dared to molest them. They held up the Tombstone stage whenever they were so inclined, and many a lonely traveler went down before their rifles that his purse and effects might become spoil for his murderers.

By their bold and open stand against the high-handed terrorism and rule of these brigands, the Earp brothers incurred their hatred. The better element of the community was on the side of the Earps.

## IKE CLANTON'S DRUNK.

A war upon the rustlers began. The Earps led it. It lasted in all five months. At the end of that time the country about Tombstone was as quiet and safe as the most peaceful section of New England. The rustlers were either dead, in the penitentiary or run out of the territory.

There was a faction of men in Tombstone who were secret friends of Curly Bill's outlaws. They sent them word when the stages would be most heavily loaded with treasure. They gave the robbers notice of the departure of this rich traveler or that, whose wealth might be had for a little sharp work and a little blood, perhaps. They aided and abetted the desperadoes and shared their plunder. Ike and Billy Clanton were the leaders of this faction.

One summer day of 1881,[14] Ike Clanton came into Tombstone and got drunk. Virgil Earp, the town marshal, arrested him, took his pistol away from him and had him fined $25. Clanton sent immediately to summon his feudsmen to his aid.

## CHALLENGE AND RESPONSE.

Toward evening four of them rode into town in answer.[15] They were Billy Clanton, Tom and Frank McLowris[16] and one who went by the peculiarly Western cognomen of Billy the Kid, although he was not that picturesque New Mexican character—rest his soul—who suddenly died one evening

☞ "IT WAS OUR BOYS who killed Stilwell. Before Stilwell died he confessed that he killed Morg, and gave the names of those who were implicated with him. When my brothers were leaving Arizona, they got dispatches from Tucson saying that Stilwell and a party of friends were watching all the railroad trains passing that way, and were going through them in search of all Earps and their friends, carrying short shotguns under their overcoats and promising to kill on sight. Our boys were bound to look our for themselves, and when they got near Tucson were very cautious. They found Stilwell near the track and killed him."

—*Virgil Earp in a May 27, 1882 interview with the* San Francisco Examiner after putting the question *"Quien es?"* to Sheriff Pat Garrett of Santa Fe, and receiving the answer not [in] Spanish, but in lead.

When his partners had assembled Ike Clanton marched them to a little open lot and from there sent word to Virgil Earp to come out and fight or else take chances on being waylaid and murdered at the first opportunity. And Virgil—.

But Wyatt Earp told the story the other night as he lounged against the bar at Austin's exchange and pulled reminiscently at a Metropole.

"Virgil came to me," he said, "and asked me what we'd better do, I told him I thought we should arrest the gang or kill them. So we called Morgan Earp and Doc Halliday[17] in to help us, and started for the lot. A hundred citizens offered to take a hand, but we did not care to have their aid.

## THE PLAY, AND MORGAN'S DEATH.

"When we reached the lot, the Clantons with their men were there ready. We filed in along the side of the building, and then stopped and faced them. We were four to five, 'I have come to put you under arrest,' said Virgil. At that Clanton's men, everyone with a six-shooter in each hand, began to fire.[18] The fight lasted until both sides had emptied their revolvers. When the smoke cleared, Tom and Frank McLowrie and Billy Clanton were dead on the ground.[19] The other two[20] had taken to their heels and got away.

"After this killing of their friends the rustlers started in to take revenge upon us. One night, while I was watching my brother Morgan play a game at billiards, a shot was fired through a window. It struck Morgan in the back and he fell over into my arms and died. I learned the names of the men who had brought about his death. Frank Stillwell[22] was the man who killed him, and there

☞ THE TRIAL OF THOSE indicted for Morgan's murder turned out pretty much as anticipated. On April 3, 1882, the *Epitaph* reported, "The case of the Territory vs. Pete Spence,[21] charged with the murder of Morgan Earp, was completed in the police court this afternoon. The prosecution asked for Mrs. Spence as a witness this morning, but the defendant objected, where upon the prosecution refused to proceed further with the case, and the court accordingly ordered the discharge of the prisoner. The same testimony was brought against Frank Bodie [Fritz Bode], who was charged with the same offense, and the court also ordered his dismissal."

☞ WHEN JOHNNY RINGO WAS 14, he witnessed his father's accidental death. This had a profound influence on the rest of the life. One eyewitness, W. Davidson, wrote in a letter that made its way into the Missouri newspaper, *Liberty Tribune*, on August 26 and September 16, 1864, "Just after daylight on the morning of the 30th July Mr. Ringo stepped outof the wagons as, I suppose, for the purpose of looking around to see if Indians were in sight and his shotgun went off accidentally in his own hands, the load entering at his right eye and coming out at the top of his head. At the report of his gun I saw his hat blown up 20 feet in the air and his brains were scattered in all directions. I never saw a more heartrending sight, and to see the distress and agony of his wife and children was painful in the extreme. Mr. Ringo's death cast a gloom over the whole company."

Writing of Ringo in a letter to Anton Mazzanovich, Big Nose Kate said he was "a fine man anyway you took him. Physically, intellectually, morally. His attitude toward all women was gentlemanly. He must have been a gentleman born. Sometimes I noticed something wistful about him, as if his thoughts were far away on something sad. He would say, 'Oh, well,' and sigh. Then he would smile, but his smiles were always sad. There was something in his life that only he, himself, knew about."

were with him Curly Bill, Apache Hank, Florentino (a Mexican), and Jack Ringo,[23] and all of them were rustlers.

"After I had shipped my dead brother's body to our home at Colton, California, I went to Virgil, who was in bed from a wound he had got in the Clanton fight.[24]

## A QUIET RESOLUTION.

"'Now, Virgil,' I said to him, 'I want you to go home. I am going to try to get those men who killed Morgan, and I can't look after you and them too. So you go home.'"

Wyatt Earp told this part of his thrilling story very simply. He had not sworn a solemn oath of vengeance over his brother's dead body, as a hero of fiction would most undoubtedly have done. He had merely formed a quiet determination. But that cool resolve was carried out with an invincible and merciless purpose. No melodramatic touches for effect's sake could have made its accomplishment bloodier or more complete.

"Virgil agreed to go," he continued, "and I went with him as far as Tucson. When I got off there a friend of mine told me that Ike Clanton and Frank Stillwell were in town and expected me. I thanked him and set out to find them. I came on them across the railroad track as it was coming on dusk. Both of them began to shoot at me.[25] I had a shotgun.

## SHOT HIM ALL TO PIECES.

"I ran straight for Stillwell. It was he who killed my brother. What a coward he was! He couldn't shoot when I came near him. He stood there helpless and trembling for his life. As I rushed upon him he put out his hands and clutched at my shotgun. I let go both barrels,[26] and he tumbled down dead and mangled at my feet. I started for Clanton then, but he escaped behind a moving train of cars.[27] When the train had passed I could not find him.[28]

"I went back to Tombstone and went to my room. The sheriff was my enemy. I knew he would try to arrest me, and I made up my mind I would not surrender myself. If I gave myself up I should have been compelled to lie in jail for a time and during my imprisonment my brother's murderers, I feared, might elude me. The sheriff called on me to surrender, and I told him I would not do it. He assembled a posse about the door of my room to take me, but I walked through the men, and none of them offered to lay a hand upon me.

"With a younger brother of mine, Doc Holliday and the others, I set out on horseback for a ranch, where I knew Apache Hank was staying. When we rode away from that ranch, Apache Hank was dead.[29] Florentino, the Mexican, we found a few days afterward and left stretched in his tracks.[30] I never succeeded in finding Ringo. He got out of the country and was killed by somebody else.[31]

## WITH CURLY BILL.

"My adventure with Curly Bill came near ending disastrously for me. With Holliday and the rest of the party, I headed for a spring in the Whetstone mountains. We proposed to rest by its waters for a few day. As we approached it in the afternoon, Curly Bill and eight of his men rose up from behind an embankment some fifteen yards ahead of us. As they rose they fired. I jumped off my horse in a jiffy, holding him by the bridle thrown over my arm. I expected Holliday and my companions to do the same thing and make a fight. I was surprised when I looked around to see them disappearing in a cloud of dust as fast as their horses could carry them. My horse reared and tugged at the bridle in such wild fashion that I could not regain the saddle, I reckoned that my time had come. But if I was to die, I proposed that Curly Bill at least should die with me.

## EXIT BILL OF THE CURLS.

"He churned several shots at me from his Winchester,[32] but he fired rapidly and his bullets went wide. I threw my shotgun to my shoulder and fixing a bead directly on his heart, turned loose both barrels. His chest was torn open by the big charge of buckshot. He yelled like a demon as he went down.

"His death struck a panic into the rest. They turned and ran for their lives and took shelter behind a clump of willows beyond the spring. I knew it would be useless for me to stand there in the open and fight eight men who were screened from my view, I backed away, using my horse's body as a bulwark against the flying lead, and firing as I withdrew. When I had got a hundred yards or so away I mounted. But I swore then that that cowardly crowd should not make me run and I walked my horse half a mile further, with Winchester bullets singing all the way thick about my ears.

"When I joined my companions Holliday came up to me and caught me gently by the arm, 'I'll help you from your horse, Wyatt,' he said, 'You must be shot all to pieces.' 'No,' I answered, 'I'm not touched.'

## SOMETHING HAD TO SUFFER.

"I told the truth, but when I got to the ground, I found that the skirts of my coat, which had been held out at my sides by my leather holsters, had been riddled into shreds. That was the closet call I ever had and how I came out alive is more than I can ever guess. Holliday and the rest, when I had told my story, wanted to charge back upon the outlaws. But for my part, I had had enough for one day. 'If you fellows are hungry for a fight you can go on and get your fill,' I said and turned my horse's head in the other direction. I had got Curly Bill and I was satisfied."[33]

Wyatt Earp's saloon.

Earp left Tombstone in 1882. For several years he ran palatial bars and gambling houses in Los Angeles and San Diego. At present his home is in San Francisco.

### IN HORSE BUSINESS NOW.

He is interested with Louis Rickabaugh[34] in a fine stable of running horses. The string passed through Denver last week bound for St. Louis. The horses were rested at Overland park for a few days. The lot includes such good performers as Lottie Mills, Pescador, Misty Morn, Rosebud and Geraldine, the famous filly about which Porter

Ashe has had so much trouble at law in California. The horses will be started at St. Louis and Chicago, and then in the fall will go back to the coast for a season of winter racing at the Bay district tracks at San Francisco.

Wyatt Earp left Denver for St. Louis last night. His brother Virgil is living at Colton, a pleasant California town in the San Bernardino valley. For a number of years he was marshal there, but is now comfortably retired.[35] Doc Holliday, the fighting Texan,[36] whose life was so intimately associated with the fortunes of the Earps, died several years ago.[37] The end of his remarkable and trou-blous career came naturally. His peaceful close was a surprise to his friends, any one of whom would have made books that he would die fighting and in his boots.

# References

1. A facsimile reproduction of this article was kindly provided for inclusion in this book by Emma Walling, author of *John "Doc" Holliday: Colorado Trials and Triumphs* (n.d.).

2. Wyatt was 45 at this time.

3. He was deputy and assistant marshal, but not for that entire period.

4. If he did, it was for a very short period. There is no record of it.

5. Sic, 1879.

6. Not true. There was little gold there and the mining companies got it, not the miners.

7. An exaggeration.

8. He was appointed deputy U.S. marshal about two years after his arrival there.

9. Virgil became city marshal the first time almost a year after his arrival. He became deputy U.S. marshal before arriving in Tombstone.

10. Sic.

11. Galeyville hotel manager Tom Thornton told the *San Francisco Examiner*, "The cowboys have no chief, nor do they run in gangs, as it generally supposed. Curly Bill...has no gang, and since his last partner shot him...Bill don't take well to partners. No, sir, the 'cowboys' don't herd together in droves, but come and go about their own personal business wherever they desire to go." (March 23, 1882)

The outlaws were a loosely formed dynamic group. Even if Curly Bill didn't head an actual gang, he did have a lot of outlaws who looked up to him and would do just about anything he asked of them.

12. Sic.

13. Beeves: the plural of beef.

14. October 26, 1881.

15. Tom was already in town. Billy and Frank arrived in town around 1 P.M. They did not receive a message from Ike. If Ike sent a message, he probably sent it to his brother Phin.

16. Sic.

17. Sic throughout this article.

18. An exaggeration. They each, except for Ike, had one pistol. It's unknown whether Billy Claiborne was armed.

19. Billy lasted about 40 minutes.

20. Ike and Billy Claiborne.

21. The case was against Spence, Stilwell, Swilling, Indian Charley, and 33-year-old German immigrant Frederick "Fritz" Bode. These men were charged because Pete Spence's wife, Maria, implicated them in a sworn statement that was presented at the coroner's inquest. Wyatt wrote to Walter Noble Burns on March 15, 1927, "I am satisfied that Spence had nothing to do with the assassination of Morgan, although he was against us."

22. Stilwell.

23. "Apache Hank" Swilling, Florentino Cruz (who may have been known as "Indian Charley"), and Johnny Ringo.

24. An ambush. Virgil didn't have a chance to fight back.

25. This is doubtful.

26. This is not accurate. One shotgun blast hit Stilwell in the thigh and the other in the chest.

27. The train Virgil was on.

28. As Pima County Sheriff Bob Paul described it in a March 3, 1898 interview in the *Tombstone Prospector*, "While the train was standing in Tucson, Frank Stilwell was seen standing on a gravel car peeking in the window of the car that Virgil was in. Wyatt Earp and the balance of the escort started after him, overtook him and killed him. The train pulled out before the shooting was over."

This happened at about 7:15 P.M. on March 20, 1882, but the body wasn't discovered until the next morning. The shots were heard, but residents thought it was just someone celebrating the town's new gaslights. One witness said he heard cheering after the shots were fired. Others said it was a scream.

When Wyatt wrote this article there was still a chance he might be arrested for this murder, so he probably worded it so he could claim it was an accident if he had to do so. According to the March 21, 1882, *Arizona Daily Citizen*:

"One load of seven buckshot had entered the left breast and ranging downward, had passed out the back. A bullet, evidently that of a pistol or rifle, had passed through the fleshy part of the left arm and entered the body just below the armpit, and passing directly through, came out in line of entrance under the right arm into which it lodged. Another load of 11 buckshot had shattered the left leg above the knee and one bullet had gone through and into the calf of the left leg, while still another bullet, evidently a downward shot, entered the right leg above the knee, passed through, and into the calf of the left leg."

The shotgun blast to the chest was fired at point blank range and the palm of Stilwell's hand was blackened and burned by powder. It makes more sense that he was shot in the legs first, perhaps to make him talk, and then in the chest, though the witnesses said the shots were fired in two groups, but fairly close together.

Stilwell was in Tucson for his trial for robbing the Bisbee stage on September 8, 1881. He and Pete Spence had been arrested for this by Wyatt and Morgan, but after producing alibi witnesses, Judge Spicer released them for insufficient evidence, so the Earps later brought a federal charge against them which required them to appear in Tucson. Stilwell and Spence were arrested again for the October 8th holdup of a stage near Charleston. That time they were arrested by Wyatt and Virgil.

29. I have yet to find out what happened to Hank Swilling.

30. Simon Acosta, a worker at Spence's camp, said in Spanish, "I immediately ran up the hill and saw them shooting at Florentino. I did not see Florentino fall; I saw them following up the hill and firing at him. I did not pay attention to the number of shots fired. They stayed on the top of the hill awhile, dismounted, and soon after went off…When I saw Florentino, he was running away. The pursuing party spread out, some on each side, and others immediately following."

Another eyewitness who did see him fall said Florentino was jumping from side to side as he ran.

31. Johnny Ringo's body was found near Turkey Creek on July 14, 1882—three months after Curly Bill was killed. The coroner's jury decided it was suicide, but the coroner wasn't convinced and, since he never saw the body, he listed, "Cause of death unknown but supposed gunshot wound." Ringo's body was found sitting against a tree. The juror's report said, "There was a bullet hole in the right temple, the bullet coming out on the top of the head on the left side. There is apparently a part of the scalp gone including a small portion of the forehead and part of the hair, this looks as if cut out by a knife." If he was partially scalped, it's doubtful he killed himself.

Some have suggested Frank Leslie was hired by Wells, Fargo & Company to kill Ringo, but Fred Dodge says he saw Leslie about the time of Ringo's death and insists he couldn't have done it. Dodge thought John "Johnny-Behind-the-Deuce" Roarke did it and that Pony Deal then killed him in revenge. Others think rancher Henry Hooker had Lou Cooley do it. It's also possible William Downing did it because he believed Ringo stole a couple of his mules and was fooling around with his 20-year-old daughter. He might have shot him in Pine (Pinery) Canyon and hauled the body to Turkey Creek so he wouldn't be implicated. Whatever happened, it's interesting that a month before he was killed, Ringo was living with Sheriff Behan. Ringo was 32 when he died.

32. Or Wells, Fargo shotgun.

33. Wyatt had come a long way since he had testified in Curly Bill's favor at hearing on the death of Marshal Fred White fifteen months earlier.

34. This is the same Lou Rickabaugh from Tombstone who was one of Wyatt's partners in the Oriental Saloon gambling concession.

35. Virgil did not retire. He continued to work in farming, mining, police-related work, and as a saloonkeeper.

36. Georgian.

37. November 8, 1887.

# CHAPTER 8

## THE VENDETTA

O N APRIL 5, 1882, the *Tombstone Epitaph* printed a letter it had received that may have been from the Earp party. The Earp party consisted of Wyatt, Doc, Warren (the youngest of the Earps), Sherm McMaster, and Turkey Creek Jack Johnson. If one of them wrote this letter, it was probably Wyatt.

# THE EARP PARTY

## Journal of Their Adventures and Wanderings

The following letter was received today written upon detached leaves from an account book, and post-marked Wilcox.[1] It may be genuine and may not be; each reader may judge for himself.[2]

IN CAMP, APRIL 4, 1882

Editor Epitaph:—In reply to the article in the Nugget of March 31, relating to the Earp party and some of the citizens of Graham and Cochise counties I would like to give you the facts in this case concerning our trip in Cochise and Graham counties. Leaving Tombstone Saturday evening, March 25.

### WE WENT INTO CAMP

six miles north of town. Next morning we were overtaken by six prospectors on their way from Tombstone to Winchester district who asked us to partake of their frugal meal, which we ate with relish, after which we travelled in company with them on the main road to Summit station, where we had dinner and awaited the arrival of the passenger train from the west, expecting

☞ "BEHAN'S POSSE BECAME ONE of the true oddities of the bizarre conflict. Backed by deputies Ringo, Fin Clanton, and other members of the cowboy-outlaw crowd, the sheriff rode out to pursue the U.S. marshals band of Wyatt and Warren Earp, the trouble maker Doc Holliday, suspected thief Sherm McMasters, and the other shady characters. It is no wonder many Arizonans would view the situation as one band of crooks against another."

*—Casey Tefertiller*, Wyatt Earp: The Life Behind the Legend, *1997*

☞ EXCERPTS FROM *The Private Journal of George Whitwell Parsons* (edited by Carl Chafin):

WEDNESDAY, MARCH 22, 1882: Excitement again this morning. Sheriff [Behan] went out with a posse supposably [*sic*] to arrest the Earp party, but they will never do it. The cowboy element is backing him strongly, John Ringo being one of the party. There is a prospect of a bad time, and there are about three men who deserve to get it in the back of the neck.

THURSDAY, MARCH 23, 1882: More killing by the Earp party. Hope they'll keep it up. [Sheriff Bob] Paul is here, but will not take a hand. He is a true, brave man himself and will not join the murderous posse here. If the truth were known, he would be glad to see the Earp party get away with all of these murderous outfits. "Tip" [Dan Tipton] and [Charlie] Smith arrested this evening,[3] while entering town. Much excitement. False charges. Behan will get it yet.

FRIDAY, MARCH 24, 1882: Mileage still counting up for our rascally sheriff. He organizes posses, goes to within a mile of his prey and then returns. He's a good one.

SATURDAY, MARCH 25, 1882: Rumors of a battle and four of Earp party killed received this A.M. Discredited. I got strictly private news though later that 'Curly Bill' has been killed at last by the Earp party and none of the latter hurt. Sheriff Behan has turned all the cowboys loose against the Earps and with this lawless element is trying to do his worst. I am heartily glad at this repulse and hope the killing is not stopped with the cutthroat named. Feeling here is growing against the ring [i.e. the county officials], sheriff, etc., and it would not surprise me to know of a necktie party some fine morning.

MONDAY, MARCH 27, 1882: Some long and continued firing right by house Saturday evening so that the whistling bullets were heard is now accounted for. It was signalling going on between the Earps' friends and themselves undoubtedly. I went out several times to see what was up. Discovered nothing. Cowboys could be seen yesterday morning trailing on mesa north of house. They had tracked the Earps that far. Lively time this.

## A FRIENDLY MESSENGER.

From here we continued our journey on the wagon road to Henderson's ranch where we had refreshments for ourselves and horses. Here we were informed that a gentlemanly deputy sheriff of Cochise county, Mr. Frank Hereford (for whom we have the greatest respect as a gentleman and officer) was at the ranch at the time of our arrival and departure and have since learned the reason for not presenting himself was fears for his safety, which we assure him were groundless. Leaving this ranch we went into camp in good grass one mile north. At seven next morning we saddled and went north to

## MR. H. C. HOOKER'S RANCH

in Graham county where we met Mr. Hooker and asked for refreshments for ourselves and stock, which he kindly granted us with the same hospitality that was tendered us by the ranchers of Cochise County. As regards to Mr. Hooker outfitting us with supplies and fresh horses as was mentioned in the *Nugget*, it is false and without foundation, as we are riding the same horses we left Tombstone on,

## FIGHT WITH CURLY BILL

☞ BEHAN AND HIS POSSE arrived at Hooker's ranch on March 28, 1882–the morning after Wyatt's posse was there. According to the *Epitaph*, "Sheriff Behan asked Mr. Hooker if he knew the whereabouts of the Earp party. Mr. Hooker replied that he did not know and that if he did he would not tell him. Sheriff Behan then said, 'You must be upholding murderers and outlaws, then.' Hooker said, 'No sir, I am not; I know the Earps and I know you and I know they have always treated me like gentlemen; damn such laws and damn you, and damn your posse; they are a set of horse thieves and outlaws.'"

and posse,[4] which we replaced by hiring a horse on the San Pedro river. In regard to the reward paid by Stock Association which the *Nugget* claims Mr. Hooker paid to Wyatt Earp for the killing of Curly Bill, it is also false as no reward has been asked for or tendered.

Leaving Hooker's ranch on the evening of that day we journeyed north to within five miles of Eureka Springs. There we camped with a freighter and was cheerfully offered the best his camp afforded. Next morning, not being in a hurry to break camp, our stay was long enough to notice the

## MOVEMENTS OF SHERIFF BEHAN

and his posse of honest ranchers,[5] with whom, if they had possessed the trailing abilities of an average Arizona ranchman, we might have had trouble, which we are not seeking. Neither are we avoiding these honest ranchers as we thoroughly understand their designs.

At Cottonwood we remained overnight and here picked up the trail of the

## LOST CHARLEY ROSS[6]

"and a hot one." We are confident that our trailing abilities will soon enable us to turn over to the "gentlemen"[7] the fruits of our efforts so that they may not again return to Tombstone empty-handed.

Yours respectfully,

ONE OF THEM.

The Earp party camped on a hill three miles from Hooker's ranch and waited for Behan's posse to come for them. Henry Hooker had told Wyatt that he and his men could wait at his ranch, but Wyatt didn't want to involve him in a battle. From the hill they watched Behan's men come and go, but Behan's men never headed in their direction. Hooker wrote in his unpublished memoirs that even though he eventually told Behan where the Earp party was, Behan's men were "willing to ride in any direction in Arizona except where [the Earps] were waiting for them."

Finally Behan and his men returned to Tombstone, where Behan presented the country with a bill for, as Earp biographer Casey Tefertiller put it, "a whopping $2,593.65, to pay for Ringo and the cowboys to ramble around the Arizona backcountry avoiding the Earps."

After Behan was gone, the Earp party returned to Hooker's ranch and spent a few more days there, during which time the money that was supposed to have been delivered to them at Iron Springs arrived, plus an additional $1,000 from Wells, Fargo & Company. They then continued with their search for outlaws.

# References

1. Willcox, Arizona.

2. They may have said this so the letter couldn't be used against them in court.

3. This happened right before Charlie Smith met with Wyatt and took Wyatt's message to E. B. Gage requesting the $1,000 loan.

4. Curly Bill and his men may have been part of Behan's posse. Curly Bill claimed they were and the *Nugget* referred to him as a deputy, but Behan later denied it. If they were, then the Iron Springs gunfight was between a deputy U.S. marshal's posse and a county sheriff's posse.

5. This is a sarcastic reference to the cowboys, who were described this way in the *Nugget*.

6. This sounds like a touch of Doc Holliday's sense of humor and has caused some to suspect this note was written by him. Charley Ross was a 4-year-old child who was kidnapped in Philadelphia in 1874. This was considered the first kidnapping for money in the United States. The kidnapper was cornered and killed. The child was never found. It was a major news story for years and new leads in the case continually surfaced, but invariably turned out to be false.

7. Behan's posse.

# CHAPTER 9

## LEAVING ARIZONA

FTER CURLY BILL'S DEATH, the Wyatt's posse searched for a couple more weeks with minimal results, though they may have had some other skirmishes and Warren apparently received a leg wound. Of the outlaws that weren't part of Behan's posses, some had fled to safer habitats, and others were laying low.

Wyatt finally decided it was probably best to leave Arizona to avoid being tried for murder or exposed to assassination, so they set off for New Mexico. A few details of their movements at this time appeared in the May 13, 1882 *Albuquerque Evening Review*. On arriving in Albuquerque, New Mexico, Wyatt gave interviews to the two papers there on the condition they didn't reveal the Earp party was in town until after they were well on their way. The *Review* waited until rumors of Wyatt's death appeared a month later before they published their interview. Unfortunately, they didn't quote Wyatt directly in their article.

# DOWNED AT LAST

## Wyatt Earp Killed Near Hooker's, Arizona

On the fifteenth of last month a party arrived in Albuquerque on the Atlantic & Pacific train,[1] whose appearance in the city speedily[2] became known among the rounders and talked about. They were the men of whose deeds the whole of Arizona was ringing, the Earp boys, as they were all together spoken of. During the month before there had been hardly a day during which a cocked revolver had not been leveled at some one, seven dead cow-boys[3] bearing witness to the accuracy of their aim. The whole story of the fights between them and their enemies is too well know to require a repetition here. They had fought well and bitterly, taking two lives for each one they lost,[4] until the law grasped them and indictment after indictment began to be found against them. Then they left Arizona and came to Albuquerque. The party as they came here was composed of Wyatt Earp, Warren Earp, "Doc" or John

> ☞ ON HEARING OF CURLY BILL'S death, the *San Francisco Exchange* said on March 27, 1882, "This makes the fourth [sic, sixth[5]] the Earp party has scored to the cowboys' one. We are beginning to doubt the courage and invincibility of that much-talked-of class, and are willing to give long odds on the murderous superiority of the Earp crowd."

Holliday, Sherman McMaster's,[6] James Johnson, John Tipton[7] and Jack Vermillion—seven, in all.

On the morning after their arrival, and before more than one or two knew of their presence, Wyatt Earp called at the Review and Journal offices, and had an interview with reporters of both papers. He stated that they had come to Albuquerque to escape persecution while awaiting the result of an effort being made by Governor Tritle to secure their pardon from the president; that they were then being sought by their foes, and that they would not given themselves up to the Arizona officers without resistance. In view of these facts, Earp requested of both papers that their temporary sojourn in Albuquerque should remain unnoticed until they could be assured that the knowledge of their whereabouts would not bring a party of cow-boy avengers down upon them. To back his assertions regarding Governor Tritle's feelings toward them, Earp presented The Review several convincing documents, and his request was accordingly granted by this paper, as it was by the Journal.

The party remained in Albuquerque for a week or more, their identity being well known to fifty people or more, leaving the city nearly two weeks ago. During their stay here "Doc" Holliday and Wyatt Earp quarreled,[8] and when Albuquerque was left the party disbanded, Holliday going with Tipton.

Notwithstanding the fact that the newspapers did not speak of their arrival here, it became known in Arizona and Tombstone supplied a party of man-hunters, who, it appears from Arizona papers received this morning at last found their prey. The Epitaph gives an account of the killing of Wyatt Earp near Hooker's, Arizona, last Monday, but a party which ambushed and attacked him, while the Citizen indorses the news, adding the statement that Tipton was killed last week while with Doc Holliday.[10] No particulars are published of the killing as both papers received their information through private sources. Wyatt met his death while returning from a visit to his wounded brother, at Colton, California, who had but the

☞ "WYATT EARP, THE FORMER Las Vegas slumgullion,[9] got his stomach full of buckshot at Tombstone three or four days ago, and has been planted for worm feed."

—*A Las Vegas newspaper following the attempted murder of Virgil* week before assured a citizen of Tombstone that all of them would, as soon as he was well, return to Arizona and stand trial on the charges preferred against them.[11]

The party, while in Albuquerque, deported themselves very sensibly, performing no acts of rowdyism, and this way gained not a few friends for their side of the fight. It appears that in Tombstone a general feeling of regret that instead of these last two murders the party were not tried fairly in open court prevails.

# References

1. The Earp party arrived in Silver City, New Mexico, on April 15, 1882. After spending the night at someone's house so they wouldn't have to register in a hotel, they took the stage to Deming and then the train to Albuquerque.

2. Sic.

3. They might be including Johnny Barnes, who may have died from wounds received at the Iron Springs gunfight, or perhaps Apache Hank Swilling.

4. Seven for the one they lost.

5. A probable seventh, Johnny Barnes, died a week later—possibly from wounds received in the Iron Springs shootout.

6. Sic.

7. John Johnson and Dan Tipton.

8. The cause of the quarrel is unclear, but it appears to have been the result of some drunken indiscretions by Doc. It wasn't very serious, because they did get together again in mid-June 1882 for a couple of weeks in Gunnison, Colorado.

9. Slumgullion: refuse from processing fish or whales. Also, the muddy deposit from mining sluices.

10. Neither report was true. This wasn't the only time Wyatt's demise was reported prematurely. On November 27, 1880, a skeptical *Dodge City Times* quoted the *Caldwell Commercial* as saying, "It is reported that Wyatt Earp, at one time a policeman at Wichita, but more recently of Dodge City, was shot and killed on Sand Creek, Colorado, by Jas. Kennedy [sic, Kenedy], of Texas, a week or two ago." Then on March 12, 1922 the *Los Angeles Times* reported, "Wyatt Earp located at [i.e. relocated to] Colton where he was killed."

11. Wyatt did not go to Colton for several years. At this time he was camped just outside of Gunnison, Colorado.

CHAPTER 10

# AFTERMATH

ROM ALBUQUERQUE, DOC and Dan Tipton found their way to Pueblo, Colorado. The day after the *Albuquerque Evening Review* article mentioning Dan's death was published, they proceeded on to Denver to see the horse races at the Denver Fair Grounds. On the following day—May 15, 1882—Doc was arrested for murder. This stirred up a whole hornet's nest and Doc suddenly found himself thrust in the limelight. That situation is discussed in more detail later in this book.

Leaving Albuquerque, Wyatt, Warren, Sherm, Turkey Creek Jack, and Texas Jack went on to Trinidad, Colorado, where Bat Masterson was city marshal. After a few days there, Sherm and Turkey Creek Jack went their own way. Wyatt, Warren, and Texas Jack set up a camp near the river just outside of Gunnison, Colorado. At first they were very cautious when they entered town, but soon it was clear they weren't going to have any trouble and Wyatt began dealing faro in one of the saloons there.

On one of their excursions into town, Wyatt and Warren were interviewed by the *Gunnison Daily News-Democrat*. The resulting article appeared on June 4, 1882.[1]

# THE EARP BROTHERS

## A Reporter Corners These Dread Enemies of the Arizona Cowboys and Makes Them Talk.

---

### Wyatt and Warren Earp Living a Quiet Life in Gunnison Preparatory to Returning to Tombstone.

---

"Do you see that man standing over there?" said a well known business man to a News-Democrat reporter yesterday, pointing to a rather tall, well-dressed, pleasant looking stranger who stood leaning against the counter, tapping his boot with his cane, while he remained a silent listener to the conversation that was going on around him. "If you want an item, tackle him. If you can get him to talk he can give 'em to you—dead oodles of 'em."

"Who is he!" asked the reporter, his curiosity somewhat aroused.

"That's Wyatt Earp, from Arizona; and there's his brother Warren, 'The Tiger' they call him,[2] sitting over there. They don't look like bold, bad men, do they? Well, they're not; but you bet your life they've got the 'sand.'[3] I've known 'em a long time now, and I'd just like you to tackle 'em once. The 'Tiger' is a good one. He's a 'square' man, but he will fight when necessary, and you just ought to see him turn himself loose. He'll just grab his two six-shooters and shut his eyes and wade in. He's a holy terror when he gets started. Wyatt is the general of the party, but the 'Tiger' is generally on hand when there's any fighting to be done.'"[4]

"What are they doing here?" asked the reporter.

"Wyatt is a Deputy United States Marshal and is here on business partly, and then Tombstone got too hot for them just now. You see, there's a big crowd of 'cowboys' out there that the Earp crowd has been fighting, and six of the 'cowboys' got killed within the last few months. Doc Holladay[5] is a friend of the Earps and was with them in their fights, and that is why some of the people in Arizona were so anxious to get him back there. They didn't want to try him; not much. All they wanted was to get hold of him once. None of these boys would object to going back and standing trial on any charges that could be brought against them, but they know that if they went back there now they would all be killed. The other party tried to have them brought back, but Governor Pitkin refused to recognize the requisition.[6] The boys are not outlaws by any means and they have lots of good, influential friends. Why, the Governor of Arizona would do anything he could for them, and the best people of Tombstone are on their side. The other crowd are a gang of cattle and horse thieves, stage robbers and cut-throats generally. They call them the 'Rustlers,' and the only people in Tombstone who stand in with them are the butchers and livery men, who buy cattle and horses cheap, and a few of the whisky men. Sheriff Behan sides with them, too. On the Earps' side are the Governor, Sheriff Paul, of Cochise county;[7] all the court officers, mining men, and nine out of ten of the respectable people of Tombstone."

"But come, I'll introduce you, and then you can get them to tell their own story."

The reporter thought he would interview the "Tiger" first. He found him a young man of perhaps twenty-eight or thirty,[8] with clear blue eyes and brown hair and moustache. He looked like anything but a fighter, and yet there was a look of firmness about the face that showed that the young man was not a man to fool with. He was neatly but plainly dressed, and walks lame from the effects of a gun-shot wound.

When asked to tell of the troubles in Tombstone, he said, "I don't know that there is much to tell beyond what has already been published; still as the Governor has refused to send us back, I don't suppose it will make any difference now. We have been here for nearly a month, and had started for the Reservation when we heard of the Governor's action and came back. This whole trouble grew out of the efforts of the 'Rustlers' to run the town. Wyatt was United States marshal, and my brother Virgil was town marshal of Tombstone.[9] My other brother, Morgan, was a policeman under him. If we had left the offices alone we could have made a barrel of money. Wyatt had the finest saloon and gambling house in Tombstone. The bar alone cost him three thousand dollars, and he was doing a rattling business. But the citizens prevailed upon him to take the office of deputy sheriff and United States marshal.[10] He used to be marshal of Dodge City, Kansas,[11] and anybody from there can tell you what kind of a marshal he made.

"The first trouble began with Ike Clanton. He made a 'gun play' and my brother Virgil disarmed him and fined him. As soon as he got out he got his brother Billy and Tom and Frank McClowry[12] and Billy the Kid,[13] and they swore they would kill us. The boys went to disarm them and they tried to stand 'em off. The fight lasted about half a minute, and Billy Clanton and Tom and Frank McClowry were killed. Virgil was shot through the shoulders,[14] but he is now recovering. After that they killed my brother Morgan by shooting him through a window while he was playing pool. There were five men in the crowd, Frank Stillwell,[15] Pete Spence,[16] 'Curley Bill' and two half-breeds. Stillwell, 'Curley Bill' and one of the half-breeds named Florantine[17] have since been killed. That makes six of the gang that have gone under."

Mr. Earp then went on to tell something of the fight in which "Curly Bill" was killed and also the particulars of Stillwell's death. He showed no anxiety to keep back anything and talked freely of the many fights in which he and his friends had engaged with the "Rustlers."

Wyatt Earp was also conversed with, but while he talked freely enough, he was yet cautious as to what he said. During the conversation he was speaking of the fight at Tuscon[18] when Stillwell and his party tried to shoot Virgil Earp, who was wounded and was being taken to his parents' home in California.

"That was when Doc Holladay killed Stillwell," broke in the reporter.

"Well, Stillwell was killed at Tuscon," was the quiet reply. He then went on to tell how he had "heard that Stillwell had been killed."

---

"EARP WAS A FINE-LOOKING man, with drooping mustaches that curled up at the ends. He was quiet in manner and never created a bit of trouble. In fact, he told us boys on the police force we could call on him any time if we needed help. He was a dead shot, wore two guns high under his arms, but he never used them here. Doc Holliday was the only one of the five that seemed to drink much and, the minute he got hilarious, the others promptly took him in charge and just disappeared."

—*Judd Riley, a Gunnison policeman quoted in the* Gunnison News-Champion, *July 17, 1930*

---

"I promised my brother to get even," he said, "and I've kept my word so far. When they shot him he said the only thing he regretted was that he wouldn't have a chance to get even. I told him I'd attend to it for him."

"Well, what are you going to do now?" asked the reporter.

"I shall stay here for a while. My lawyers will have a petition for a pardon drawn up. Everybody in Tombstone knows that we did nothing but our duty. Anyway I'd do it over again under like circumstances, and all the best people there will sign the petition. Governor Pitkin knows the facts pretty well and will sign it too. We look for a pardon in a few weeks, and when it comes I'll go back; but if no pardon is made I'll go back in the fall anyway and stand trial. I'd go now, but I know we would have no show. They'd shoot us in the back, as they did my brother."[19]

"You didn't get Spence," said the reporter.

"No," answered Earp, "I would sooner have met him than any _____.[20] I had a letter from Tombstone yesterday, saying that he was seen near there lately with a bunch of stolen cattle."

"Do you anticipate further trouble when you go back?"

"I don't know," was the quiet reply, "I suppose so. I'm going to run for sheriff this fall. Behan knows he can't get it again, and that's what makes him so hot towards me. I hear the gang is breaking up and a good many are going to other parts of the country. I sold out my place, but we have some mining property back there yet. Doc Holladay is in Pueblo now and he may come over here."

The conversation finally drifted into other channels and, thanking Mr. Earp, the reporter withdrew, thanking his stars that he was not an Arizona "Rustler."

Wyatt never did return to Tombstone. He and Warren remained in Colorado until late 1882 and then they moved on to San Francisco, where Wyatt caught up with Sadie. The two of them returned to Colorado the following year.

# References

1. A facsimile reproduction of this article was kindly provided for inclusion in this book by Emma Walling, author of *John "Doc" Holliday: Colorado Trials and Triumphs* (n.d.).

2. Wyatt is often called "the Lion of Tombstone." Since Warren's nickname was "the Tiger," one has to wonder if Wyatt's was "the Lion."

3. Sand: courage.

4. Warren was constantly getting into fights—many of which he provoked—but usually not when Wyatt was around.

5. Sic throughout this article.

6. The attempt to extradite Doc is covered in detail later in the book.

7. Pima County.

8. Warren was 27 at this time.

9. Virgil was city marshal and deputy U.S. marshal. Wyatt had been deputy sheriff and later deputy U.S. marshal.

10. Deputy U.S. marshal.

11. Deputy and assistant city marshal.

12. Sic throughout this article.

13. Billy Claiborne.

14. Morgan was shot through the shoulders during the gunfight. Virgil was shot in the calf. Then two months later Virgil was shot in the left arm and back.

15. Sic, throughout this article.

16. Later Wyatt said Spence wasn't involved in Morgan's death, but that Johnny Ringo was.

17. Florentino Cruz. The other "half-breed" was Hank Swilling.

18. Sic throughout this article.

19. Wyatt probably did intend to return. In a March 28, 1882 interview with the *Los Angeles Times*, James said they had too much property in Tombstone to leave and they were going to return and fight it out to the bitter end. But Wyatt was too much of a political hot potato for a pardon and as time passed he eventually realized there was no point in going back.

20. Two or three words here are too faint to be read, but it's probably "sons of bitches."

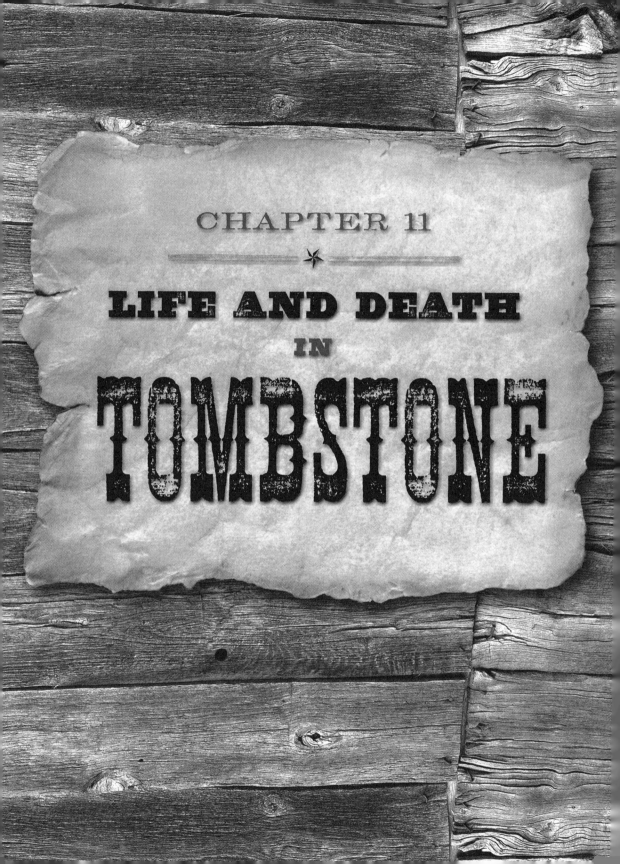

# CHAPTER 11

✦

## LIFE AND DEATH
### IN
# TOMBSTONE

I N APRIL 1926 Wyatt gave a deposition in the Lotta Crabtree Estate Case, which was reported in newspapers all across the nation. At stake was the disposition of almost $4 million, and it all hinged on what had happened in Tombstone in 1880.

Lotta Crabtree was a household name for twenty-five years in the late 1800s. Practically everyone had heard of this famous actress and comedienne whose fame peaked in the 1880s.[1] As one of the highest paid actresses of the time, she had earned a large fortune by the time she retired at the age of 45. Much of this was invested by her mother in municipal bonds and vacant land near cities in areas she foreshadowed expanding and developing. When Lotta died in 1924 at the age of 77, she left a tremendous estate. Having come from near poverty, her will set up a charitable trust to put her fortune to good use, plus there were small annuities to her closest surviving relatives—her five first cousins.

The will was challenged by over a hundred people who claimed to be related to Lotta. These were whittled down to a single person—Carlotta Cockburn claimed to be the daughter of Lotta's brother, Jack, born in Tombstone on March 19, 1881. At the trial, her lawyer, Jim Hoy, told how John "Jack" Crabtree, Jr., met Anne Leopold in San Francisco on his way to Tombstone and they got married, or at least decided to live together as husband and wife. Six months after Carlotta was born, Jack abandoned Anne and Carlotta, and six months after that Anne left as well, leaving Carlotta with May Leslie, the wife of "Buckskin" Frank Leslie. She turned the girl over to Ed Bullock, who had been Jack's partner in a corral in Tombstone. The girl eventually ended up in a Catholic orphanage in Tucson. There was considerable evidence to support her claim.

The attorney for the defense, Judge Frederick Chase,[2] insisted Jack and Anne didn't actually get married and that common law marriages were meaningless in Tombstone. They also tried to prove that Jack didn't meet Anne early enough to be Carlotta's father. He implied that Ed Bullock was actually her father and didn't want to admit it.

Wyatt testified for Carlotta and was considered her best witness. Parts of Wyatt's deposition are a bit tedious, but it does contain some very interesting information. And of course they had to talk about the shootout. His deposition has never been published before. Until now, only a handful of people have ever read it.

In the end, the judge of the case, William Priest, ruled against Carlotta and the trust remained intact. Both judges Chase and Priest later became two of the three trustees administering Lotta Crabtree's fortune.

☞ IN LATER YEARS, WYATT assisted the Los Angeles Police Department in some special missions that were not quite legal, such as retrieving fugitives from Mexico. A former policeman who was Wyatt's assistant, Arthur M. King, said, "Earp was a very quiet fellow—a fine man, one of the coolest I've ever seen. He was afraid of nothing. When he'd get angry the corner of his right eye would twitch just a little. He...was an artist at swearing, and he took to drinking pretty heavily when he reached fifty. You see, Earp never used to drink at all."[3]

They had considerable discretion in interpreting Lotta's wishes—such as diverting money she had specified to help animals.

Since the trial, further evidence surfaced supporting Carlotta's claim and disproving much of the defense's testimony. Unfortunately, it appeared too late to help Carlotta.[4]

Below is Wyatt's deposition. This could be the only transcript that exists that depicts how Wyatt spoke.

(Under stipulation, the further hearing of depositions was continued on this day, to No. 1818 Fourth Avenue, Los Angeles, California, at the hour of 3 P.M.)

## WYATT S. EARP[5]

produced as a witness on behalf of the Contestant, having been first duly sworn, was examined and testified as follows:

### DIRECT EXAMINATION
### BY MR HOY:

**Q** You live, ordinarily, where?

**A** I have been summering in Los Angeles for the last 20 years.

**Q** In the winter where do you live?

**A** Down at some mines I have got on the Colorado River.

**Q** Vidal?[6]

**A** Yes.

**Q** Now, Mr Earp, were you in Tombstone in the early days?

**A** I went to Tombstone in October, 1879.

**Q** How long did you stay?

**A** I lived there until the 23nd of March, 1882.[7]

**MR CHASE** May we have the same stipulation as to objections and motions to strike out?

**Mr Hoy**  Yes, but I want to add to the stipulation that I have the same objection and motion regarding your cross-examination.

**Mr Chase**  Yes.

**Q by Mr Hoy**  What position did you hold while you were there, if any?

**A**  I was deputy sheriff from about the 1st of October 1879 up to the latter part of April, just before the election came off in 1880.[8]

**Q**  Then what position did you hold?

**A**  I was Deputy United States Marshal and Wells Fargo private man.

**Q**  Was your brother or brothers or your father any officer down there in the early days?

**A**  I had a brother who was chief of police.

**Q**  What was his name?

**A**  Virgil.

**Q**  Was your father down there at all?

**A**  No.

**Q**  Where are you from?

**A**  Do you mean where was I born?

**Q**  Yes.

**A**  Monmouth, Warren County, Illinois.

**Q**  When did you strike the West?

**A**  1864.[9]

**Q**  How old are you now?

**A**  I am in my seventy eighth year. I was 77 the 19th of last month.[10]

**Q**  While you were in Tombstone do you remember any of the people you used to know back there?

**A**  Yes.

☞ "This [Tombstone] is a terribly out of the way place. It is farthest from New York by rail and telegraph than any other city in the United States, a fact I was not aware of until recently."
—*George Parsons in his journal, April 17, 1880*

**Q** Who do you remember?

**A** Well—that is while I was still living in Tombstone?

**Q** No. Who do you remember among the old timers back there?

**A** A man by the name of Young, a man by the name of Hunsaker, who is a lawyer here, John P. Clum and his son, and there is quite a few here—a man named Oscar Roberts,—but a lot of them have died in the last four or five years.

**Q** Do you remember anybody down there in the early days by the name of Crabtree?

**A** I did.

**Q** Will you tell what you know about him, where you met him and how you met him and everything that you know about him?

**A** Well, I met Crabtree when he first came to Tombstone. He came there with a man named Bullock, Ed Bullock and his wife.

**Q** Where did you meet him?

**A** They started a corral[11] in Tombstone and I met him at that corral, but I used to see them often from the street. They were right on the street and passing by I would see them. Of course I would look in and see them around the corral and after they had been there a short time I got acquainted with Crabtree. I went up one time to try to buy a three seated hack that he had. I had 12 or 15 horses that I had taken to Tombstone with me from Kansas and I had a coach and he had a three seated hack and I thought I could turn that hack into a pretty good coach and I intended to start a stage line from Tombstone to Benson. I went into the corral to try to buy that hack. There is where I first met Mrs Crabtree to know who she was. Of course I was satisfied before that that she was the wife of Crabtree but I met her there and I was introduced to her by Crabtree.

**Q** Later on did you hear of any family coming to them?

**A** She had a child later on.

**Q** Do you remember where they were living then?

**A** They were living east of Fremont.[12] I don't know what the name of the street was that they were living on and I am not positive as to whether it was Fourth or Fifth, but I have always though it was Fifth Street they were living on. I know it was east[13] of Fremont. Those streets east[14] of Fremont, there was no business on those streets at all and they were cut up with washes pretty bad and that made it kind of a residential part of town and I never got down in that part of town very often, very seldom.

**Q** Was anybody with you when Crabtree introduced you to his wife?

**A** My brother Virgil. He went with me. We were partners at the time, or had the horses together.

**Q** How many times in all did you see Mrs Crabtree in Tombstone, do you think?

**A** Well, I couldn't say positively, but I have met her—afterwards I met her at a family's that I went to see with a man by the name of Johnson.[15] They were friends of his and he asked me to go and visit the family with him.

**Q** Did you go?

**A** I went, and I met Mrs Crabtree there. The first time I made the visit to these people[16]—I was there probably six or eight times alltold.[17]

**Q** At that time when you went there did they have a baby?

**A** She had a baby.

**Q** What kind of a baby was it, boy or girl?

**A** I don't know that.

**Q** Don't you remember?

**A** I don't recollect.

**Q** When you became acquainted with Crabtree, or after you knew him, did you know that he was in any way related to Lotta Crabtree, the actress?

**A** Well, no, I didn't know it at that time.

**Q** Did you at a later time?

**A** At that time I didn't know anything about Lotta Crabtree.

**Q** You are not a Californian, you came from Kansas?

**A** The first time I heard of Lotta Crabtree was after I left Tombstone and went to San Francisco in the latter part of 1882 and of course there I heard of Lotta Crabtree because they had a fountain there that she had erected, or had had erected in front of the Chronicle Building. That is the first time I ever heard of her.

**Q** When did you hear of, or did you connect your acquaintanceship with Crabtree in Tombstone with her, or did you hear anything to lead you to know that there was any connection?

**A** No, I don't think I heard anything.

**Q** Did you know where the San Jose rooming house was in those early days?[18]

**A** Yes.

**Q** Did you ever see Mrs Crabtree there?

**A** I have.

**Q** Did you know the lady who ran that?

**A** Yes.

**Q** Who was it?

**A** Mrs Falloon.[19] Afterwards she married a man named Taylor. I met Mrs Crabtree at Mrs Falloon San Jose rooming house on two or three occasions. I recollect one occasion very well, where there had been a man shot, by the name of Storms, and he had a room at the San Jose rooming house and we took Storms down there to his room. The doctor was going to hold a post mortem[20] and they wanted me to stick around, and being there I met Mrs Crabtree. She had her baby with her then and I had quite a long talk with her with regard to the shooting and how it came up and what it was about, and all that. On two or three other occasions I met here there. I used to take my prisoners down to the San Jose rooming house. They had no jail in Tombstone at that time. That was before the county was divided.[21] It was all Pima County and we had to take our prisoners to Tucson. In holding them in Tombstone I used to get a room in the San Jose and put a guard over them and in that way I met Mrs Crabtree on two or three occasions.

**Q** How old a woman was she, would you say?

**A** Oh, I would put her anywhere between 16 and 18 years old at that time, quite young.

**Q** How old was Crabree in those days?

**A** Around 25 I should think.

**Q** What kind of a looking fellow was he?

**A** Smallsized[22] man, a man about the size of—oh, to the best of my knowledge about 5 feet 9 or 9$\frac{1}{2}$ and weighed about 135 or 140.

**Q** Did you hear something about his being in some connection with Ed Bullock?

**A** He was supposed to be a partner of Bullock.

**Q** In what?

**A** In the corral.

**Q** Who told you that?

**A** I don't know.

**Q** How did you know it?

**A** By seeing them together and doing business with each other.

**Q** Did you do business—did you ever do any business with them or see them doing business with each other?

☞ "DURING THE 365 DAYS of my official administration as mayor of the City of Tombstone there were but three murders committed within the city limits. That is as near as we came to having 'a dead man for breakfast every morning.' It is my recollection that in each of the above instances the murderer was arrested by Deputy Marshal Wyatt Earp. The above total of violent deaths for the year does not include the three men killed in the street battle with the police."
—*John Clum, 1929. He was Tombstone's fourth mayor, serving from January 4, 1881 to January 3, 1882*

**A** Well, you see they were both there at the corral and when I went to buy that hack or try to buy that hack, we had all of our talk with Crabtree.

**Q** Did he talk as if he was the proprietor and interested in it?

**A** Yes.

**Q** Some one has said in connection with this case and the taking of these depositions that that was a pretty rough city up there, a very rough town, very little law and order and that law and order was more observed in the breach than in the observance thereof. What have you got to say about that?

**A** I say it is wrong.

**Q** What are the facts?

**A** The facts are there. I arrested pretty nearly every man that done any killing there. I don't think there was only a couple of people that ever got into trouble and killed any one—just about two outside of what I arrested myself and I can mention all the killings on my fingers.

**Q** Ten killings?

**A** Not that many.

**Q** How many?

**A** Oh, I will tell you—let's see. The first man killed was Killeen, Mike Killeen.

**Q** Who killed him?

**A** Well, I know who killed him.

**Q** Did Frank Leslie kill him?

**A** No.

**Q** Who was the next one—by the way you were there and saw the shooting?

**A** I was on the ground not a half a minute afterwards. I arrested Frank Leslie and also this other man.[23]

**Q** There is one.

**A** Then City Marshal White. He was killed by Curley Bill. I arrested him and took him to Tucson and put him in jail. Then the next man was killed by a man by the name of Bradshaw. He killed his partner McIntyre.[24] Bradshaw had bought a kind of a funny looking shirt, a red striped shirt and he went up the street and everybody was making fun of it and saying "Where did you get that shirt?" And he got hot over it and he says "The next man that kids me about this shirt I am going to kill him." The next man he met was his partner, the man that he was sleeping with and rooming with[25] and of course he said to Bradshaw—we called him "Brad" he said "Where did you get that shirt?" and he jerked his gun out and killed him.[26] That is three. That is Killeen, the Marshal and McIntyre. The next man killed was Storms and he was killed by Luke[27] Short. That was four. That is all I can recollect outside of the trouble that I had, the Clanton and McLowry boys.

**Q** Those men were men that were outlaws and you representing law and order, you had to shoot them?

**A** Yes.

**Q** By the way, what do you say as to that community's condition regarding law and order and morality and living, according to the ordinary customs of civilization as it was in that mining camp in those days, in 1878 and '83?[28]

**A** State that over again.

**Q** I would like to ask you to state your observation of those times and tell us what the condition of this community was for law and order?

**A** It was not half as bad as Long Angeles.[29]

**Q** Tell us whether it was good or bad or whether it was a lawless outpost?

**A** I called it good.

**Q** You were in charge?

**A** I called it good.

**Q** Did you ever hear a breath of scandal about reputation, illrepute,[30] against the name of Mrs. Crabtree?

**A** No sir, I did not.

**Q** I think you have answered this, but I will ask it again. You said that they lived in the residence portion of town?

**A** They lived on the same street.

**Q** I never knew the name of those streets up there. They run the same as Fremont, but they lived east[31] of Fremont.

**Q** Over towards the Dragoons?[32]

**A** In that direction. It could not have been more than a block away.

**Q** Did you ever hear it mentioned that Mr and Mrs Crabtree were living in any other relationship than as husband and wife?

**A** No sir.

**Q** Your understanding was what, as to the relationship?

**A** That they were man and wife.

**Q** And you got it from whom?

**A** I got it from their actions more than anything else.

**Q** And what else?

**A** From the introduction he gave me.

**Q** What else?

**A** And her having a child by him and everything went to show that they were man and wife.

**Q** Did you ever hear it questioned that that child was Jack Crabtree's child, in Tombstone?

**A** No.

**Q** Did you ever hear otherwise?

**A** No.

**Q** Did you ever see him with that child on the street or any place else?

**A** I have seen him with the child on the street several times and then several times I have seen him in the restaurant run by a man by the name of Brown—Doughnut Brown. He had a restaurant there.

**Q** With that child?

**A** Yes, and with his wife.

The conflict between the Earps and the outlaws flared up very quickly. Things were so calm in Tombstone prior to the storm that just a few weeks before the gunfight, Virgil asked that his police force be reduced from six to two.

**Mr Hoy**  Your witness, Judge Chase.

**A**  This Doughnut Brown had a restaurant on Fifth Street between Allen and Fremont. I have seen him there. I used to take my meals there myself.

**Q** BY MR HOY  While you were there and saw him there what was his attitude towards the child? Can you say that it was other than the normal fatherly attitude, or what was it?

**A**  The same as any other father would be. I never did see anything else.

### CROSS EXAMINATION BY MR CHASE:

**Q**  When did you first see Crabtree?

**A**  Well, I cannot say just what time, but I was under the impression it was along the latter part of 1880. It might have been a little earlier than that, or later.

**Q**  When did you first see Bullock?

**A**  Just about the same time.

**Q**  You didn't see them come to Tombstone?

**A**  No I didn't see them come to Tombstone but I was under the impression that they both came there together.

**Q**  When did you first see the woman that you have called Mrs Crabtree?

**A**  Well, the first time that I met the woman, that is just to see her, was around the corral.

**Q**  How long after you saw Bullock and Crabtree was that?

**A**  Oh, they were around the corral the same time.

**Q**  How long after you first saw them at Tombstone was it that you saw her around the corral?

**A**  Why, I saw them all about the same time.

**Q** Do you remember when the baby was born?

**A** No.

**Q** When did you first see the baby?

**A** I saw the baby at the corral.

**Q** At the corral?

**A** Yes.

**Q** About how long after you first saw Bullock and Crabtree was it that you saw the baby, first?

**A** Well, it was two or three months after I first saw him.

**Q** How old was the baby then?

**A** The first time I saw it?

**Q** Yes.

**A** It didn't look to me like it was over a week or ten days old.

**Q** Do you know where the baby was born?

**A** No, I do not.

**Q** Had you heard?

**A** No, I know it was born in Tombstone, but I don't know at what time.

**Q** Or where?

**A** That I could not swear to, but it was supposed to have been born where they were living. I couldn't swear to that.

**Q** You mean you don't know?

**A** I don't know.

**Q** Have you heard that it was born in a carriage at the corral?

**A** No sir, I never heard that.

**Q** Do you know Colonel Breckenridge?[33]

**A** Yes.

**Q** Has he talked with you about this?

**A** Yes.

**Q** Didn't you tell him that you had heard that it was born in a carriage?

**A** No sir. Breckenridge knows nothing about it except what I told him.

**Q** Didn't you tell him that you had heard something about it being born in a carriage?

**A** I told him at one time when he was here, one time, that some how or other I had got it into my mind that it was born in a carriage.

**Q** Because you had heard it?

**A** No.

**Q** Well, how did you get it in your mind?

**A** By seeing her around this carriage before, and a short time after.

**Q** Was that carriage fitted up as a sleeping place?

**A** Yes.

**Q** Who fitted it up?

**A** Crabtree, I suppose.

**Q** Was that carriage in the corral?

**A** It was in the front part of the corral.

**Q** At the time the carriage was there, fitted up as a sleeping place, you say the woman that you called Mrs Crabtree, you saw her around the corral constantly?

**A** Yes.

**Q** Even after the baby was born you saw her around the corral?

**A** Yes.

**Q** You understood that she lived there at that time?

**A** I seen her around the corral quite often after the baby was born, but they were living then down east[34] on Fremont Street.

**Q** At the time you saw her around the corral she had the little baby with her?

**A** She had a baby with her. I had seen her there. She would come down quite frequently.

**Q** You say you saw her in the San Jose house quite frequently also?

**A** Yes sir.

**Q** Before or after you saw her around the corral?

**A** It was afterwards. It was after.

**Q** She lived there at one time, did she?

**A** Huh?

**Q** At the San Jose?

**A** Not that I know of.

**Q** Didn't she—

**A** As I say I have seen her there quite often when I would pass by the San Jose rooming house I would see her there. Several times I saw her there. But whether she lived there or not I don't know.

**Q** Do you know Mrs Warnerkres, whose maiden name was Henson?[35]

**A** No, I don't recollect her.

**Q** Don't remember her at all; a woman who kept a rooming house near there, not far away?

**A** I don't recollect her.

☞ "I WAS ASKED TO go to Tombstone in my capacity as [Deputy] United States Marshal, and went. My brother Wyatt and myself were fairly well treated for a time, but when the desperate characters who were congregated there, and who had been unaccustomed to troublesome molestation by the authorities, learned that we meant business and were determined to stop their rascality if possible, they began to make it warm for us."

—*Virgil Earp in an interview with the* San Francisco Examiner, *May 27, 1882*

**Q** Never heard of her?

**A** I have heard the name.

**Q** As a woman keeping a rooming house?

**A** I have heard that name, but now—whether it was there or whether it was since this case come up I don't quite know. I think it is since this case come up I have heard that name. I heard some one speak of her since this case come up.

**Q** You spoke about a man named Storm having been killed and you say you took him to the San Jose House?

**A** Yes sir.

**Q** Where he lived?

**A** He had a room there.

**Q** You say that you saw this lady whom[36] you called Mrs Crabtree at the San Jose House then?

**A** She was there at that time.

**Q** Did she have her baby with her?

**A** Yes.

**Q** What time of day was it?

**A** That was about 2 o'clock in the afternoon.

**Q** What year was it in?

**A** 1881.

**Q** What part of 1881?

**A** The fore part.

☞ "WYATT EARP, ONE OF the most efficient officers Dodge ever had, has just returned from Fort Worth, Texas. He was immediately appointed Asst. Marshal, by our city dads, much to their credit."

—Ford County Globe *on Wyatt's return to Dodge City, May 14, 1878*

**Q** How early in 1881?

**A** I don't recollect.

**Q** Can you remember when Storms was killed?

**A** No, I don't recollect the month.

**Q** I wish you would fix it for us as well as you can?

**A** I know it was in 1881 but so far as the month is concerned I don't know.

**Q** The early part of the year 1881?

**A** No.

**Q** The latter part of the year 1881?

**A** No; it might have been about the middle. It was not the latter part nor the fore part.

**Q** You say you also saw the woman whom you called Mrs Crabtree at another house?

**A** I saw Mrs Crabtree at two or three other houses.

**Q** I understood you to say and to refer particularly to one where you saw her in company with a man named Johnson?[37]

**A** Yes. I went with a friend of mine named Johnson—he wanted to see this family.

**Q** What family?

**A** I don't know who they were. I never had met them. He wanted me to go with him and I went with him. I made my first visit there and that is when I met Mrs Crabtree again.

**Q** Did she then have a baby?

**A** Yes, she had a baby with her.

**Q** What time of the day did you go?

**A** About 8 o'clock at night.

**Q** Was Crabtree there?

**A** No sir.

**Q** What was the name of that family?

**A** I have been trying to think of it ever since I was first interviewed by Bess and Breckenridge. I cannot think of it. It was something like Mahoney or Maroney—something like that: I never have been able to think what it was. I never did get well acquainted with the family.

**Q** Where was the house?

**A** It was on Fifth Street, and on one of those streets east[38] of Fremont, about a block from Fremont and half way down the street.

**Q** Those two streets east of Fremont. Now, who did Johnson go to see?

**A** The wife of Mahoney, if that was his name?

**Q** What did you go for?

**A** Well, I had this Johnson with me and the thing was getting pretty warm between me and the rustlers and Johnson had joined my party, and he had been identified with this other party for a while and they got on to him. I was using Johnson at that time the same as Chief Heath would use a stool pigeon, but we didn't call them stool pigeons in those days. I was letting him get information for me. They had got on to him and of course it was a little dangerous for a man like that to get out alone and I went with him.

**Q** Did he go down there to this house?

**A** I went with him, yes. That is the first time I ever met this family, was this time.

**Q** Did Johnson go down there to get information as an officer?

**A** Oh, no.

**Q** He went to make a call?

**A** I don't know what he went there for.

**Q** What did he do?

**A** There was two rooms to the house, a front room and a back room and a kitchen. I never was in there of course. I sat down in the front part of the room, and they would go into this back room and do the talking.

**Q** Who was "they?"

**A** Johnson and this man's wife. They never closed the door.

**Q** What man's wife? Who are you now referring to?

**A** Mahoney, or whatever his name was.

**Q** This lady called Mrs Crabtree would stay in the other room.

**A** No sir.

**Q** What did she do?

**A** She went off with her child after we came. She was there a few minutes and then went home. She lived just a short ways from there. She went out. So I was set down there and they went into this back room but they never closed the door. I went there with him about 6 or 8 times all told inside of 5 or 6 months and that door never was closed, so I know there was nothing wrong between them.

**Q** Between Johnson and this Mrs Mahoney?

**A** Yes.

**Q** You never saw Mrs Crabtree there again?

**A** Just once after that.

**Q** And that is all?

**A** Yes. I saw her just twice at that house. I met her at other times at an ice cream parlor.

**Q** What ice cream parlor?

**A** On Fourth Street between Allen and Fremont.

**Q** Whose place?

**A** A woman named Hinkley. She afterwards married a man named Fay, a reporter on the Nugget.[39]

**Q** What was she doing?

**A** I don't know. I used to go there pretty often. I liked ice cream and I met her over there. At one time I thought maybe she worked there.

**Q** Was she behind the counter?

**A** No, I don't know as they had a counter. They had tables around the room and another room in back.

**Q** Did you ever know what her maiden name was, her first name?

**A** No.

**Q** Never heard of it?

**A** I have heard it since this case came up.

**Q** Did you ever hear that it was Anna Leopold, or Annie?[40]

**A** No.

**Q** Did you ever hear anybody referred to as native daughter?

**A** No.

**Q** Nobody in Tombstone?

**A** No. As a native daughter did you say?

**Q** Yes.

**A** No.

**Q** Was Johnson the man's name?

**A** That is the name that he was going by but I don't think it was his right name.

**Q** What was his right name?

**A** I don't know. I never found out.

> ☞ "YOU ASK FOR MY impressions about
> Wyatt Earp in Tombstone as a Peace
> Officer and as a man. As a man he was
> Ace high, and as a Peace Officer he
> WAS the peace."
>
> —*Fred Dodge in a letter to Stuart Lake,*
> *October 8, 1928*

on in Kansas City and he was going

there was some parties[42] that had has

street fight and several people got

the country, so I made up my mind

was in this trouble and I knew they

it they came to Prescott, Arizona,

re. Some prize fighter slugged the

cifully, and he went off and got a

n for four years. There was Bud

he went to the penitentiary. But this

d I got acquainted with him and he

o and picking up a herd of cattle,

d I knew that he could give me a lot

the other side so I took him in with

my posse. After he had been there awhile he asked me to help get Bud Blunt out of
the penitentiary. He said that if I would get up a petition in Tombstone and one in
Leadville and one in Prescott he thought that the governor would pardon him. I had
heard all about Blunt killing this fellow after he had been pounded up, and I had
made up my mind that he was about half way right and I helped him get this petition up and he was pardoned by the governor. He went back to Missouri and I never
heard of John Blunt again. I had made up my mind, putting[43] everything together
afterwards, that this man Johnson was John Blunt a brother of Bud's, and also a
brother of this man's wife.

**Q** Do I understand that you used Johnson or Blunt or whatever his name was as a stool pigeon because he knew the people that you were after and was familiar with the facts you wanted?

**A** That was what I wanted.

---

☞ "A MAN LATELY ARRIVED from the East received a close call from a stray bullet, and concluded he wouldn't stay any longer in Tombstone. He left for home on the next train, and will probably convey the impression that the notorious camp is a den of cut throats, when, in reality, a man had not been shot for many months prior to this tragedy."
—*Clara S. Brown, Tombstone correspondent to the* San Diego Union, *November 3, 1881*

---

**Q** And had been associating with them?

**A** Yes. I wanted to get information.

**Q** Was that the reason why you used him?

**A** Yes.

**Q** Did he know this woman that you referred to as Mrs Crabtree?

**A** Who?

**Q** Johnson?

**A** Did he know Mrs Crabtree?

**Q** Yes.

**A** He knew her quite well I think.

**Q** Do you remember when she went away?

**A** No. She disappeared all at once.

**Q** Do you know a man named Rabb?

**A** I do not.

**Q** Never heard of him?

**A** No, not until this case came up.

**Q** Do you know where she went from Tombstone?

**A** Where who went?

**Q** This woman who called herself Mrs Crabtree?

**A** No, I do not.

**Q** Never heard?

**A** Never heard where she went and at that time I didn't know anything about where she went.

**Q** You said you didn't go down in that part of town very often?

**A** No, not very.

**Q** Any particular reason for that?

**A** Well, there was no business on those streets, there was no business I think at all. It was a residential part of town now that I call to mind—my lawyer lived in that part of town and I went to his place several times and I met Mrs Crabtree at his house on two or three different occasions. His name was Jones, Harry Jones and he was my lawyer. They lived in that vicinity, but that part of town had no business outside of residential purposes and I had no business down there, much. Of course the San Jose house, that was on one of the principal streets, on Fremont.

☞ "THE LESS YOU BET, the more you lose when you win."

—*Wyatt's creed*

**Q** You never heard the relations between Mr Crabtree and this woman discussed, did you?

**A** Between what?

**Q** You never heard the relations between them discussed, did you?

**A** No.

**Q** It was not a matter of talk about the town was it?

**A** I never heard it discussed at all, they were supposed to be man and wife.

**Q** That is your supposition?

**A** Yes I never heard anything to the contrary.

**Q** Or to that point either?

**A** No sir.[44]

**Q** You drew your own conclusions to that effect from the fact that you say you saw them together and there was a baby?

**A** Yes.

**Q** It was not a matter of gossip about the town, was[45] it?

**A** Never heard any.

**Q** You cannot think of anybody you ever heard discussing what they were to each other?

**A** No.

**Q** For the most of the time you were there you were deputy marshal, weren't you?

**A** I was deputy sheriff. I was made deputy sheriff on my way to Tombstone.[46] I stopped off in Tucson.[47] I had some friends in Tucson from Kansas. I had left Dodge City, Kansas, where I had been chief of police of Dodge City for four years[48] before and I went to Tombstone and quite a number of my friends were living in Tucson. I had quite a big outfit and I camped out in the edge of town. I went up town and met some of those friends and the sheriff there, his name was Chabelle,[49] I was camped down there and he and another man came down there to see me and the Sheriff prevailed upon me to take the deputyship. I told him I had just got away from that kind of a life at Dodge City and I didn't want to go back to it, but he told me—put it up to me in a glowing way that it would be just the same as being sheriff of the county. He said "You have got all that country over there and there is money in it." Finally I accepted the deputyship and I went over there as a deputy sheriff.

**Q** How long were you deputy sheriff?

**A** Well, that was in the later part of October, 1879, and I served until 1880.[50]

**Q** Then you became United States Marshal or Deputy United States Marshal?

**A** I went to Tucson late in 1880 and put in my resignation to Sheriff Chabelle and he wanted to know why I done that, and I told him that a friend of mine by the name of Bob Ball[51] was running for sheriff and running on my ticket and that I was going to support him and I didn't feel like working for Ball and being his deputy.[52] So he accepted the resignation.

**Q** You then became Deputy United States Marshal?

**A** Then I was appointed Deputy United States Marshal.

**Q** And were such until you left?

**A** I was Deputy United States Marshal until I left.

**Q** After you became Deputy United States Marshal there was not the best of feeling between your office and the office of the sheriff?

**A** No.

**Q** The sheriff's name was Behan?

**A** Yes.

**Q** You were allied with one faction and he with another?

**A** Yes.

**Q** With you was allied Doc Holliday?

**A** Yes.

**Q** He was somewhat of a notorious character in those days?

**A** Well, no. I couldn't say that he was notorious outside of this other faction trying to make him notorious. Of course he killed a man or two before he went there.

**Q** Didn't he have the reputation of being a holder-up of stages?

**A** I never heard of it until I left.

**Q** With the Behans were allied the Clandens?[53]

**A** Yes. And the Behan side whenever they got a chance to hurt me over Holliday's shoulders they would do it. They would make a lot of talk about Doc Holliday.

**Q** Because he was allied with you?

**A** He never had no trouble in Tombstone outside of being in this street fight with us. Then on one occasion he got into some trouble with part of the combination that was against me, Joyce, and his partner, and he shot Joyce in the hand and the other fellow[54] in the foot and of course that made them pretty sore against Holliday.[55] But they knew that I was Holliday's friend and they tried injure me every way they could.

**Q** Didn't that feud finally culminate in what you have referred to as a streetfight?
**A** No sir.

**Q** What was that and where did it take place and when?
**A** It took place in October on Fremont Street.

**Q** October of what year?[56]
**A** 1881.

**Q** How many were killed in that fight?
**A** Three.

**Q** Who were they?
**A** Billy Clandon and the two McLowreys.[57]

**Q** Was one of your brothers injured at that time?
**A** I had two brothers wounded in that fight, and Doc Holliday.

**Q** Was one of them killed?
**A** No, not then.

**Q** Was Doc Holliday in that fight?
**A** Yes.

**Q** Was one of your brothers subsequently killed?
**A** Not in that fight.

**Q** In another fight?
**A** No other fight. He was killed afterwards by being assassinated, but not in a fight. He was shot through a window.

**Q**  You left after that?

**A**  Yes.

**Q**  You said you left Dodge City for Tombstone?

**A**  Yes.

**Q**  What were you going to do in Tombstone?

**A**  I intended to start a stage line when I first started out from Dodge City, but when I got there I found there was two stage lines and so I finally sold my outfit to one of the companies, to a man named Kinnear.[58] But I intended to start this stage line when I went there.[59]

**Q**  What did you do besides being deputy sheriff and marshal?

**A**  What did I do?

**Q**  Yes.

**A**  Well, I dealt awhile in pasteboard and ivory.

**Q**  Well, you are talking to people who don't know what those things are.

**A**  Dealing faro bank.

**Q**  Where was that?

**A**  In Tombstone.

**Q**  What place?

**A**  That was the Oriental.

**Q**  Was that on the main street?

**A**  On the business street.

**Q**  On Allen Street?

**A**  Yes.

**Q**  Was the Bird Cage open while you were there?

**A**  Yes.

**Q** Do you remember when that was opened?

**A** Some time in 1880. I don't recollect just when, just what month. It was about the later part of 1880.[60]

**Mr Chase** I think that is all.

**A** After this trouble came up, this fellow Behan, he intended to run for sheriff and he knew that I did, and if I do say it myself I was a pretty strong man for the position. He knew that he had to do me some way and he done everything in the world that he could against me. He stood in with this tough element, the cow boys and stage robbers and others, because they were pretty strong and he wanted their vote. Whenever they would get a chance to shoot anything at me over Holliday's shoulders they would do it. So they made Holliday a bad man. An awful bad man, which was wrong. He was a man that would fight if he had to but—

**Q by Mr Hoy** Did you hear any more or any less about other married people in Tombstone than you heard about Jack Crabtree and his wife?

**A** I didn't hear anything.

**Q** Did you hear anything more or less about Jack Crabtree and his wife than you did about any other married people?

**A** I did not.

**Q** It was just the same—they were treated just the same as married people by everybody?

**A** Yes.

**Q** And everybody understood they were married?

**A** Yes.

**Q** And were according to your understanding?

**A** Yes.

**Q** What I am getting at is this. Were there or not many people in Tombstone going as husband and wife that you didn't know whether they were married or not. You had never seen their marriage license, but you took them as man and wife?[61]

**A** Yes.

**Q** Were Jack and Anna Crabtree taken the same way?

**A** Yes.

**Q** Were they any different than any others?

**A** No sir, none at all. There was lots of good married people there.

**Mr Hoy** All right, Mr Earp, that is all. We are very much obliged to you.

---
[62]

# References

1. Some people have claimed that Lotta performed at the Bird Cage Theater, but there is no credible evidence she ever went to Tombstone.

2. He was a retired Superior Court justice.

3. Wyatt wasn't known to swear either while he was in Tombstone, but he was a different man after the Vendetta. Prior to the Vendetta he had tried to avoid killing, unlike many other peace officers who were quick to shoot troublemakers. After the events leading to the Vendetta, he was willing to shoot on sight. Wyatt also said he had his first drink of hard liquor during the Vendetta while he was at Henry Hooker's ranch. It was in San Francisco in the 1890s that he really began to drink.

4. More information on this trial can be found in David Dempsey and Raymond P. Baldwin's *The Triumphs and Trials of Lotta Crabtree* (William Morrow & Co., 1968).

5. Wyatt usually used just one middle initial. His full name was Wyatt Berry Stapp Earp. He was named after his father's neighbor and commanding officer in the Mexican War, Wyatt Berry Stapp.

6. California.

7. March 25, 1882.

8. Wyatt has the months confused here. He left Dodge City for Tombstone in September 1879. In his statement at the hearings following the shootout, he said he arrived in Tombstone on December 1, 1879. The document of his taking the oath of office for deputy sheriff is dated July 17, 1880 and his resignation is dated November 9, 1880.

9. Wyatt was 16 years old when his father led a wagon train from Council Bluffs, Iowa, to San Bernardino, California. Wyatt was placed in charge of the Earp wagons and stock. The journey—from May 12th to December 19th—took seven months and one week. Virgil was still fighting in the Civil War. James had already returned home, but was permanently disabled.

10. Wyatt was in his 79th year. He turned 78 in 1926.

11. The Lexington Livery Stable.

12. Fremont runs east and west. The Crabtrees lived on Fremont at Fifth Street.

13. North.

14. North.

15. Turkey Creek Jack Johnson, who accompanied Wyatt on the Vendetta.

16. Sic.

17. Sic.

18. It was on the northwest corner of Fremont and Fifth, next door to Crabtree and Bullock's Lexington Livery Stable.

19. Mrs. Fallon. Her maiden name was Samantha Elizabeth Hale. She was also known as Kate Taylor, Kate Logie, and as Samantha Taylor she was a dancer at Tombstone's Bird Cage Theater. She then ran the San Jose House for it's owner, Ed Schieffelin. One old Tombstoner later described it as "the sportingest boardinghouse in Tombstone," which is a polite way of calling it a brothel. The police also sometimes used it as a place to hold prisoners.

Brothels were still essentially legal at this time. They were regulated and closely monitored by the police. In many cities the madams and working girls were brought before a judge on a regular basis and fined, but this was just one of the ways cities taxed the red light district. Occasionally this was also done to the owners of gambling establishments. Sometimes the only time fines were levied was when the city treasury was getting low. Some police departments issued brothel licenses as a way of raising money for city coffers. The brothels usually just looked on it as a business expense. In return, the police generally made sure the customers didn't get out of line. Brothel licensing and protection by the police still goes on today in some parts of Nevada.

James Earp's wife, Bessie, was a madam and probably a prostitute in 1894 and 1875 while they were living in Wichita, Kansas.

20. Sic.

21. Pima County was divided into Pima and Cochise Counties on February 1, 1881.

22. Sic.

23. This happened on June 22, 1880. Wyatt arrested N. F. "Buckskin Frank" Leslie and George Perine. Originally Leslie claimed he'd killed Killeen in self-defense and they were both released. Then it was revealed that Killeen had made a deathbed statement saying it was actually Perine who shot him and Perine was tried for murder. Killeen's statement was printed in the *Epitaph* on August 24, 1880. It said:

At the ball I wanted to see my wife. I heard that she had gone home with Leslie, and when I was told she had gone home I went down to the hotel [the Cosmopolitan Hotel] with the expectation of finding both of them in Leslie's room, but they were not there; meanwhile, I started towards the porch [actually it was more of a balcony as it was on the second floor], having heard voices, and I thought it might be them; I got to the door of the porch and satisfied myself she and Leslie were sitting side by side, his arm around her waist; that settled it; I thought I would go off now, started back again; Perine came along pistol in hand and knowing him to be a particular friend of Leslie I looked for trouble as in the early part of the evening he went into Tasker & Hoke's and bought a box of cartridges and filled all the chambers of his pistol and deposited the

remainder of the box with me; I started away from the porch when Perine came along and yelled out "Look out Frank, there is Mike," with that Leslie rose from his chair in a half standing position, pulling his pistol; he fired the pistol at me and I fired one shot at him; I saw I was in for it and I made a jump and caught the pistol and beat him over the head with mine, which I had in my hand at the time; I happened to look and saw Perine standing in the door with his pistol leveled at me; he pulled the trigger, which he repeated twice, firing in all three shots; by this time I had used up Leslie pretty well; then turned and jumped and caught Perine's pistol, and did the same to him; by this time people commenced to congregate and I dropped this man not thinking of my own wounds; all I knew was I was shot in the nose somewhere. I fired two shots myself intentionally, and every time I would strike the pistol went off accidentally; fired at Perine when he fired at me; one shot was at Perine and one was at Leslie; fired at Leslie when he pulled his revolver first and stood in a half stooping position; this was right after he first fired at me.

M. D. Killeen.

At his trial, Perine insisted the only weapon he had that night was a pocket knife, Leslie insisted he shot Killeen, and May Killeen—who was now May Leslie—testified that Perine wasn't even on the scene. The Grand Jury decided he was innocent. Obviously Wyatt thought otherwise. This May Leslie is the one with whom the one-year-old Carlotta Crabtree Cockburn was left by her mother.

Frank Leslie was about 37 years old at this time. Originally from Texas, it's said he was a deputy under James Butler "Wild Bill" Hickock in Kansas in the early 1870s. It's also said he spent some time as a rough rider in Australia and a ship's pilot in Fiji before he came to Tombstone. On November 14, 1882, Frank Leslie killed Billy the Kid Claiborne, one of the surviving outlaws from the O.K. Corral gunfight. May Leslie eventually left him and he became involved with a prostitute named Mollie Williams. He murdered Williams in drunken rage in 1889 and was sent to the territorial prison in Yuma for twenty-five years, though he was released eight years later after being pardoned by the governor. He died in Oakland, California around 1939.

24. Actually it was J. T. Waters.

25. These were very different times. Friends often shared the same bed in total innocence. Necessity made this common practice and there was no implication of homosexuality. In fact, for several years Abraham Lincoln as a young man lived with his friend, Joshua Speed, sharing a double bed with him in a room above a general store that Speed ran.

26. Wyatt was slightly off on this. On July 25, 1880, E. L. Bradshaw did kill J. T. Waters, but it was Waters who wore the shirt. The *Epitaph* reported:

Yesterday morning Water's purchased a blue and black plaid shirt, little dreaming that the faded garment would hurl his soul into eternity before the sun had set. It so happened that several good natured remarks were made about the new shirt during the day until Waters had taken sufficient liquor to make the joking obnoxious to him, and he began to show an ugly resentment and was very abusive, concluding with, "Now, if anyone don't like what I've said let him get up, G–d d—m him. I'm chief. I'm boss. I'll knock the first s— of a b—— down that says anything about my shirt again." This happened in the back room at Corrigan's Saloon and as Waters stepped into the front room Bradshaw happened in, and seeing the new shirt his friend was wearing made some pleasant remark about it, whereupon Waters, without a word, struck Bradshaw a powerful blow over the left eye which sent him senseless to the floor. Waters then walked over to Vogan & Flynn's, to see, as he said, "if any s— of a b—— there don't like this shirt." He had just entered the street when Ed Farris made some remark about the new shirt, which Waters promptly resented in his pugilistic style. After some more rowing Waters went back to Corrigan's Saloon. As soon as Bradshaw recovered from the knockdown he went into the back room, washed off the blood, went down to his cabin, put a bandage on his eye and his pistol in his pocket. He then came up to Allen Street and took his seat in front of Vogan's and Flynn's Saloon. Seeing Waters in Corrigan's door, Bradshaw crossed towards the Eagle Brewery, and walking down the sidewalk until within a few feet of Waters, said: "Why did you do that?" Waters said something whereupon Bradshaw drew his pistol and fired four shots, all taking effect, one under the left arm probably pierced the heart, two entered about the center of his back between his shoulders and one in the top of the head ranged downward toward the neck, any one of which would probably have resulted fatally. Water's fell at the second shot and soon expired. Bradshaw was promptly arrested and an examination will be had in the morning before Justice Gray.

27. The name they have here is difficult to read, but it should be Luke Short. This happened on February 25, 1881, and Bat Masterson was there. He wrote about it in his April 1907 article on Short that appeared in *Human Life* magazine.

The spring of 1881 found Luke Short in Tombstone, Arizona, dealing faro in a house managed by Wyatt Earp.

One morning I went into the Oriental gambling house, where Luke was working, just in time to keep him from killing a gambler named Charlie Storms. There was scarcely any difference between this case and the one with the bad man in Leadville, a couple of years previous. Charlie Storms was one of the best-known gamblers in the entire West and had, on several occasions, successfully defended

himself in pistol fights with Western "gun-fighters."

Charlie Storms and I were very close friends,—as much as Short and I were—and for that reason I did not care to see him get into what I knew would be a very serious difficulty. Storms did not know Short, and, like the bad man in Leadville, had sized him up as an insignificant-looking fellow, whom he could slap in the face without expecting a return.

Both men were about to pull their pistols when I jumped between them and grabbed Storms at the same time requesting Luke not to shoot,—a request I knew he would respect if it was possible without endangering his own life too much. I had no trouble in getting Storms out of the house, as he knew me to be his friend. When Storms and I reached the street I advised him to go to his room and take a sleep, for I then learned for the first time that he had been up all night, and had been quarreling with other persons.

He asked me to accompany him to his room, which I did, and after seeing him safely in his apartment, where I supposed he could go to bed, I returned to where Short was. I was just explaining to Luke that Storms was a very decent sort of man when, lo and behold! there he stood before us. Without saying a word, he took hold of Luke's arm and pulled him off the sidewalk, where he had been standing, at the same time pulling his pistol, a Colt's cut-off, [.]45 calibre, single action; but like the Leadvillian, he was too slow, although he succeeded in getting his pistol out. Luke stuck the muzzle of his pistol against Storms' heart and pulled the trigger. The bullet tore the heart asunder, and as he was falling, Luke shot him again. Storms was dead when he hit the ground. Luke was given a preliminary hearing before a magistrate and exonerated.

28. The defense tried emphasizing Tombstone's lawlessness so they could say that Tombstone was not the sort of place a newlywed couple would go to and that a common law marriage would mean nothing in such a Sodom and Gomorrah. Hoy was trying to counteract those arguments here.

29. Sic.

30. Sic.

31. North.

32. The Dragoon Mountains.

33. Billy Breckenridge, Behan's deputy. He went on to become the U.S. marshal for Arizona.

34. North.

35. Carrie Hanson Warnecros. Carrie was a "wild flower" who worked for Mrs. Fallon (a.k.a. Samantha Taylor, etc.) at the San Jose House. She later married Paul Warnecros, who was a dentist in Tombstone until Howard Herring—Colonel Herring's son—died in his dentist's chair from an overdose of cocaine, which they used as an anesthetic in those days. Many people wanted to try the dentist for

murder, but the D.A. decided not to prosecute, probably because it wasn't intentional. Warnecros fled Tombstone and apparently took prostitute Carrie Hanson with him to Los Angeles.

36. Sic.

37. Turkey Creek Johnson.

38. North.

39. Artemus Emmett Fay was the *Nugget*'s first publisher. He had previously been the editor of the *Tucson Star*.

40. Mrs. Crabtree, Carlotta Crabtree Cockburn's mother.

41. Sic.

42. Sic.

43. Sic.

44. Sic.

45. Sic.

46. He didn't become deputy sheriff until July 27, 1880.

47. Sic.

48. This is a big exaggeration.

49. Sic throughout this deposition. Sheriff Charles A. Shibell.

50. He was deputy sheriff from July 27, 1880 to November 9, 1880.

51. Bob Paul, the man who was riding as shotgun messenger when Bud Philpott was murdered.

52. When Wyatt resigned, Bob Paul had already lost the election through fraud. Wyatt resigned so he could help Paul prove the fraud had taken place. They were successful and Paul became the sheriff of Pima County.

53. Sic throughout, Clantons.

54. This was 19-year-old William Crownover Parker, Jr., whose wealthy father financed his ventures in Tombstone.

55. Milt Joyce leased the bar and restaurant concessions at the Oriental Saloon, where Wyatt and his partners leased the gambling concession. On October 11, 1880, less than a month after Doc's arrival in Tombstone and shortly after Wyatt threw Johnny Tyler out of the Oriental, Tyler was back in the Oriental having a confrontation with Doc. Doc challenged Tyler to draw his weapon and fire, but Tyler decided to back down and soon left town.

After Tyler retreated from the Oriental, Doc handed his gun over to the bartender and it was placed behind the counter. Joyce then began in on Doc for his bloodlust. Doc was in no mood for Joyce's abuse, so he stepped outside and borrowed a gun. According to the *Nugget*, he "walked toward Joyce, who was just coming from behind the bar, and with a remark that would not look good in print, turned loose with a self-cocker. Joyce was not more than ten feet away and jumped for his assailant and struck him over the head with a six-shooter, felling him to the floor and lighting on top of him. Officers [Fred] White and Bennett were near at hand and separated them, taking the pistols from each. Just how many shots were fired none present seemed able to tell but in casting up accounts Joyce was found to be shot through the hand, his partner, Mr. Parker, who was behind the bar, shot through the big toe of the left foot, and Holliday with a blow of the pistol in Joyce's hands." Wyatt and Behan were also present when all this took place. Joyce sided with the outlaws in the Earp-outlaw war.

56. Sic.

57. Sic.

58. It was on a Kinnear & Co. stage that Wyatt rode as shotgun messenger for Wells Fargo. This was also the stage on which Bud Philpott was killed.

59. Sic.

60. December 1881.

61. Wyatt probably didn't even have a marriage license for himself and his second wife, Celia Ann "Mattie" Blaylock.

62. The copy of Wyatt's deposition in the court records is a carbon and is unsigned.

Tombstone in 1881 facing east.

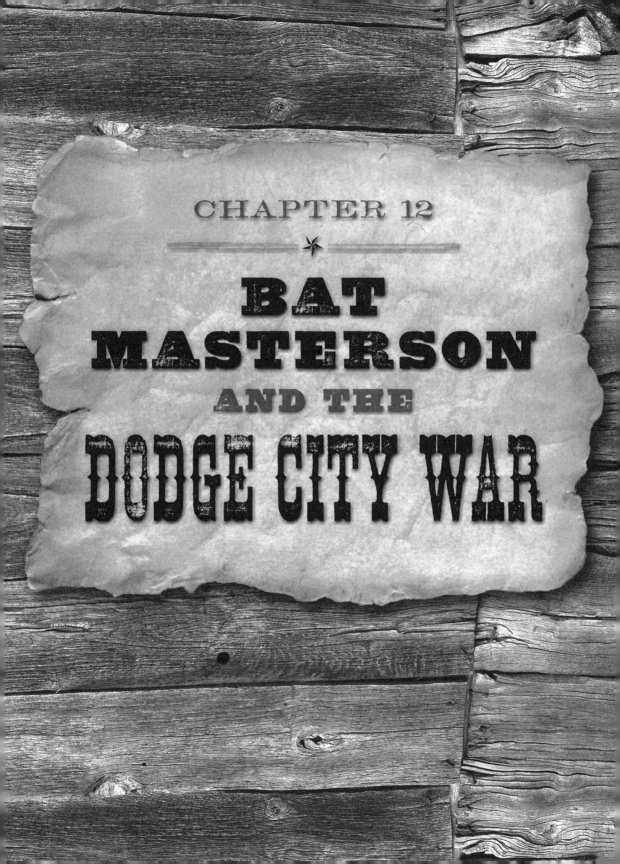

# CHAPTER 12

✦

# BAT MASTERSON AND THE DODGE CITY WAR

WHEN BAT MASTERSON was born in Canada in 1853, his name was Bertholomiew, but he grew to hate it as he got older, and when he was able to, he changed his name to William Barclay Masterson, but the diminutive form of his original name stayed with him. Bat went on to be marshal of Dodge City and Ford County's second sheriff. He was a friend of President Theodore Roosevelt, who in 1905 appointed him deputy U.S. marshal of the southern district of New York state. Roosevelt later tried to make him U.S. Marshal of Oklahoma, but Bat refused the position. He remained a close friend to Wyatt until he died in 1921.

This article on Bat was Wyatt's third for the *San Francisco Examiner*. It was published on Sunday, August 16, 1896.

# WYATT EARP'S TRIBUTE TO BAT MASTERSON THE HERO OF 'DOBE WALLS.

Five men, riding to the summit of a knoll, caught sight of a deserted adobe house in a hollow at their feet. As the sun sank toward the edge of the prairie they found their refuge for the night.[1]

The solitude of the building was more painful than the solitude of the plains; the yellowish walls glimmered like the walls of a vault in the gloom that had settled in the hollow as sediment settles in a glass. But these things did not matter, for there was water close by, and those grim walls were thick to stop bullets as well as arrows.

The five men watered their weary horses at the creek, and then drove picket-pins into the ground within a stone's throw of the house, where there was plenty of grass, and tethered the animals thereto with their lariats. Next they unlimbered their heavy saddles and carried them into the house. The plainsman's saddle is more precious to him than jewels. In this case, bacon, coffee and army biscuits were involved. More important still, there was ammunition, and plenty of it.

It was a quarter of a century ago.[2] The five men were scouts, carrying dispatches from Dodge City to Camp Supply,[3] through a country depopulated and laid waste

Bat Masterson in about 1876. He would have been around 23 years old
when this picture was taken in Dodge City.

by the Cheyennes.[4] Their camping place was within forty miles of Camp Supply, in
the heart of that No-Man's-Land known as the Panhandle of Texas.

When the first rays of the sun came slanting over the prairie one of the men went
out to water the horses, while his comrades prepared breakfast. Ping! A rifle shot
startled the solitude. The four men rushed to the door. The fifth was lying face down-

ward two hundred yards from the house.[5] The horses were plunging and tugging at the ropes. In another second or two they had broken lariats or torn up picket-pins and galloped madly away. A horse can smell an Indian.[6]

Another moment, and a hail of bullets and arrows spattered against the 'dobe walls. Then five hundred yelling Indians[7] galloped from behind a knoll and charged the building.

The four surviving scouts were ready for them. Everything was orderly and precise. It did not need that many words should be spoken. What few laconic orders that were given came from the youngest man in the party. He was a mere boy—a bright, sturdy boy,[8] whose wide, round eyes expressed the alert pugnacity of a blooded bull-terrier. To look at him one could not doubt that nature had molded him for a fighter.

The plan of defense was very simple. Like all buildings in that wild country, the old 'dobe house was provided with portholes on every side. It was a question of shooting fast and shooting straight through those portholes, and the scouts knew how to shoot both fast and straight. The fire was more than the Cheyennes could stand.[9] With a baffled yell they wheeled and retreated, picking up their killed and wounded as they galloped to cover behind one of the many knolls that encompassed the house like the mighty billows of a frozen ocean.

That one charge was the history of the day.[10] It was repeated again and again, first on one side of the house and then on another.[11] Each charge found the scouts prepared, and each time the Indians carried a dozen or more of their dead off the field.

Toward evening there was a brief breathing spell.

"I'm going to bring him," said the youngest scout—the boy with the bull-terrier eyes—pointing at the body lying on its face near the stampeded picket.

"Better not try, Bat, they'll get ye sure."

"We can't leave him lying there like that."

And taking his rifle in his hand the boy went. He ran out under fire and he staggered back under fire with the body in his arms.

More charges, followed by a sleepless night, to guard against surprises. And at daybreak the fighting began again. Never before were Indians known to make such a stubborn fight. Never before did such a handful hold such a horde at bay. The face of the plain was befreckled with blood up to a radius of fifty yards of the house, but how many dead Indians had been carried off the beleaguered men had no means of knowing.[12] One of them had his leg half shot away and all were sick from exhaustion, when at midafternoon a company of cavalry came riding over the plain and the Indians fled.[13]

Thus was fought the "battle of 'dobe walls," the event which made young Bat Masterson a hero on the frontier.

It was not long afterward that Bat drifted to Sweetwater,[14] where he became a lively citizen of as lively a town as ever subsisted on the patronage of a frontier army post. Bat was no more a laggard in love than he was a dastard in war, and Annie Chambers[15] was as proud of her handsome little hero as he was fond of his dashing, red-haired beauty. I had never met Bat at that time, but I had known Annie both in Leavenworth and Ellsworth. She was as fine a girl as ever set in a frontier town by the ears, and she was better educated than most women of her kind.

Sergeant King,[16] one of the most notorious bullies and gun fighters in the army, wanted to dance with Annie one night and because she refused he pulled his six-shooter and shot her in the breast. Even as she fell, dying, into Bat's arms the latter jerked his gun on the soldier and shot him dead, but not before King had pumped some lead into Bat's groin.

That was one of the killings for which Bat Masterson has been held up by some ignorant writers as a shocking example of ferocity and lawlessness. But of the many men he killed there was not one who was not in the wrong, and not one who did not start in with the best of the fight. Shocking as it may seem to civilized souls, we had our crude code of honor on the frontier. When I speak of a fair fighter I mean a man who will not fight for what he knows to be a bad cause, and who will not take his enemy at a disadvantage. Such a man is Bat Masterson.

Bat was acquitted, of course, and soon afterward came over to Dodge City, where I had just been installed as City Marshal.[17]

His fame as the hero of 'dobe walls and the slayer of Sergeant King had preceded Bat to Dodge, and he attracted no end of respectful attention as he limped from one gambling house to another, still pale and weak from the effect of King's bullet. Bat was somewhat of a dandy in those days, but before all else he was a man. Not that his physique entitled him to attention beyond other men, for in his case nature had packed a big consignment of dynamic energy into a small compass and corded it up tight. But there was something in the way his bullet-shaped head was mounted on his square shoulders, something in the grain of his crisp, wiry hair, something in the tilt of his short nose that bespoke an animal courage such as not every man is endowed withal.

Mere animal courage has made many a man a brute and an assassin, but Bat Masterson had a wealth of saving graces which shone from the honest fullness of his face. I have already spoken of his eyes. They were well-nigh unendurable in conflict—so bold, to[18] bright, so unmitigable was their gaze; but in moments of peace they danced with mischief, with generosity, with affection. A small and carefully nurtured coal-black mustache half hid a mouth which was readier to soften in mirth than to harden in anger, and the stubborn chin beneath was cleft with the dimple that physiognomists interpret as the symbol of a kindly heart.

In moving from Wichita to take the Marshalship of Dodge City at my own salary I had stipulated that I should have the appointment of my own police force.[19] A fair judge of manhood as I esteemed myself, what wonder that I should have fastened hungry official eyes upon the hero of 'dobe walls?

"Bat," said I, "will you join the force?"

"I'd like it first-rate," he replied.

"Then throw away that cane and get to work," I said.

And forthwith Bat was sworn in to protect the peace.[20]

During the summer that he served with me—before he ran for Sheriff and was elected[21]—stirring events came to pass in Dodge City. And like the Arizona feud of which I have already written,[22] they all arose out of one small incident. That incident was the killing of "The Nightingale."

One night a Texas desperado named Kennedy[23] was diverting himself at a dance-hall by flourishing his six-shooter. Mayor Kelly happened to be there, and as there was no officer present to restrain the Texan he took it upon himself to interfere.[24]

"You'd better give them guns to the bartender, my boy," he said kindly, "or some of my men will arrest ye."

Kennedy resented the suggestion and there was a dispute. But there was no word or thought of killing at that time. The Mayor's remonstrance rankled in Kennedy's mind, however, and at 2 o'clock in the morning[25] he started out to kill the Chief Executive.

Mounting his horse, so as to be in readiness for flight, the Texan rode down to the house where Kelly lived. The room where the Mayor and his wife slept opened on to the street,[26] and Kennedy knew the direction in which the bed lay at the opposite end of the room. On the other side of a slender partition was another bed, occupied by Willett and his wife. Willett was a clerk for a neighboring grocer; his wife was a vaudeville woman of varied experiences on the frontier, and so sweet a singer that she was called "The Nightingale."[27] Ask any man who knew Deadwood or Dodge in its prime to tell you how she sang "Killarney."

And so, making a careful estimation of the elevation of the Mayor's bed, Kennedy began to empty his Winchester through the panels of the door. He calculated well, for two bullets went through the down comforter under which the Kellys slumbered. Nearly all the shots penetrated the partition behind their bed.[28]

About that time Willett half awoke and turned over on his side, throwing his arm around his wife. At his touch her body fluttered like that of a wounded bird, and something bubbled in her throat. Willett was wide awake in an instant—he did not know why. His hand touched something wet upon her breast and he asked her what it was; but there was no reply. Willett jumped out of bed and lit a match. It was blood upon his hand. It was blood upon the woman's breast. A bullet had torn its way clear through her body. The Nightingale was dead.

Poor Willett ran over to me and I pulled on my clothes in a hurry. The only house where there was a light was the Long Branch saloon, so I went in there for information. Kennedy was there, sitting on a monte[29] table, swinging his legs.

"Was he here when the shots were fired?" I whispered to the bartender.

"For God's sake don't say anything here," was the reply. "Come into the back room and I'll tell you all about it."

"Kennedy's the man," he continued excitedly, when we had retired out of earshot. "He left here with another man just before the shooting and immediately afterward he came in the back way and took a big drink of whiskey."

I ran back to the bar, but Kennedy had gone.

Bat joined me just then. He had been down to the house and the Mayor had told him all about the trouble in the dance hall.[30] In searching the town for Kennedy we ran across the man in whose company he had left the saloon, and this fellow more than confirmed our suspicions of the Texan's guilt. Moreover, he led us to the alley where the murderer had tied his horse, and from there we picked up a clear trail leading out of the city.

☞ TOM THORNTON, WHO RAN a hotel in Galeyville, described the cowboys to the *San Francisco Examiner*, saying, "There are some who have followed the frisky longhorn herds over the Texas plains, but nine-tenths of them never saw Texas. They were wild, reckless men from all over the world. They do not work, and they are never without money. They live in a style that you city folks would despise no doubt, but still they are never actually without food, a good horse, arms, ammunition and blankets. They are not all brave, and often sneak away from danger, but in my twenty years' intercourse with them I never knew one them to whine and squeal when he knew he had to die. They will run away from death, but when cornered will look into the muzzle of a six-shooter with defiant indifference."

At daylight Bat, Bill Tillghman[31] and I started out on the trail, taking this man along with us.[32] For two days we followed it across the prairie toward the Texas border, and then a heavy rainstorm came up and swept away all vestige of a hoofprint.[33]

At a distance of nearly 100 miles from Dodge we made a circuit of fifteen miles in order to get to a ranch for the night.

"Some of these here Texans are going home pretty early ain't they?" was the ranchman's greeting. "Kennedy was here yesterday afternoon, and he seemed in a hurry too."

Thus we picked up another trail, only to lose it again next day, when we were overtaken by more rain. In this predicament we made for a ranch twenty miles further on and reached the place at 3 o'clock in the afternoon. Our horses were fagged out, so we turned them out to grass and prepared to rest ourselves. After a while we caught sight of a horseman four or five miles away across the prairie, evidently making for the ranch. We watched him with idle curiosity, and when he came within a couple of miles of us Bat said, with conviction: "That's Kennedy. I know him by the way he rides; and besides, I know his horse." And when the stranger had arrived within a mile of the ranch we all knew that Bat, who had the eye of a hawk, was right.

Our horses were scattered over the pasture and it was too late to attempt to capture them. We agreed that it would be unwise to wait until Kennedy should get too close, least he should recognize our horses and wheel in his tracks. So we ambushed ourselves behind a heap of earth that had been thrown up from a new well, first agreeing that if he should scent danger and turn to make a run for it I should kill the horse and Bat attend to the man.

When he came within seventy-five yards of us we rose up and called him to halt. He whipped out his gun, firing at us as he wheeled his horse.[34] True to our agreement I shot the horse, which dropped just as Bat landed a bullet in Kennedy's shoulder.[35]

Well, we took away his six-shooters and his Winchester, hired a team and drove him back to Dodge. But the brute was never convicted. He was a son of a multi-millionaire cattleman by a Mexican mother, and his father's money procured him endless delays, and finally an acquittal.[36]

But the incidents connected with the wounding and capture of Kennedy for the murder of the Nightingale deepened the hatred bestowed upon Bat Masterson and myself by the Texan rustlers from whose violence we tried to protect the citizens of Dodge. Dodge had become the center of the cattle trade then, and the periodic incursions of cowboys, whose chief ambition was to be able to go back to Texas and boast of having "killed an orf'cer" were the curse of the community. The townspeople hated the Texans,[37] and the Texans despised the townspeople. In the vernacular of the feud the Southerners were "long horns," the Northerners "short horns."[38]

It was after Bat Masterson had been returned as Sheriff that I paid the visit to Mexico, during which I first met Doc Holliday and his Big-nose Kate, as told in a previ-

☞ "MOST COWBOYS THINK IT'S an infringement on their rights to give up shooting in town..."
  —An old cowman quoted by Andy Adams in his novel, Log of a Cowboy (1903)

ous story.[39] During my absence Ed Masterson, Bat's elder brother, acted as my deputy.[40] A crowd of cowboys started shooting in the Birdcage dance hall[41] one night and Ed went over to see about it. He disarmed them all and made them pile their guns behind the bar. Then he returned across the deadline—the avenue formed by the railroad tracks, which divided the decent from the disreputable part of the town. Not long afterward, however, the cowboys recovered their six-shooters and began firing again. Ed went back to restore order and tried to disarm the first cowboy he encountered. The two men were scuffling for possession of the gun, when another cowboy fired at Ed Masterson and killed him.

Just at that moment Bat Masterson had appeared, attracted by the shooting. He saw his brother fall and with a quick drop killed the man who had fired the shot. The rest began to run away, shooting, and Bat winged the man with whom Ed had been scuffling. He died a few days later, while they were taking him back to Texas.[42]

Thus was perpetrated another of the so-called atrocities with which the hero of 'dobe walls was to be reproached in after years by writers whose knowledge of the frontier was derived from Bowery melodramas.

In view of the bloody complications closing in on my narrative it is high time that I introduced Bob Wright,[43] the deus-ex-machina[44] of much of the violent work that followed. Bob Wright was a tower of strength to the Texas faction.[45] He had lived in their country and he depended on their patronage for the prosperity of his store, which was one of the largest in the city. He was a legislator, too—a duly elected representative from the county.

Bob Wright sought to interfere with me one night because I was taking one ill-behaved cattleman, who happened to be worth some millions of dollars, to the calaboose. My prisoner had tried to kill an inoffensive Dutch fiddler for not playing his favorite tune often enough to please him. The cattleman appealed to Wright, and Wright threatened to have me put off the city force if I persisted in the arrest. The upshot of it was that I threw Wright into the calaboose to keep his friend company for the night. It was soon after that incident that the Texans began to hatch plots to kill me by foul means or fair—preferably the former.[46]

The first attempt fell to the lot of a desperado named Hoyt,[47] who was no 'prentice in the art of assassination. I was standing on the sidewalk outside a saloon one bright moonlight night,[48] talking to Eddie Foy, who was leaning against the doorway, when Hoyt came riding down the street on a white horse. I noticed that he had his right hand by his side, but did not suspect anything until he came within ten steps of where I was standing. Then he threw his gun over like lightening and took a shot at me. By the time he was on a level with me he had taken another shot, but both missed.

I ran out, intending to pull him off his horse, and, failing that, I tried to grab his horse's tail as it passed me. But the horse was too quick for me, and as Hoyt dug in his spurs he wheeled in his saddle and fired at me again. With that I crouched down in the middle of the road for a steady aim, and emptied my gun after him as he tore down the road. I saw him disappear over the bridge that spanned the Arkansas river, and made sure I had missed him. But five minutes later, when I was telling the story to Bat Masterson and a crowd of citizens, the white horse came galloping back, mounted by a boy, who told us that its rider was lying, badly shot, just beyond the bridge. Half suspecting an ambush, Bat and I took shotguns and went back with the boy. There, sure enough, was Hoyt, full of lead and remorse, and groaning most dolefully. Two or three days later he died.[49]

This episode was not without its humorous side, for to this day Eddie Foy, the comedian, is fond of telling how, at the first shot, he threw himself under a monte table and stayed there till the shooting was over.[50]

Undeterred by Hoyt's fate, the plotters sent Clay Allison,[51] and the noted Colorado gun-fighter hastened to Dodge City to kill the City Marshal.[52] Let not the gentle reader, unused to frontier ways, jump to the conclusion that Allison was a hired bravo. He would probably have resented the imputation with deadly alacrity. It was reputation he was after, not money. To have killed me would meant for him to bask in the chaste effulgence of frontier fame for the rest of his days.

And so Clay Allison came to town, and for a whole day behaved like a veritable Chesterfield.[53] But the next morning one of my policemen woke me up to tell me that the

The Long Branch saloon in Dodge City. Owned by Luke Short and
Bill Harris, it was the focal point of the Dodge City War.

The interior of the Long Branch saloon in Dodge City.

bad man from Colorado was loaded up with rum and searching for me everywhere with a pair of six-shooters and a mouthful of threats. Straightway I put my guns on and went down the street with Bat Masterson. Now, Bat had a shotgun in the District Attorney's office, which was behind a drug store just opposite Wright's store. He thought the weapon might come in handy in case of trouble, so he skipped across the street to get it. But not caring to be seen with such a weapon before there was any occasion for it, he stayed over there, talking to some people outside the drug store, while I went into Webster's saloon looking for Allison. I saw at a glance that my man wasn't there, and had just reached the sidewalk to turn into the Long Branch, next door, when I met him face to face.

We greeted each other with caution thinly veiled by insouciance,[54] and as we spoke backed carelessly up against the wall, I on the right. There we stood, measuring each other with sideway glances. An onlooker across the street might have thought we were old friends.

"So," said Allison truculently, "you're the man that killed my friend Hoyt."

"Yes, I guess I'm the man you're looking for," said I.

His right hand was stealing round to his pistol pocket, but I made no move. Only I watched him narrowly. With my own right hand I had a firm grip on my six-shooter, and with my left I was ready to grab Allison's gun the moment he jerked it out. He studied the situation in all its bearings for the space of a second or two. I saw the change in his face.

"I guess I'll go round the corner," he said abruptly.

"I guess you'd better," I replied.

And he went.

In the meantime ten or a dozen of the worst Texans in town were laying low in Bob Wright's store, with their Winchesters, ready to cover Allison's retreat out of town, or help him in the killing, if necessary. From where he had stationed himself Bat Masterson could see them, but I did not know they were there. After the encounter with Allison I moved up the street and would have passed Bob Wright's door had not Bat, from across the street, signaled to me to keep out of range. A moment later Allison, who had mounted his horse, rode out in front of Webster's and called to me.

"Come over here, Wyatt," he said, "I want to talk to you."

"I can hear you all right here," I replied. "I think you came here to make a fight with me, and if you did you can have it right now."

Several friends of mine wanted me to take a shotgun, but I thought I could kill him all right with a six-shooter. At that moment Bob Wright came running down the street to urge Allison to go out of town. He had experienced a sudden change of heart because Bat had crossed over to him with these portentous words: "If this fight comes up, Wright, you're the first man I'm going to kill."[55] Allison listened to the legislator's entreaties with a scowl.

"Well, I don't like you any too well," he said. "There were a lot of your friends to be here this morning[56] to help me out, but I don't see them round now.

"Earp," he continued, turning to me and raising his voice. "I believe you're a pretty good man from what I've seen of you. Do you know that these coyotes sent for me to make a fight with you and kill you? Well, I'm going to ride out of town, and I wish you good luck."

And so Clay Allison made his exit. Ten days later he reappeared within a mile of town and sent a messenger asking my permission to come into Dodge and attend to some business regarding his cattle. I sent him word that he was welcome to come so long as he behaved himself. He availed himself of the offer, and for two weeks he behaved like an exemplary citizen. It was a fourteen day's wonder, for Allison had never in his life before conducted himself like a Christian. Indeed, it had been his practice to force every store, saloon and bank other than those he patronized to close up during such time as he honored a frontier town with a visit.

☞ "WYATT DIDN'T SWEAR, OR call names. He didn't have to raise his voice."

—*Jack Archer, stagecoach driver*

A year or so later Allison came to an ignominious end by falling off a wagon and breaking his neck.[57]

It was a day or two after my bloodless encounter with the famous Colorado fighter that Wright came to me with the olive branch, made a clean break of the Hoyt and Allison conspiracies, and offered me his friendship in return for my protection from his erstwhile friends, the Texans.

Even the Allison adventure was topped off with an epilogue of a grimly humorous kind, which I cannot forbear telling. Bat Masterson was speculating on the havoc his shotgun would have wreaked in the ranks of the cowboys if he had enjoyed a chance to use it that morning, and for the sake of a change of air and a little target practice he and I rode out of town, upended a broad plank and began firing at it. First of all Bat fired both barrels of his shotgun, which was loaded just as he had picked it up in the District Attorney's office when I was looking for Allison. Walking up to the board he found to his dismay that the gun had been loaded not with buckshot, as he thought, but with the finest of birdshot. Somebody, he learned afterwards, had borrowed the gun for a day's sport, and had left it loaded on returning it to its place.

"It would have been just the same,"[58] grumbled Bat, "if a good man's life had depended on that charge in that gun."

And now for the last, but not the least dramatic episode by which Bat's memory and mine are linked with Dodge City—not the Dodge City of cowboy revelry and bloodshed, but the Dodge City of what I can't help thinking a decadent if more decorous era.

As the town grew civilized Bat Masterson and I drifted to Tombstone. Jim Masterson,[59] another of Bat's brothers, remained in Dodge, a partner with Uptograph[60] and Peacock in the possession of a saloon and gambling house. Jim had a dispute with his partners about the division of profits, and three or four of their creatures jumped on him. He escaped to his room with the intention of getting a gun and they surrounded the place, keeping him prisoner a whole day. Some of his friends telegraphed for Bat, and he traveled the 1,500 miles to make a fight with his brother's enemies.

He arrived in Dodge at 9 o'clock, one morning,[61] and had hardly stepped from the train when the other faction, who knew of his coming, started across the deadline to meet him. When they got within fifty yards of him they gave him a shot or two by way of welcome, and he returned the fire with such effect as to inflict a mortal wound on Uptograph.[62]

Thereupon Mayor Webster[63] appeared with a double-barreled shotgun and arrested Bat, who was afterwards fined $10 and ordered to leave Dodge for the rest of his life.[64] You see, Dodge had become so civilized that it had no further use for the men who had been its best protectors in the days of the Texas Terror.

☞ Greatly exaggerating the accomplishments of Short's friends, a local paper reported:

> "A brief history of these gentlemen who will meet here tomorrow will
> explain the gravity of the situation. At the head is Bat Masterson. He is
> credited with having killed one man for every year of his life. This may be
> exaggerated, but he is certainly entitled to a record of a dozen or more, He
> is a cool, brave man, pleasant in his manners, but terrible in a fight. Doc
> Holliday is another famous killer. Among the desperate men of the West,
> he is looked upon with the respect born of awe, for he has killed in single
> combat no less than eight desperadoes. He was the chief character in the
> Earp war at Tombstone, where the celebrated brothers, aided by Holliday,
> broke up the terrible rustlers. Wyatt Earp is equally famous in the cheer-
> ful business of depopulating the country. He has killed within our personal
> knowledge six men, and he is popularly accredited with relegating to the
> dust no less than ten of his fellow men. Shotgun Collins was a Wells,
> Fargo & Co. messenger, and obtained his name from the peculiar weapon
> he used, a sawed-off shotgun. He has killed two men in Montana and two in
> Arizona, but beyond this his exploits are not known. Luke Short, for whom
> these men have rallied, is a noted man himself. He has killed several men
> and is utterly devoid of fear."

It was not long after Bat's banishment that this very Webster, the Mayor,[65] fell foul
of another frontiersman—no less redoubtable a gambler and gun fighter than Luke
Short.[66] Luke and a man named Harris[67] kept a gambling house next door to one kept
by the Mayor, and as Luke was well known in Texas and all over the frontier they
enjoyed most of the patronage. In order to harass his rivals the Mayor had an ordinance
passed denying women free access to the saloons—a prerogative which they had heretofore enjoyed in Dodge.[68] Moreover, he secured a piano to add to the attractions of his
own place and imported a professor to play it.

Short and Harris promptly furnished themselves with a handsomer piano and
hired two girls to play and sing. Webster ordered a policeman to arrest these two girls,
and they were taken to the calaboose.[69] Luke went over to bail them out, but the policeman refused to accept his bonds. In the argument that ensued the policeman fired at
Luke and Luke shot the policeman in the leg.[70]

Bat Masterson.

Thereupon Webster organized a shotgun brigade among his friends, and in the morning they marched Luke down to the depot, bundled him on board a train, and warned him never again to return to Dodge City.[71] Apart from the ignominy of the thing and the natural desire to get square with his enemy, this was a serious matter for Luke, who had been dragged away from a profitable business in the city. So he telegraphed to Bat Masterson,[72] and the pair of them, inspired by mutual friendship and a common grievance, tried to devise measures by which they could force the authorities of Dodge to receive them with the distinguished consideration which they conceived to be their due. Among other measures, they laid their grievance before the Governor of the State, who expressed his entire sympathy with them, and advised them to fight their way into the city if necessary.[73]

In this extremity they resorted to get my assistance, and Bat jumped on a train for Silverton, Col., where I was living at the time. (It should be understood that all this happened subsequent to the vendetta which resulted in my leaving Arizona).

Well, I was only too ready for anything with a spice of adventure in it, and especially for a chance to help two old friends. In particular I was indignant at the ingratitude with which Bat Masterson had been served by the city he had protected so well in its darkest hours. So I gathered around me a company of rough diamonds who had seen me through many a tough fight in Arizona, and started for Dodge City. Bat stopped off at Trinidad, for it was agreed that I and my merry men should go alone to make terms with the enemy. Luke Short was at Wichita.

Our train got to Dodge at 10 o'clock in the morning[74] and we marched up the street to Luke's Saloon, I with my Wells-Fargo shotgun and my men with their Winchesters. Body of Bacchus! No wonder Dodge City rubbed its eyes. There was Milsap,[75] there was Shotgun Collins,[76] there was Shoot-Your-Eye-Out Jack, who wore his hair down to his waist; and there was Crooked-Mouth Green,[77] whose features had been so mutilated by a bullet that his mouth extended round to the back of his head. Faithful followers and quick fighters, every one of 'em.[78]

We met the District Attorney[79] going up the street and his face wore a careworn, "come ye in peace now or come ye in war" look as he exclaimed:

"My God, Wyatt! Who are these people you've got with you?"

"Oh," said I, carelessly, "they're just some bushwackers I've brought over from Colorado to straighten you people out."

"In whose interests?" he asked.

"Luke Short's and Bat Masterson's"[80] I replied.

A few paces further on I met Mayor Webster, who shook hands with me with an air of cordiality that the yellowish pallor of his cheeks belied. We all filed into Luke's saloon and there we were sworn in as deputies by Prairie Dog Dave,[81] the Constable, who was with us blood and bones, as all the good people in town were. Indeed, the city was sick of the Webster reign of terror and glad to see a way out of it, and I soon had a following of a hundred or more fighters ready to do my bidding. It was no mean advantage to be deputized by Prairie Dog Dave, for that enabled us to carry our arms without violating the law concerning which Dodge had become so sensitive.

The town council convened a hurried meeting and sent for me to ask my intentions. I told them that I wanted Luke Short and Bat Masterson to return to Dodge at their pleasure. I added that if this were accomplished peacefully I would be so much better pleased, but that if necessary I was prepared to fight for my demands. In reply they offered to compromise. They would permit Luke to return for ten days to wind up his business. Bat Masterson they would not permit to enter the town. To this proposition I made no reply, but walked out of the council room. Soon afterward they sent for me again, and I again assured them that there could be no compromise—that Luke and Bat must be free to live in Dodge as long as they wanted to, provided they obeyed the laws.

Before the council had made any decision I wired to Luke Short to meet me at Kingsley,[82] thirty miles away. I had an idea he might decide to return with me, so I gave orders to my followers to post themselves in front of Wright's and at other strategic points in case of disturbance. Luke and I dined together at Kingsley and, as I had anticipated, he resolved to come back with me. But we agreed that we would let the other fellows begin the fighting.

Luke and I jumped off the rear platform of the sleeper as the train slowed up, each with a double-barreled shotgun in readiness and advanced up the street, fully expect-

The Dodge City Peace Commission.

ing to make a stiff fight for it.[83] But the enemy didn't appear. That night I telegraphed to Bat, telling him to come on the next train. He arrived in the morning and had no sooner alighted than a deputy sheriff demanded his shotgun, but I would not let him give it up.

I had hard work to persuade Bat to go into Webster's and shake hands with the Mayor,[84] but he consented at last and the trouble was over in a few minutes. We had conquered Dodge City without firing a shot. It was a great moral victory, for Bat and Luke were unmolested from that time forth.[85] Not that Bat stayed long to enjoy the fruits of his vindication, for he was then City Marshal of Trinidad.[86]

Among other manifestations of exuberance at the successful issue of our invasion the citizens dubbed us "the Dodge City Peace Commission" and had us photographed in a group, which is hereby reproduced. Crooked-Mouth Green and my other picturesque henchmen did not figure in this group, as they felt sensitive about submitting their physiognomies to the fierce light of frontier history. Which is really a pity.

As everybody knows, Bat Masterson has now for many years been identified with Denver, where he is appreciated at his true worth. His association with the prize ring and other forms of sport all over the country has brought his name prominently before a younger and more effete generation. And he has fallen into flesh. But to me he will always be Bat Masterson, the quick fighter, the square gambler, the staunch friend and generous foe—the fastest of my frontier friends.

WYATT S. EARP.

By the time of the Dodge City War, Wyatt was trying to keep a low profile, especially since Doc Holliday had been arrested in Denver the previous year on the outstanding warrants for the murders of Frank Stilwell and Florentino Cruz. It took considerable maneuvering to get him released. No doubt Wyatt desired to avoid this. Still, he wanted to help his friends Bat and Luke, so when his name began appearing in newspapers across the country, he apparently decided to spread some disinformation about his involvement and his whereabouts. This would explain a letter that appeared in the *Denver Tribune*, which was reprinted in the *La Plata Miner* on May 26, 1883. Wyatt arrived in Dodge the following week on the May 31st.[87]

MR. WYATT EARP, new of this city sends the following card to the Denver *Tribune*:

"Silverton, May 18.—Noticing the article in your issue of the 16th regarding a visit of a party of eight men to Dodge City, in which I am made to appear as one of said party, I write this to refute all such charges. For the past year my residence has been in San Francisco, and I have but recently come to this city, where I expect to remain the present summer. I knew nothing of any invasion of Dodge City, and have no idea of participating in such a step. For the benefit of my friends in Dodge and elsewhere will you kindly publish?

WYATT S. EARP.

This ploy seems to have worked to some extent, since the *La Plata Miner* wrote in a June 23, 1883 article on Luke's problems in Dodge City, "We are inclined to think that the facts are somewhat exaggerated, as the name Wyatt Earp has constantly been associated with the trouble, when the facts are that Earp has been a resident of Silverton for some months."

# References

1. Adobe Walls in the Texas panhandle was a small settlement that was little more than two stores, a storehouse, a corral, a blacksmith's shop, and a saloon with a restaurant in the back. All the buildings were in a line facing east. It was primarily a frontier outpost for groups of buffalo hunters.

   Wyatt probably got much of his information for this account from Bat many years earlier, which would explain the inaccuracies in his version of events.

2. The attack was on the morning of June 27, 1874.

3. Camp Supply (later Fort Supply) was in Indian Territory, or what would later be known as Oklahoma.

4. There were actually twenty-eight men and one woman—most of them buffalo hunters, including Bat. The country had been depopulated and laid waste by white hunters, settlers and the U.S. Army. Most of the remaining Native Americans had been forced onto desolate reservations with almost nothing to eat while their main source of food and clothing—the buffalo—was being decimated. In the three years from 1872 through 1874, 3.7 million buffalo were killed. Only four percent of this was by Native Americans. Army policy at the time was to allow the hunters to drive the buffalo to extinction in order to solve the "Indian problem." As General Philip Sheridan told a group of Texans who were concerned about the wholesale slaughter by hunters, "Let them kill, skin, and sell until the buffalo is exterminated, as it is the only way to bring lasting peace and allow civilization to advance." The buffalo were virtually gone by the following year. They were replaced by the Texas Longhorn and the land was repopulated by whites.

5. Four men were killed in the first few minutes—two were freighters that were caught outside the settlement. One of the other casualties accidentally shot himself.

6. Possibly, but they can definitely hear bullets.

7. Estimates of the number of Native Americans in the attack range all the way up to 1,000. Probably the best figure is found in the note Fred Leonard sent while under seige. He said there were about 200.

   The attackers were primarily Cheyennes, Kiowas, and Arapahos under the leadership of Chief Quanah Parker. Upset that the U.S. government was not keeping its promises to keep the buffalo hunters from trespassing onto lands that by treaty were for their sole use, the frustrated Chief Parker and his men decided to take care of the problem themselves.

8. Not hardly. Bat was 21.

9. One warrior later said, "The buffalo hunters were too much for us. They stand behind adobe walls. They had telescopes on their guns." The hunters also had long-range repeating rifles.

10. The initial attack lasted three hours.

11. The attackers were able to reach the buildings, where they tried breaking down the doors and shooting through holes they made in the roofs.

    Fred Leonard wrote, "At the height of the attack above the crash of the guns the besieged hunters were amazed to hear a clear urgent bugle call. Through the firing loopholes they watched amazed as the painted braves wheeled and swung into formation, answering the bugler's command as precisely as a trained regiment of troopers."

    Bat also wrote of this, saying:

    > We had in the building I was in [Hanrahan's Saloon], two men who had served in the United States Army and understood the bugle calls. The first blown call was a rally which our men instantly understood. The next was a charge and that also was understood, and immediately the Indians came

rushing forward to a fresh attack. Every bugle call he blew was understood by the ex-soldiers and was carried out to the letter by the Indians, showing the bugler had the Indians thoroughly drilled.

The bugler was killed late in the afternoon of the first day's fighting as he was running away from the wagon owned by the Shadler brothers both of whom had been killed in the same wagon. The bugler had his bugle with him at the time he was killed by Harry Armitage. Also, he was carrying a tin can filled with sugar and another filled with coffee, one under each arm. Armitage shot him through the back with a .50 caliber Sharps rifle, as he was making his escape.

12. Between fifteen and thirty were killed.

13. Chief Parker withdrew his warriors when he saw there was little chance of success and continued his raids elsewhere. Small bands remained behind and harassed the settlement for five or six days. Bat and several others set off to alert Dodge, but found that news of the attack had already reached there and a relief party of forty hunters was already on the way. Federal troops didn't arrive in Dodge until the first week in August. Bat signed on as one of the scouts to lead them to Adobe Walls. More than a dozen hunters were still there when the troops arrived, but they decided to abandon the place when the troops arrived.

14. Texas.

15. Documentation of this incident is slim. Most accounts give her name as Molly Brennan, but one of these names could be an alias. It happened on January 24, 1876, and all that's known for sure is that she and King were killed and Bat was wounded.

16. Corporal Melvin A. King. His real name was Anthony Cook. It's not known why he changed it.

17. Wyatt was deputy city marshal in May 1876, but by the next month he was a deputy sheriff.

18. Sic, so.

19. Wyatt was deputy marshal and then assistant marshal. The marshal at this time was 300-pound Lawrence "Larry" Deger, who held the post largely for political reasons. As assistant marshal, Wyatt would have been Dodge's top officer in all but title only. Wyatt would have been appointed by the mayor, but he may have been able to choose his own deputies.

20. If Bat served under Wyatt, it was for a very short period. There is no record of it.

21. Bat was elected sheriff of Ford County on November 6, 1877. He was 23 at the time.

22. In the first of Wyatt's *San Francisco Examiner* articles.

23. James "Spike" Kenedy, the son of a major Texas rancher who was part owner of a 390,000-acre ranch in what is now Kenedy County, Texas.

24. Mayor James "Dog" Kelley, who was part owner of the Alhambra Saloon in Dodge City, had ejected Kenedy from his establishment. Kenedy returned with a gun and threatened Kelley, but was arrested by City Marshal Charles "Charlie" Bassett. Kelley refused to press charges for attempted murder, so Kenedy was fined for carrying a concealed weapon. This was on July 29, 1878.

25. This happened three months later on October 4, 1878, at around 4:30 A.M.

26. Contemporary newspaper accounts say Kelley went to a hospital in Fort Dodge for treatment several days earlier. His bed was occupied by dance hall girl Fannie Garrettson.

27. This was 34-year-old Dora Hand, who went by the name Fannie Keenan. The newspapers fail to mention whether she was in bed with a clerk named Willett. If she was, they weren't married, as one paper said she had applied for a divorce from Theodore Hand. They may have been living together, but it seems more likely that Wyatt or his editor cleaned the story up a bit for their Sunday newspaper readership.

28. Kenedy fired two shots from his .44 caliber pistol. Both went through the partition. One passed through two quilts just above Miss Garrettson.

29. Monte: a card game using a deck of forty cards. Two layouts of two cards each are drawn from either the top or bottom of the deck and turned face up. Players place bets on one of the pairs that it will match the suit of the next card dealt.

30. Perhaps the story of the mayor being in the hospital was a cover and he actually was in his bed with the dance hall girl after all.

31. Noted lawman Bill Tilghman, who was one of Bat's deputies at this time.

32. Also in the posse were City Marshal Charlie Bassett and Deputy Sheriff William Duffy. Wyatt was assistant marshal at the time and Bat was sheriff.

33. The posse left at 2 P.M. on the day of the shooting and the storm hit that night. The *Dodge City Times* on October 12, 1878, said, "They started down the river road, halting at a ranch below the Fort, thence going south, traveling 75 miles that day. A heavy storm Friday night delayed the pursued and pursuers; but Saturday afternoon found the officers at a ranch near Mead City [now Meade], one hour in advance of Kennedy [sic] who said he was delayed by the storm in his proposed hasty exit to his cattle ranch at Tuscosa, Texas."

34. The *Times* said he stopped a few hundred yards off. After three commands to throw up his hands, he "raised his arm as though to strike his horse with a quirt he held in his hand."

35. The horse fell on Kenedy, pinning him to the ground. When Bat dragged Kenedy out from under the horse by grabbing Kenedy's wounded arm, Bat said he could hear the bones "craunch," but Kenedy only said, "You sons of bitches, I will get even with you for this."

36. On October 29, 1878 the *Ford County Globe* said, "His trial took place in the sheriff's office, which was too small to admit spectators. We do not know what the evidence was, or upon what grounds he was acquitted. But he is free to go on his way rejoicing whenever he gets ready."

Kenedy was hardly rejoicing. His shoulder had been destroyed by a .50 caliber slug from a Sharps rifle. Several inches of bone had to be removed from his useless arm. It was a while before he was well enough for his father to take him back to Texas. He died of typhoid six years later while under indictment for another murder.

37. That is, the townspeople who weren't making a load of money off the cowboys.

38. Just as in Tombstone, the Civil War wasn't quite over.

39. While Wyatt may have gone to Mexico, he primarily went to Texas and met Doc in Fort Griffin.

40. Edward "Little Ed" Masterson was appointed city marshal on December 4, 1877. The incident Wyatt describes here happened on April 9, 1878, at about 10:00 P.M.

41. The Lady Gay Dance Hall and Saloon. The Bird Cage Theater was in Tombstone.

42. On April 12, 1878, the *Topeka Commonwealth* quoted an extra edition of the *Ford County Globe* as saying:

> At 10 o'clock last night, City Marshal Edward Masterson, discovered that a cowboy who was working for Soburn of Kansas City, named Jack Wagner, was carrying a six-shooter contrary to the city ordinance. Wagner was at the time under the influence of liquor, but quietly gave up the pistol. The Marshal gave it to some one of Wagner's friends for safe keeping and stepped out into the street. No sooner had he done so than Wagner ran out after him pulling another pistol, which the Marshal had not observed. The Marshal saw him coming and turned upon Wagner and grabbed hold of him.
>
> Wagner shot Marshal Masterson at once through the abdomen, being so close to him that the discharge set the Marshal's clothes on fire.
>
> Marshal Masterson then shot Wagner.
>
> About this time a man named Walker got mixed up in the fight. He, it appears, was boss herder for Oburn, and Wagner was working under him. He also got shot once through the left lung and his right arm was twice broken.

The Masterson who did the shooting was Bat. The newspapers at the time were confused on this and mistakenly reported that Ed had shot his assailants, but Bat and other old timers were clear that Bat shot Wagner and Walker. Bat was standing about sixty feet away when he fired.

Additional information was added by the *Dodge City Times* of April 13th, "Early in the evening, Marshal Masterson disarmed Wagner; later Marshal Masterson and Deputy Marshal Nat Haywood tried the second time to disarm Wagner. While in the act, Masterson was shot in the abdomen. Walker in the meantime snapped a pistol in the face of officer Haywood. [Bat] Masterson fired four shots one of them striking Wagner in the bowels, Walker was struck three times, and his right arm partially shattered with the other shot."

Ed died within the hour, Wagner died twenty-one hours later, and Walker survived for awhile before he finally succumbed. The mayor sent a message to Wyatt asking him to return to Dodge and take over the job of assistant marshal. Ed was 26 when he was killed.

43. Bob Wright was one of the founders of Dodge City. He was also part owner of one of the stores at Adobe Walls and was there when it was attacked.

44. Deus-ex-machina: the unexpected agent.

45. The veracity of this story has yet to be established, but it sounds suspiciously like an incident that took place in the summer of 1877 where Mayor Kelley ordered Marshal Deger to release a prisoner. Deger refused, so the mayor fired him. Deger then threw the mayor in jail for interfering with an officer. Several months later the mayor and city council fired Deger and replaced him with Ed Masterson.

46. Apparently Wright wasn't too upset with Wyatt, because four years later he was the first to sign the statement by Dodge citizens supporting Wyatt after the O.K. Corral gunfight. After all, Wright was a businessman, not a cattleman.

47. George Hoy. Bat Masterson also wrote of this incident, which occurred on July 25, 1878. The next day an article in the *Dodge City Times* said:

> It seems that three or four herders were paying their respects to the city and institutions, and as is usually their custom, remained until about 3 o'clock in the morning, when they prepared to return to their camps. They buckled on their revolvers, which they were not allowed to wear around town, and mounted their horses, when all at once one of them conceived the idea that to finish the night's revelry and give the natives due warning of his departure, he must do some shooting, and forthwith he commenced to bang away, one of the bullets whizzing into a dance hall nearby, causing no little commotion among the participants in the 'dreamy waltz' and quadrille. Policemen Earp and [James] Masterson made a raid on the shootist who gave them two or three volleys, but fortunately without effect. The policemen returned the fire and followed the herders with the intention of arresting them. The firing then became general, and some rooster who did not exactly understand the situation, perched himself in the window of the dance hall and indulged in a promiscuous shoot all by himself. The herders rode across the bridge, followed by the officers. A few yards from the bridge one of the herders fell from his horse from weakness caused by a wound in the arm which he had received during the fracas. The other herder made good his escape. The wounded man was properly cared for and his

wound, which proved to be a bad one, was dressed by Dr. [T. L.] McCarty. His name is George Hoy, and he is rather an intelligent looking young man.

48. This incident happened about 8 P.M.

49. He died almost a month later. He was under bond for rustling at the time.

50. Eddie Foy was, at that time, a famous frontier comedian and vaudevillian. In his book, *Clowning Through Life* (1928), Foy said he was calling out a square dance when the shooting started.

> We were going merrily on with the dance when suddenly "Bang! Bang! Bang!" came a roar of eight or ten big pistols from the outer darkness, the crash from our windows and shrieks from the women.
> Everybody dropped to the floor at once, according to custom. Bat Masterson was just in the act of dealing a game of Spanish monte with Doc Holliday, and I was impressed by the instantaneous manner in which they flattened out like pancakes on the floor. I had thought I was pretty agile myself, but those fellow had me beaten by seconds at that trick."

Soon after this, Bat Masterson saved Foy's life when he was almost shot by English gambler and gunfighter Ben Thompson.

51. Robert "Clay" Allison was a famous gunfighter with a clubfoot and a mean streak. The number of deaths attributed to him is similar to the numbers that are often cited for Wyatt, Bat and Doc.

52. Charles Bassett was city marshal at this time. Wyatt was assistant marshal.

53. Chesterfield: elegant, urbane, or suave. So far no other documentation for the following story can be found. It's not the sort of thing that would make it into the papers unless a reporter happened to be on the scene. It is recorded that Clay Allison stopped off in Dodge in late July or early August of 1878 and again on September 5th.

54. Insouciance: indifference.

55. It's known Bat and Wright were good friends at a later date and Wyatt does say later in this article that Wright made things up with them.

56. Sic.

57. On July 1, 1887 he fell from his wagon and one of the wheels crushed his skull.

58. This is apparently a typo and should be "a shame."

59. Bat's younger brother was also a lawman. He became city marshal of Dodge after Wyatt left. He was part owner of the Lady Gay Dance Hall and Saloon with Al Updegraff and A. J. Peacock. Jim couldn't get along with Updegraff, who was an alcoholic and was consuming a large portion of the profits. Updegraff was Peacock's brother-in-law, so Peacock took his side.

60. Sic throughout this article, Updegraff.

61. On April 16, 1881 from Tombstone.

62. Updegraff was shot through the lung, but he survived. Bat was along the railroad tracks firing south. Peacock and Updegraff were around the corner of the jail, firing north toward the businesses on Front Street. Others joined the fight and several of the businesses had their windows shot out.

63. Alonzo B. Webster was Dodge's mayor from April 4, 1881 to April 3, 1883. When he gave up the job, he was replaced by one of his friends, Larry Deger—the same 300-pound Deger who was city marshal when Wyatt was a deputy.

Both Webster and Deger were part of a reform movement that was ostensibly against alcohol, gambling and prostitution, but they were really after power and control of the city. This is why, in spite of the anti-alcohol, etc. stance, Webster owned two saloons, among other things.

Bat had decided to leave Dodge shortly after he was defeated as sheriff in 1879 by another reform candidate, who happened to also be a saloon owner and bartender, though he was considered to be more of a merchant. Shortly after taking office, Webster had fired Jim Masterson as city marshal and turned the job over to one of his bartenders.

64. Bat took Jim with him after a financial settlement was reached over his share of the saloon.

65. It was two years later, just after Webster left office and Deger took over.

66. Twenty-nine-year-old Texan Luke Lamar Short was a good friend of Wyatt's. When Wyatt obtained part interest in the gambling concession at Tombstone's Oriental Saloon in late 1880 or early 1881, two of the dealers he recruited were Bat Masterson and Luke Short. True to his name, Luke was short. Bat described him as being 5' 6" and weighing about 140 pounds. "It was a small package," he wrote, "but one with great dynamic force."

67. William "Bill" Harris had been one of Wyatt's partners in the Oriental. He and Luke now owned the Long Branch Saloon in Dodge. He was also in the cattle business and founded Dodge's first bank. In the 1883 race for mayor, he had been Deger's opponent.

68. On April 26, 1883, the new mayor and city council passed two ordinances. One "for the suppressing of vice and immorality" levied fines from $5 to $100 on prostitutes and brothel keepers and the other against vagrancy carried fines from $10 to $100 for anyone "loitering, loafing or wandering" in the city without a job or visible means of support.

69. Whether they bought pianos is uncertain, but this was really over entertainment of a more intimate sort. On April 28, 1883, police raided the Long Branch and arrested three ladies of the evening. It appears the customers preferred the women at Luke's saloon over those at Webster's, and Webster was losing money. When Luke discovered none of the women in the other saloons had been arrested, he put on his pistols and headed for the jail.

70. Stories are conflicting as to who fired first, but neither were hit. Policeman Louis C. Hartman tripped and fell as

he was running away and apparently Luke thought he had killed him. Luke returned to the Long Branch and barricaded himself in. The next morning he was persuaded to come out and was promptly arrested and released on $2,000 bond.

71. A couple of days after his arrest, Luke was arrested again, along with five other gamblers, as being undesirables. They were held in jail while an armed crowd of vigilantes prevented their lawyers from seeing them. The next day the vigilantes, led by the mayor, escorted them to the station, where they were given the choice of east or westbound trains.

72. Bat, at this time, was the city marshal at Trinidad, Colorado.

73. Kansas Governor George Washington Glick telegraphed Dodge's sheriff to find out what was going on and sent for the county clerk of Ford County, who affirmed Luke's story. By this time, newspapers across the country were starting to call it "the Dodge City War." The governor wasn't pleased with the sheriff's response, saying:

> The accounts of the way things have been going on there are simply monstrous, and it requires that the disgrace that is being brought upon Dodge City, and the State of Kansas, by the conduct that is represented to have occurred there, should be wiped out. Your dispatch to me presents an extraordinary state of affairs, one that is outrageous on its face. You tell me that the mayor has compelled several parties to leave the town for refusing to comply with the ordinances. Such a statement as that if true, simply shows that the mayor is unfit for his place, that he does not do his duty, and instead of occupying the position of peace maker, the man whose duty it is to see that the ordinances are enforced by legal processes in the courts, starts out to head a mob to drive people away from their homes and their businesses.

As Wyatt's heavily armed men began arriving, city officials asked the governor to send in the militia, instead he said he was sending his attorney general to check out the situation. He also ordered the sheriff to meet Luke at the train station and guarantee his protection. When word of the governor's response got out, Luke's enemies began to fade into the woodwork.

74. On May 31, 1883.

75. Johnny Millsap.

76. George "Shotgun" Collins.

77. Johnny "Crooked-Mouth" Green.

78. Others who reportedly showed up included Dan Tipton, Texas Jack Vermillion, Charlie Bassett, Jim Calhoun, Rowdy Joe Lowe, Mysterious Dave Mather, Six-Toed Pete, Three-Fingered Dave, Dirty Sock Jack, and Dynamite Sam. There were also rumors Doc Holliday was in the area, but Wyatt probably would have mentioned him if he was. If there was a chance of some action he no doubt would have been right up front with Wyatt.

79. Thirty-five-year-old Michael "Mike" Sutton was a Reformer. He was married to ex-Mayor Webster's niece, but he was also a friend of Bat's. He didn't care much for Luke though and was part of the movement to run him out of town. It's said he went into hiding when Wyatt's army began to arrive.

80. Sic. The comma is missing here.

81. "Prairie Dog Dave" Morrow.

82. Kinsley, Kansas.

83. This was on June 3, 1883.

84. He was the former mayor, but he still dominated Dodge politics.

85. Things had quieted down by the time Attorney General Thomas Moonlight arrived in town. A compromise was struck that gambling would continue in areas screened off from dance halls and barrooms and women would be allowed, but they had to be more discreet. Also Short and his friends agreed to help chase off crooked gamblers and swindlers.
Short and Harris sold the Long Branch on November 19, 1883, and Short moved on to Fort Worth, Texas. The following year he reached an out-of-court settlement with the city of Dodge for having been run out of town.

86. Bat had been Trinidad's marshal for about a year, but he was defeated for re-election on April 3, 1883—almost two months before the Dodge City War. Three days after Bat arrived in Dodge City, he and Wyatt moved on.

87. This article was kindly provided for inclusion in this book by Emma Walling, author of *John "Doc" Holliday: Colorado Trials and Triumphs* (n.d.)

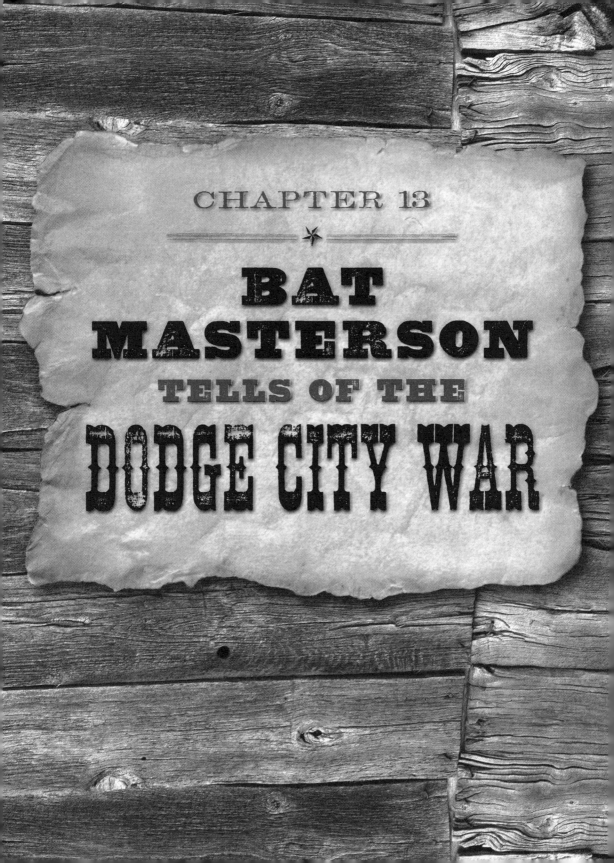

# CHAPTER 13

★

# BAT MASTERSON

## TELLS OF THE

# DODGE CITY WAR

at Masterson wrote about the Dodge City War in his biographical article on Luke Short, which appeared in the April 1907 issue of *Human Life* magazine. Only the section on the Dodge City War is presented here.[1.]

# THE STORY OF TWO RIVAL SHOWS

In the spring of 1883 Luke formed a partnership with Harris and Beeson[2] of Dodge City, and operated the Long Branch saloon, the biggest and best paying gambling house in Dodge at the time. The mayor of Dodge, whose name was Webster,[3] was also running a gambling house and saloon next door to that operated by Short. At this time Dodge City was the shipping point for the Texas cattle driven every summer from the great cattle ranges of western Texas to the northern markets.

A fortune was to be made every season by the gambling house that could control this trade and, as Short was from Texas and had once been a cowboy himself, he held the whip hand over the mayor, so far, at any rate, as the patronage of the cattlemen was concerned. This the mayor did not relish and, as he was a stubborn and strong minded man himself, who would brook no opposition if he could help it, he set to work to put Luke out of business.

He had an ordinance passed by the City Council, prohibiting music[4] in all the gambling houses and saloons of the city. Short employed a band in his place of business and Webster did likewise; but the latter was the mayor and therefore in control of the situation, so he thought. The city marshal was instructed by the mayor to notify Short that the music in his place must be discontinued.

"That suits me," Luke is reported to have told the marshal. "I don't need music in my house in order to do business, and besides, maintaining a band is quite an item of expense."

The following night the only house in the city in which there was music was that operated by the mayor. Luke then smelt a mouse.

"We'll see about this," remarked Luke to his partners, Beeson and Harris.

The next night he re engaged the band and instructed it to go ahead grinding out the old familiar melodies, so dear to the heart of the Texas cowboy. Luke remained about the place for several hours to see what move, if any, was to be made by the mayor. As he saw nothing to cause alarm, he concluded to go away for a while and pay a visit to a sick friend. He had not left the place more than ten minutes before all the members of the band, among them one woman, the pianist, were arrested and locked up in the city calaboose.[5]

## FORCED TO LEAVE THE TOWN

Luke was notified, and came hurriedly down to the saloon. He learned the facts of the arrest and went out to hunt up the officer who was in charge of the squad, in order that he might furnish bail for the musicians and have them released. But he could not find him or any other person who was considered competent to accept a bail bond.

All the time Luke was trying to get his employees out of the calaboose, the music in the mayor's place was in full swing. This, as can well be imagined, did not tend to help matters in the least. About the time Luke had made up his mind that nothing could be done that night towards the release of the prisoners, he saw the officer whom he had been looking for standing some little distance away. Luke started towards him.

The officer, who was standing on the sidewalk, which was a foot or so above the street, saw Luke coming, and instantly pulled his pistol and fired point blank at him. The shot missed and Luke returned the fire; but just as he pulled the trigger the officer started to run, and in leaving the sidewalk for the dark street he fell.

Luke, thinking he had hit him, went then to his place of business, secured a shot gun and stood off the town until morning. He accomplished this by refusing to submit to arrest that night."

The next morning he was prevailed upon to lay aside his weapons, go over to the police court, plead guilty to creating a disturbance, pay a fine and have the whole thing ended. That was what had been promised him if he would take off his arms and surrender to the officers. He accordingly gave up his pistols and started for the police court

Luke Short.

☞ IN 1902, A MINING company had hired Wyatt as "caretaker" to protect their property in Tonopah, Nevada, from claim jumpers. John Hays Hammond, a consulting engineer for the company, wanted to avoid any gunfighting. He later wrote in an article for *Scribner's Magazine* (March 1925):

> I ASKED EARP TO DO everything he could to avoid gun-play, meanwhile I said;
> "I want you to promise me that you will not shoot except in self defense."
> He put out his hand and we shook. He said;
> "I'll go through with you on that, Mr. Hammond. But—I must be the judge of when the self-defense starts."
> So prettily outplayed, I of course accepted the compromise.

with the officers. But instead of them taking him to the police court, as they promised, they took him to the city jail and kept him locked up until the noon trains arrived.[6]

The passenger trains going East and West passed each other at Dodge, and Luke was marched to the depot by an escort armed with shotguns and told to choose which train he would take. There was nothing left for him to do. They had him, and were only waiting for an excuse to riddle him with buckshot if he offered the least resistance.

He took the East bound train and landed in Kansas City.

## LINING UP FOR A BIG FIGHT

I was in Denver at the time, and he wired me to come to Kansas City at once, which I did. We talked the matter over when we met, and concluded to go up to Topeka and place the matter before the Governor. The next day we did so. The Governor denounced the conduct of the Dodge City authorities, but said that he could do nothing, as the local authorities at Dodge had informed him that they were amply able to preserve the peace and did not desire state interference.

We stated to the Governor that we believed we were able to rehabilitate ourselves in Dodge, but did not care to run afoul state authorities, in case we concluded to do so. The Governor told us to go ahead and re establish ourselves, if we could; that he would keep off, and wished us luck.

Immediately I started for Silverton, Colorado, where Wyatt Earp was located at the time, and enlisted him in our cause. Luke went to Caldwell, Kansas, where he had a couple of staunch friends, who were willing to take the bit in their mouths and go to the front and fight his battles whenever called upon. Inside of a week from the time Luke and I separated in Kansas City, we had our forces organized and were on the way to Dodge. It was decided that if a fight was all that would satisfy the mayor of Dodge—a fight he would have.

Wyatt was selected to land in Dodge first. With him, but unknown to the Dodge authorities, were several desperate men. Several more dropped into town unobserved by the enemy. It finally became whispered about that Wyatt Earp had a strong force of desperate men already domiciled in town in the interest of Luke Short.[7]

The mayor called a hasty meeting of his friends, and after they had all assembled in the council chamber of the city hall, informed them solemnly of what he had heard about the Earp invasion. Anyone who was present at that meeting could easily have seen that anything but a fight was what the mayor and his friends were looking for, now that such a thing was not altogether improbable.

Someone present suggested that Wyatt be invited to attend the meeting and state, if he would, his position in the matter. The suggestion met with the instant approval of all present, and the mayor proceeded to forthwith appoint a committee to call upon Earp and inform him of its action. Wyatt was soon found, and told of the wishes of the assembled patriots.

## A CONFERENCE WITH THE ENEMY

"It will afford me great pleasure to attend your meeting," was the laconic reply of the noble Warwick, and he was soon the central figure of as fine a collection of cut-throats as ever scuttled ship.

The mayor, addressing Wyatt, made inquiry as to the truth of the report that he and numerous other desperate men were in the city for the purpose of reinstating Short in Dodge.

"Mr. Mayor, and gentlemen of the meeting," said Wyatt; "I guess the report is true.

I came here some days ago," said he; "and, thinking that perhaps something might happen where I would need assistance, brought along some other gentlemen who signified a willingness to join in whatever festivities might arise."

"Moreover," continued Wyatt, "Luke and Bat will each arrive at noon tomorrow, and on their arrival we expect to open up hostilities."

"Now, look here, Wyatt," said the mayor, "you have no better friends anywhere than we are, and we don't want any more fighting in this town. There has already been enough shooting and killing in Dodge to do for a while. Now, why can't this thing be fixed up before it goes any farther?"

"It can," said Wyatt, "If you are willing to allow Luke to return and conduct his business unmolested as heretofore."

"I am perfectly willing to agree to that," said Webster.

"And so are we," sung out the meeting in a chorus.

"All right, gentlemen," replied the phlegmatic Mr. Earp, "there shall be no conflict. I will proceed to inform both Mr. Short and Mr. Masterson of your decision in the case, and I will guarantee that if you keep your part of the agreement there shall be no bloodshed."

Wyatt immediately notified Short and I by wire of the complete backdown of the enemy, and when we reached the city next day we were cordially received by our friends.[8] The enemy, not being sure that Wyatt could control the situation, kept in the background until he had received assurances from both Short and I that the peace terms made by Earp would be faithfully lived up to by us.

As soon as things quieted down a little, Short sent for the mayor and sheriff to meet him and some of his friends at his place of business for the purpose of talking over the situation and arriving at a better understanding. The mayor and sheriff came and with them the city attorney and the prosecuting attorney of the county. Short's party consisted of himself, his two partners, Beeson and Harris, Wyatt Earp and myself.

### HUMILIATING HIS HONOR THE MAYOR

Luke addressed the mayor something after this fashion, after we had all settled down in our chairs:

"Mr. Webster, you have on the police force of this city two men who, without any reason known to me, showed themselves during the late trouble to be bitter enemies of mine. I want them removed from the force."

The mayor assured Luke that he need not give himself any further concern on that score, as both men complained of had already handed in their resignations and left town.

"Very well," said Luke. "There is, however, another thing I wish to call to your notice. You had an ordinance passed by the city council prohibiting music in saloons. I want that ordinance repealed."[9]

"It shall be done," said the mayor, and turning to the city attorney, instructed him to prepare a call for a special meeting of the council and to draw up an ordinance calling for the repeal of the objectionable one.

This ended Short's business with the mayor. He then turned to the sheriff and said in substance:

"Mr. Sheriff, you also have two men in your office that are objectionable to me and I would like to have you remove them." He then named the men, and the sheriff promised that they would have to go.

"Here are the names of the men you can appoint in their place;" and he handed the sheriff a piece of paper containing the names of the men he desired appointed.[10]

"All right, Luke," said the sheriff, "they are good enough for me."

Luke then turned around to the prosecuting attorney of the county and said, "I furnished bail for Mr. Blank in the sum of $2,000 before I was ordered to leave town, and I want the bail bond containing my name returned to me and all record of it destroyed."[11]

"That will be easy," said the prosecutor.

"Now, gentlemen," said Luke, "there being nothing further to do, suppose we return to the bar and take a little something just for old times' sake."

"All right," said everybody present, and the procession to the bar started. Luke had won a bloodless battle, but that such was the case was no fault of his, for he had been willing to fight at any and all stages of the proceedings.

## SHORT OWNS THE TOWN AGAIN

We subsequently found that when Mayor Webster learned how he had been trapped by Earp, he hunted up the sheriff and prosecuting attorney and sent a hurry up telegram to the Governor, which was signed by all three of them requesting him to send with as little delay as possible two companies of militia, assuring him that unless that was immediately done, a great tragedy would surely be enacted in the streets of Dodge City.

The Governor, anticipating just such a move as this one on the part of the authorities at Dodge as soon as they got frightened—and the telegram calling for the militia strongly indicated that the time had arrived, refused point blank to send the militia, and reminded the senders of the message that they had already repeatedly assured him that they were sufficiently able to handle the situation and did not need the militia; "and," said the Governor, in concluding his reply, "I expect you to do it."

When it became known in Dodge the sort of a reply the Governor had sent back to the appeal for militia, something of a consternation took possession of the mayor's followers. Those who had lately been the loudest in their declarations of hostility to Short were now for peace at any price.

Webster, himself no coward, saw that the yellow streak he knew was in the makeup of his followers was giving unmistakable signs of recrudescence.[12] He knew that when the time came he would have to fight the battle alone. He remembered that those very men upon whom he would now have to rely for support had already hid themselves from Short the night of the arrest of the musicians, and he could well imagine what they were likely to do now that Short had been strongly reinforced.

It was at this stage of affairs that Webster concluded to send for Wyatt, and if possible bring about a settlement of the difficulty without an appeal to arms. In making this move the mayor acted both wisely and timely; for had the case gone over to the next day there would have, in all probability, been bloodshed on both sides.

Luke, soon after his restoration to Dodge, concluded to settle up his affairs and move to Texas. He somehow could not bring himself to like those with whom he had so recently been on the outs, and that fall sold all his interests in Kansas to his partners, and went to Texas.

Wyatt and his friends arrived in Dodge on June 3, 1883 and cleared the way for Bat, who then was able to re-enter the city. By that point, the situation had largely been defused. Bat wrote of his return in a letter to the *Daily Kansas State Journal*, which they reprinted on June 9th.

I arrived here yesterday and was met at the train by a delegation of friends who escorted me without molestation to the business house of Harris & Short. I think the inflammatory reports about Dodge City and its inhabitants have been greatly exaggerated and if at any time they did "don the war paint," it was completely washed off before I reached here. I never met a more gracious lot of people in my life. They all seemed favorably disposed, and hailed the return of Short and his friends with exultant joy I have been I unable as yet to find a single individual who participated with the crowd that forced him to leave here at first.

# References

1. There is little doubt Bat wrote these articles himself. In 1903 he became a columnist for the *New York Morning Telegraph* and he continued writing his columns right up to the day he died. While some have suggested Bat's *Human Life* articles were ghostwritten by his editor and friend Alfred Henry Lewis, the writing styles of these two men were very different.

2. Chalkley McArtor Beeson sold his interest in the saloon to Luke on February 3, 1883.

3. Webster had just left office. The new mayor was Deger.

4. This was about entertainment of a more sensuous nature, not music.

5. There were three women.

6. They released him on bond and later arrested him again. Then he was taken to the depot.

7. One newspaper reported Wyatt had forty to fifty men at his command.

8. Short returned first, then Masterson.

9. There was a compromise.

10. David "Mysterious Dave" Mather was appointed assistant city marshal. He killed Tom Nixon and another man in two separate incidents the following year and was run out of town by Marshal Bill Tilghman.

11. The bond was for himself.

12. Recrudescence: renewed activity.

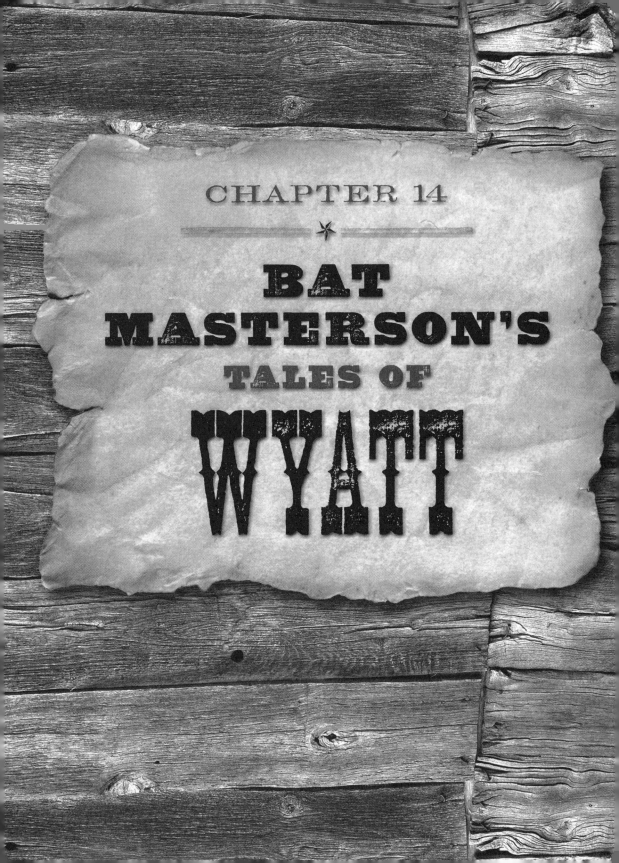

# CHAPTER 14

✴

# BAT MASTERSON'S TALES OF WYATT

emory tends to play tricks on people and the passage of time tends to exacerbate this. Things get much worse when one didn't witness the event and all they know about it is what others told them. Unfortunately, all three of these influences were at work when Bat Masterson wrote this article about Wyatt.

This is an interesting piece and it does have historical value, but it is very inaccurate. I believe Bat was sincere when he wrote this and he was trying to be accurate, though I think he was more interested in telling a good story. He obviously wanted to present his friend in a good light, but a quarter of a century had passed since most of these events occurred and Bat wasn't present when many of them happened. He also didn't have the books, articles, documents, or copies of the contemporary newspaper reports to refer to like we have today. He had to rely on his memory, so it's really not surprising he got much of it wrong. What is surprising is how accurate Wyatt's testimony and articles are by comparison. Still, Bat's assessment of Wyatt and his character seems pretty accurate.

Bat wrote six articles in a series for *Human Life* magazine. They were on Ben Thompson, Wyatt Earp, Luke Short, Doc Holliday, Bill Tilghman, and Buffalo Bill Cody. The magazine's editor, Alfred Henry Lewis, wrote one article in the series and it was about Bat Masterson. The article presented here was the second in the series and it appeared in the February 1907 issue.

# FAMOUS GUN FIGHTERS OF THE WESTERN FRONTIER

## Second Article. Wyatt Earp

### By W. B. (Bat) Masterson

EDITOR'S NOTE:—Mr. Masterson's articles began with one on Ben Thompson in the last issue. He will, from month to month, tell the stories of Doc Holliday, Buffalo Bill, Wild Bill Hickok, Charlie Ford, Frank James, Clay Allison, Luke Short, and others once foremost among this hard riding, quick shooting chivalry of the plains. These men were the personal friends of Mr. Masterson. They have slept in his blankets, cooked by his campfire.But the country has changed materially since Tombstone was a booming mining camp and Dodge was the toughest town on the cattle trail from

Texas. It is consequently no more than natural that Wyatt Earp's attire should have changed too as well as his associations and manner of life.

Mr. Masterson himself has witnessed stirring times, and stood for years a central and commanding figure in a dangerous day that has gone. His life on the plains began when he was seventeen years old. He has been buffalo hunter, Indian trader, Indian fighter. He was a scout for Miles under the great Ben Clarke—in the Indian war of 1874. Later, at the age of twenty two, Mr. Masterson was elected sheriff of Ford County, Kansas, with headquarters at Dodge City. Dodge then was reckoned the roughest camp on the border. That day is now past and Mr. Masterson is no longer a queller of "bad men," but a resident of New York and a contributor to the press. Also he is a warm personal friend of President Roosevelt, who caused him to be named a Deputy United States Marshal for the Southern district of New York.

Thirty five years ago that immense stretch of territory extending from the Missouri River west to the Pacific Ocean, and from the Brazos River in Texas north to the Red Cloud Agency in Dakota,[1] knew no braver nor more desperate man than Wyatt Earp,[2] the subject of this narrative.

☞ "THROUGH ALL THE trying times I never knew Wyatt Earp to be other than quiet, cool, and courageous. His head was always clear, which showed that he was absolutely devoid of fear."

—*Fred Dodge in a letter to Stuart Lake, October 8, 1928*

Wyatt Earp is one of the few men I personally knew in the West in the early days, whom I regarded as absolutely destitute of physical fear. I have often remarked, and I am not alone in my conclusions, that what goes for courage in a man is generally the fear of what others will think of him—in other words, personal bravery is largely made up of self respect, egotism, and an apprehension of the opinion of others.

Wyatt Earp's daring and apparent recklessness in time of danger is wholly characteristic; personal fear doesn't enter into the equation, and when everything is said and done, I believe he values his own opinion of himself more than that of others, and it is his own good report that he seeks to preserve. I may here cite an incident in his career that seems to me will go far toward establishing the correctness of the estimate I have made of him.[3]

## CLAIMED THE CARDS WERE CROOKED.

He was once engaged in running a faro game in Gunnison, Colorado, in the early days of that camp; and one day while away from the gambling house, another gambler by the name of Ike Morris, who had something of a local reputation as a bad man with a gun, and who was also running a faro game in another house in the camp, went into Wyatt's game and put down a roll of bills on one of the cards and told the dealer to turn.

The dealer did as he was told, and after making a turn or two, won the bet and reached out on the layout and picked up the roll of bills and deposited them in the money-drawer. Morris instantly made a kick and claimed that the cards were crooked, and demanded the return of his money. The dealer said he could not give back the money, as he was only working for wages, but advised him to wait until Mr. Earp returned, and then explain matters to him, and as he was the proprietor of the game he would perhaps straighten the matter up.

In a little while Wyatt returned, and Morris was on hand to tell him about the squabble with the dealer, and incidentally ask for the return of the money he had bet and lost.

Wyatt told him to wait a minute and he would speak to the dealer about it; if things were as he represented he would see what could be done about it. Wyatt stepped over to the dealer and asked him about the trouble with Morris. The dealer explained the matter, and assured Wyatt that there was nothing wrong with the cards, and that Morris had lost his money fairly and squarely.

By this time the house was pretty well filled up, as it got noised about that Morris and Earp were likely to have trouble. A crowd had gathered in anticipation of seeing a little fun. Wyatt went over to where Morris was standing and stated that the dealer had admitted cheating him out of his money, and he felt very much like returning it on that account; but said Wyatt—"You are looked upon in this part of the country as a bad man, and if I was to give you back your money you would say as soon as I left town, that you made me do it, and for that reason I will keep the money."

Morris said no more about the matter, and after inviting Wyatt to have a cigar, returned to his own house, and in a day or so left the camp.

Wyatt in his early twenties, photographed at about
the time he was a constable in Lamar, Missouri.

## LOST HIS REPUTATION IN THE CAMP.

There was really no reason why he should have gone away, for so far as Wyatt was concerned the incident was closed; but he perhaps felt that he had lost whatever prestige his reputation as a bad man had given him in the camp, and concluded it would be best for him to move out before some other person of lesser note than Wyatt Earp took a fall out of him.

This he knew would be almost sure to happen if he remained. He did not need to be told that if he remained in town after the Earp incident got noised about, every Tom, Dick and Harry in camp would be anxious to take a kick at him, and that was perhaps the reason for his sudden departure for other fields where the fact of his punctured reputation was not so generally known.

The course pursued by Earp on this occasion was undoubtedly the proper one—in fact, the only one, and preserve his reputation and self respect. It would not have been necessary for him to have killed Morris in order to have sustained his reputation, and very likely that was the very last thing he had in mind at the time, for he was not one of those human tigers who delighted in shedding blood just for the fun of the thing.

He never, at any time in his career, resorted to the pistol excepting in cases where such a course was absolutely necessary. Wyatt could scrap with his fists, and had often taken all the fight out of bad men, as they were called, with no other weapons than those provided by Nature.

There were few men in the West who could whip Earp in a rough-and tumble fight thirty years ago, and I suspect that he could give a tough youngster a hard tussle right now, even if he is sixty one years of age.[4]

☞ "IN SOME OF the so-called colorful tales of the Southwest the Earp boys have been classed as 'gunmen,' and occasionally Wyatt has been dubbed a 'two-gun-man.' These terms exaggerate the facts, although it is admitted that Wyatt was a better man with one gun than most of the blustering bad men would have been with a half dozen, but if my memory is loyal, neither Wyatt nor Virgil, even when serving as peace officers, ever made a conspicuous display of their weapons unless the attitude of the disturbers of the peace made such a display desirable. It is a remarkable fact that, to the best of my knowledge and belief, none of the Earp boys ever fired a single shot within the city limits during their entire residence in Tombstone—excepting in the fight with the rustlers on the afternoon of October 26, 1881."

—*John Clum, Tombstone's fourth mayor, 1929*

I have known Wyatt Earp since early in the seventies, and have seen him tried out under circumstances which made the test of manhood supreme. He landed in Wichita, Kansas, in 1872, being then about twenty six years old,[5] and weighing in the neighborhood of one hundred and sixty pounds, all of it muscle. He stood six feet in height, with light blue eyes, and a complexion bordering on the blonde. He was born at Monmouth, Illinois, of a clean strain of American breeding, and served in an Iowa regiment the last three years of the Civil War, although he was only a boy at the time.[6]

He always arrayed himself on the side of law and order, and on a great many occasions, at the risk of his life, rendered valuable service in upholding the majesty of the law in those communities in which he lived. In the spring of 1876 he was appointed Assistant City Marshal of Dodge City, Kansas,[7] which was then the largest shipping point in the North for the immense herds of Texas cattle that were annually driven from Texas to the northern markets. Wyatt's reputation for courage and coolness was well known to many of the citizens of Dodge City—in fact it was his reputation that secured for him the appointment of Assistant City Marshal.

☞ "WYATT EARP, WHO WAS on our police force last summer, is in town again. We hope he will accept a position on the force once more. He had a quiet way of taking the most desperate characters into custody which invariable gave one the impression that the city was able to enforce or mandate and preserve her dignity. It wasn't considered policy to draw a gun on Wyatt unless you got the drop and meant to burn powder without any preliminary talk."

—Dodge City Times, *July 7, 1877*

He was not very long on the force before one of the aldermen[8] of the city, presuming somewhat on the authority his position gave him over a police officer, ordered Wyatt one night to perform some official act that did not look exactly right to him, and Wyatt refused point blank to obey the order.[9] The alderman, regarded as something of a scrapper himself, walked up to Wyatt and attempted to tear his official shield from his vest front where it was pinned.

When that alderman woke up he was a greatly changed man. Wyatt knocked him down as soon as he laid his hands on him, and then reached down and picked him up with one hand and slammed a few hooks and upper cuts into his face, dragged his limp

To the Editor of the Times.

In answer to the publication made by Bob Fry of the Speareville News, asserting that I made threats that I would lick any s— of a b— that voted or worked against me at the last election, I will say it is as false and as flagrant a lie as was ever uttered; but I did say this: that I would lick him the s— of a b— if he made any more dirty talk about me; and the words s— of a b— I strictly confined to the Speareville editor, for I don't know of any other in Ford county.

W. B. MASTERSON.

This letter appeared in the *Dodge City Times* on Saturday, November 15, 1879. During Bat's campaign for re-election as sheriff, Bob Fey had hinted Bat was guilty of fraud and just before the election he claimed Bat had threatened to shoot to him. Bat's advisors recommended he not answer the charges in print; it was bad advice as Bat was trounced in the polls. After the election Bat wrote this letter.

form over to the city calaboose, and chucked it in one of the cells, just the same as he would any other disturber of the peace.

The alderman's friends tried to get him out on bail during the night, but Wyatt gave it out that it was the calaboose for the alderman until the police court opened up for business at nine o'clock the following morning, and it was. Wyatt was never bothered any more while he lived in Dodge City by aldermen.

While he invariably went armed, he seldom had occasion to do any shooting in Dodge City, and only once do I now recall when he shot to kill, and that was at a drunken cow boy, who rode up to a Variety Theatre[10] where Eddie Foy, the now famous comedian, was playing an engagement.[11] The cowboy rode right by Wyatt, who was standing outside the main entrance to the show shop, but evidently he did not notice him, else he would not in all probability have acted as he did.

## AN INCIDENT NOT ON THE PROGRAM.

The building in which the show was being given was one of those pine board affairs that were in general use in frontier towns. A bullet fired from a Colts 45[12] calibre pistol would go through a half dozen such buildings, and this the cow boy knew. Whether it was Foy's act that angered him, or whether he had been jilted by one of the chorus we never learned; at any rate he commenced bombarding the side of the building directly opposite the stage upon which Eddy[13] Foy was at that very moment reciting that beautifully pathetic poem entitled "Kalamazoo in Michigan."

The bullets tore through the side of the building, scattering pieces of the splintered pine boards in all directions. Foy evidently thought the cow boy was after him, for he did not tarry long in the line of fire.

The cow boy succeeded in firing three shots before Wyatt got his pistol in action. Wyatt missed at the first shot, which was probably due to the fact that the horse the cow boy was riding kept continually plunging around, which made it rather a hard matter to get a bead on him. His second shot, however, did the work, and the cow boy rolled off his horse and was dead by the time the crowd reached him.

Wyatt's career in and around Tombstone, Arizona, in the early days that bustling mining camp was perhaps the most thrilling and exciting of any he ever experienced in the thirty five years he has lived on the lurid edge of civilization. He had four brothers besides himself who wagoned it into Tombstone[14] as soon as it had been announced that gold[15] had been discovered in the camp.

Jim was the oldest of the brothers,[16] Virgil came next, then Wyatt, then Morgan, and Warren, who was the kid of the family. Jim started in running a saloon as soon as one was built.[17] Virgil was holding the position of Deputy U. S. Marshal. Wyatt operated a gambling house,[18] and Morgan rode as a Wells Fargo shot gun messenger on the coach that ran between Tombstone and Benson, which was the nearest railroad point. Morgan's duty was to protect the Wells Fargo coach[19] from the stage robbers with which the country at that time was infested.

## STAGE ROBBERS OF SAN SIMON VALLEY.

The Earps and the stage robbers knew each other personally, and it was on this account that Morgan had been selected to guard the treasure the coach carried. The Wells Fargo Company believed that so long as it kept one of the Earp boys on their coach their property was safe; and it was, for no coach was ever held up in that country which one of the Earp boys rode as guard.

A certain band of those stage robbers who lived in the San Simon Valley, about fifty miles from Tombstone and very near the line of Old Mexico, where they invariably took refuge when hard pressed by the authorities on the American side of the line, was made up of the Clanton brothers, Ike and Billy, and the McLowry brothers, Tom and Frank.

This was truly a quartette of desperate men, against whom the civil authorities of that section of the country at that time were powerless to act. Indeed, the United States troops from the surrounding posts, who had been sent out to capture them dead or alive,[20] had on more than one occasion returned to their posts after having met with both failure and disaster at the hands of the desperadoes.[21]

Those were the men who had made up their minds to hold up and rob the Tombstone coach;[22] but in order to do so with as little friction as possible, they must first get rid of Morgan Earp. They could, as a matter of course, ambush him and shoot him dead from the coach; but that course would hardly do, as it would be sure to bring on a fight with the other members of the Earp family and their friends, of whom they had a great many.

☞ "FROM THE HYGIENIC point of view, whiskey and cold lead are mentioned as the leading diseases at Tombstone. What with the leisure that seems to prevail, the constant drinking and gambling at the saloons, and the universal practice of carrying deadly weapons, there is but one source of astonishment, and that is that the cold-lead disease should claim so few victims."

*—William Henry Bishop,*
Harper's Monthly, *March 1883*

Bat Masterson and Wyatt Earp in 1876 while they were in Dodge City.
This is the only known photograph of Wyatt wearing a badge.

They finally concluded to try diplomacy. They sent word to Morgan to leave the employ of the Wells Fargo Express Company, as they intended to hold up the stage upon which he acted as guard, but didn't want to do it as long as the coach was in his charge. Morgan sent back word that he would not quit and that they had better not try to hold him up or there would be trouble. They then sent word to Wyatt to have him induce Morgan, if such a thing was possible, to quit his job, as they had fully determined on holding up the coach and killing Morgan if it became necessary in order to carry out their purpose.[23]

☞ "THE PEOPLE OF Tombstone have reason to congratulate themselves that they have not only courageous Marshals but Marshals who are dead shots. That performance yesterday, wherein three cowboys were left dead on the field and one lodged in jail, is among the happiest events Tombstone has witnessed, and especially so as it was attended with so little injury to the law vindicators."

—San Francisco Exchange, *October 27, 1881*

Wyatt sent back word that if Morgan was determined to continue riding as guard for Wells Fargo he would not interfere with him in any way, and that if they killed him he would hunt them down and kill the last one in the bunch. Just to show the desperate character of those men, they sent Virgil Earp, who was City Marshal of Tombstone at the time, word that on a certain day they would be in town prepared to give him and his brothers a battle to the death.[24]

Sure enough, on the day named Ike and Billy Clanton and Tom and Frank McLowry rode into Tombstone and put their horses up in one of the city corrals.[25] They were in town some little time before the Earps knew it.[26] They never suspected for a moment that the Clantons and McLowrys had any intention of carrying out their threat when they made it.

When Virgil Earp fully realized that they were in town he got very busy. He knew that it meant a fight and was not long in hustling up Wyatt and Morgan and "Doc" Holliday, the latter as desperate a man in a tight place as the West ever knew. This made the Marshal's party consist of the Marshal himself, his brothers Wyatt and Morgan, and "Doc" Holliday. Against them were the two Clantons and the two McLowrys, an even thing so far as numbers were concerned.[27]

As soon as Virgil Earp got his party together, he started for the corral, where he understood that the enemy was entrenched, prepared to resist to the death the anticipated attack on the Earp forces.[28]

## THE TOWN TURNED OUT FOR THE BATTLE

Everybody in Tombstone seemed to realize that a bloody battle was about to be fought right in the very center of the town, and all those who could, hastened to find points of vantage from which the impending battle could be viewed in safety.[29] It took the City Marshal some little time to get his men together, as both Wyatt and Holliday were still sound asleep in bed,[30] and getting word to them and the time it took for them to get up and dress themselves and get to the place where Verge[31] and Morgan were in waiting, necessarily caused some little delay.

The invaders, who had been momentarily expecting an attack, could not understand the cause of the delay and finally concluded that the Earps were afraid and did not intend to attack them, at any rate while they were in the corral. This conclusion caused them to change their plan of battle.

☞ "WE ARRESTED FRANK STILWELL and Pete Spence. On our way in to Tombstone Stilwell and Spence both swore they would get Wyatt, Morg, and myself for this arrest."

—*Fred Dodge in a letter to Stuart Lake, September 18, 1930*

They instantly resolved that if "The mountain would not come to Mahomet—Mahomet[32] would go to the mountain." If the Earps[33] would not come to the corral, they would go and hunt up the Earps. Their horses were nearby, saddled, bitted and ready for instant use. Each man took his horse by the bridle line and led him through the corral gate to the street where they intended to mount.

But just as they reached the street, and before they had time to mount their horses,[34] the Earp party came round the corner. Both sides were now within ten feet of each other. There were four men on a side, every one of whom had during his career been engaged in other shooting scrapes and were regarded as being the most desperate of desperate men. The horses gave the rustlers quite an advantage in the position. The Earps were in the open street, while the invaders used their horses for breastworks.[35] Virgil Earp, as the City Marshal, ordered the Clantons and McLowrys to throw up their hands and surrender. This order was replied to with a volley from their pistols.[36]

The fight was now on. The Earps pressed in close, shooting as rapidly as they could. The fight was hardly started before it was over, and the result showed that nearly every shot fired by the Earp party went straight home to the mark.[37]

☞ "MORG EARP'S BODY sent to Colton yesterday, and today Virgil Earp and wife left for that place. A bodyguard well armed accompanied Virg Earp, and tonight came news of Frank Stilwell's body being found riddled with bullets and buckshot. A quick vengeance and a bad character sent to Hell where he will be the chief attraction until a few more accompany him."

—George Parsons in his journal entry, dated March 20, 1882, though he actually wrote it a few days later

## FURTHER DEVELOPMENTS OF THE FEUD

As soon as the smoke of battle cleared away sufficiently to permit an accounting being made, it was seen that the two McLowrys and Billy Clanton were killed. They had been hit by no less than a half dozen bullets each,[38] and died in their tracks.[39] Morgan Earp was the only one of the Marshal's force that got hit. It was nothing more, however, than a slight flesh wound in one of his arms.[40]

Ike Clanton made his escape, but in doing so stamped himself as a coward of the first magnitude. No sooner had the shooting commenced than he threw down his pistol and with both hands high above his head, he ran to Wyatt Earp and begged him not to kill him. Here again Wyatt showed the kind of stuff that was in him, for instead of killing Clanton as most any other man would have done under the circumstances, he told him to run and get away, and he did.[41]

The Earp party were all tried for the killing, and after a preliminary examination lasting several weeks, during which more than a hundred witnesses were examined, they were all exonerated.

There were at this time two other outlaw bands in the country, who, when they heard of the killing of the McLowery brothers and Billy Clanton, swore to wipe out the Earp family and all their friends.[42] They had no notion, however, of giving the Earps any more battles in the open. In the future, killings would be done from ambush, and the first one to get potted by this guerrilla system of warfare was Virge Earp, the City Marshal.

As he was crossing one of the most prominent corners in Tombstone one night he was fired upon by some one not then known, but who was afterwards learned to be "Curly Bill,"[43] who was concealed behind the walls of a building that was then in course of construction on one of the corners.[44] A shot gun loaded with buck shot was the weapon used.[45]

Most of the charge struck Verge in the left arm between the shoulder and elbow, shattering the bone in a frightful manner. One or two other shots hit him but caused no serious injury. He was soon able to be about again, but never had any use afterwards of his left arm.[46] As a matter of course the shock he sustained when the buck shot hit him caused him to fall, and the would be assassin, thinking he had turned the trick successfully, made his escape in the dark to the foot-hills.

The next to get murdered was Morgan Earp, who was shot through a window one night while playing a game of pin-pool with a friend.[47]

Wyatt then realized that it was only a question of time until he and all his friends would be killed in the same manner as his brother, if he remained in town. So he organized a party consisting of himself, "Doc" Holliday, Jack Vermillion, Sherman McMasters and Bill Johnson,[48] and after equipping it with horses, guns and plenty of ammunition, started out on the war path intending to hunt down and kill every one he could find who had any hand in the murder of his brother Morgan and the attempted assassination of Verge.

Wyatt had in the meantime learned that Pete Spence, Frank Stillwell, and a Mexican, by the name of Florentine, were the three men interested in the killing of Morgan.[49] Pete Spence had a ranch[50] about twenty five miles from Tombstone near the Dragoon Mountains, which was in reality nothing more than a rendezvous for cattle thieves and stage robbers.

Wyatt and his party headed straight for the Spence ranch as soon as he left Tombstone on his campaign of revenge. He found only the Mexican when he reached the ranch, and after making some inquiry as to the whereabouts of Spence, and learning that he had left early that morning for Tombstone by a different route from the one the Earps had traveled, proceeded, without further ceremony, to shoot the Mexican to pieces with buck shot.

They left the greaser's body[51] where it fell, and returned to Tombstone, where they expected to find Spence.[52] He was there all right enough, but seeming to anticipate what Wyatt intended doing, had gone to the sheriff, who was not on friendly terms with the Earp faction, and surrendered, having himself locked up in jail.

Of course, Wyatt had to let him go for the time being, and was getting ready to start out on another expedition when he received word from Tucson that Frank Stillwell and Ike Clanton were there.[53] Wyatt and "Doc" Holliday immediately started for Benson, where they took the

Pete Spence.

train for Tucson which was about sixty miles farther south.[54] Both were armed with shot guns, and just before the train came to a stop at the Tucson station, Wyatt and Holliday, from the platform of the rear coach, saw Clanton and Stillwell standing on the depot platform.

They immediately jumped off and started for the depot, intending to kill them both, but they were seen coming by the quarry who had evidently been made aware of Earp's movements and were on the lookout at the station. Clanton and Stillwell started to run as soon as they saw Wyatt and Holliday approaching, Stillwell down the railroad track and Clanton towards town.

Wyatt and Holliday immediately gave chase to Stillwell and succeeded after a short run in overtaking him. He threw up his hands and begged not to be killed, but it was too late. Besides, Wyatt had given instructions that no prisoners should be taken, so they riddled his body with buck shot and left it lay where it fell, just as they had the Mexican. Wyatt and Holliday then returned to Tombstone, thinking there might still be a chance to get a crack at Pete Spence, but the latter still clung to the jail.[55]

## WYATT'S BODY COUNT

☞ "WYATT EARP, OF CALIFORNIA, is the celebrity who about two years ago went on the warpath at Tombstone, Arizona, against a mob of desperadoes who had assassinated his brother, Morgan Earp. In the terrible encounter which ensued he killed not less than eight of the assassins."

—National Police Gazette, *July 21, 1883*

☞ "ONE OF THEM IS Wyatt Earp...famous in the cheerful business of depopulating the country. He has killed within our personal knowledge six men, and is popularly accredited with relegating to the dust no less than ten of his fellow men."

—Kansas City Journal, *May 15, 1883*

☞ "WYATT EARP IS CREDITED with ten men, one of them his own brother-in-law."

—Seattle Post-Intelligencer, *July 22, 1900*

☞ "[WYATT EARP] HAS KILLED more than a dozen stage robbers, murderers, and cattle thieves."

—G. W. Caldwell in the introduction to his interview with Wyatt, *1888*

☞ "[WYATT] EARP HAS A cemetery which he has stocked with over 30 men, and no one seemed desirous of questioning his word."

—Los Angeles Tribune, *June 2, 1888*

## DEFYING THE SHERIFF OF TOMBSTONE

Meanwhile the sheriff of Tombstone had received telegraphic instructions from the sheriff of Tucson to arrest Wyatt and Holliday as soon as they showed up,[56] for the murder of Stillwell. When Wyatt got back to town he hustled his men together for the purpose of going out after Curly Bill, whom he believed to be the man who had shot Verge from ambush.[57] When the sheriff and his posse reached Wyatt, the latter and his crowd were about to mount their horses preparatory to going on the "Curly Bill" expedition.

"Wyatt, I want to see you," said the sheriff.

"You will see me once too often," replied Wyatt as he bounded into the saddle.

"And remember," continued Wyatt to the sheriff, "I am going to get that hound you are protecting in jail when I come back, if I have to tear the jail down to do it."

The sheriff made no further attempt to arrest Wyatt and Holliday. The next night Wyatt killed Curly Bill at the Whetstone Springs,[58] about thirty miles from Tombstone, and just to make his word good with the sheriff, he and his party returned to town.[59] The sheriff, however, had during his absence released Spence and told him to get across the Mexican border with as little delay as possible if he valued his life, for the Earp gang would surely kill him if he didn't.[60]

This ended the Earp campaign in Arizona for the time being.

Much has been written about Wyatt Earp that is the veriest rot, and every once in a while a newspaper article will appear in which it is alleged that some person had taken a fall out of him, and that when he had been put to the test, had shown the white feather.[61] Not long ago a story was

Sheriff John H. Behan.

published in the different newspapers throughout the country that some little Canadian police officer somewhere in the Canadian Northwest had given Wyatt an awful call down; had, in fact, taken his pistol from him and in other ways humiliated him.

The story went like wild fire, as all such stories do, and was printed and reprinted in all the big dailies in the country. There was not one word of truth in it, and the newspaper fakir who unloaded the story on the reading public very likely got no more than ten dollars for his work.

Wyatt, to begin with, was never in the Canadian Northwest, and therefore was never in a position where a little Canadian police officer could have taken such liberties with him as those described by the author of the story.

Take it from me, no one has ever humiliated this man Earp, nor made him show the white feather under any circumstances whatever. While he is now a man past sixty, there are still a great many so called bad men in this country who would be found, if put to the test, to be much easier game to tackle than this same lean and lanky Earp.

Wyatt Earp, like many more men of his character who lived in the West in its early days, has excited, by his display of great courage and nerve under trying conditions, the envy and hatred of those small minded creatures with which the world seems to be abundantly peopled, and whose sole delight in life seems to be in fly specking the reputations of real men. I have known him since the early seventies and have always found him a quiet, unassuming man, not given to brag or bluster, but at all times and under all circumstances a loyal friend and an equally dangerous enemy.

# References

1. The Red Cloud Agency was close to Dakota, but was actually in Nebraska.

2. It sounds strange today to see Bat refer to his friend as "desperate." We're more used to hearing outlaws described this way, but back then the word also meant "fearless" or "without care for danger."

3. The accuracy of this story has yet to be established.

4. On March 19, 1907, Wyatt turned 59.

5. Wyatt was 24.

6. Bat is confusing Wyatt with Virgil and Newton. Virgil served the last three years of the war in an Illinois regiment, while Newton served three and a half years in an Iowa regiment. James served two years in an Illinois regiment before he was wounded and disabled. Wyatt was too young to serve. He had just turned 17 when the war ended.

7. Wyatt appears to have become assistant marshal in the fall of 1876.

8. Alderman: a councilman.

9. Documentation of this story has not yet been found. Wyatt's account can be found in the chapter "Bat Masterson and the Dodge City War."

10. Ben Springer's Comique Variety Hall.

11. Wyatt's account of this incident can be found in the chapter "Bat Masterson and the Dodge City War."

12. Sic, .45.

13. Eddie.

14. Wyatt, Virgil and James rode their wagons into Tombstone. Morgan arrived later and Warren after that.

15. Though there was some gold there, Tombstone was primarily a silver camp.

16. Newton was the oldest.

17. There were already saloons in Tombstone when the Earps arrived there. James started out as a bartender in the Sampling Room Saloon.

18. At first, Wyatt rode as shotgun messenger for Wells, Fargo & Company. Then he became deputy sheriff for Pima County. Wyatt didn't get his gambling concession going until about January of 1881.

19. The coaches weren't owned by Wells, Fargo & Company.

20. Dead or alive rewards were never issued for the Clantons or the McLaurys. Some soldiers did go to the McLaury's ranch to retrieve some stolen mules. The rustlers said they would return the mules if the soldiers sent the Earps away. After the Earps left, the rustlers made a promise to deliver the mules a couple days later, but they didn't do it.

21. Bat is exaggerating.

22. Tom and Frank's only known illegal activities were acting as fences for stolen cattle. It's doubtful Billy was involved in any holdups, but Ike apparently was. The outlaws in general were involved in everything from theft to murder.

23. It's unlikely the robbers would reveal their plans to the Earps, but then again, some of the robbers did some pretty stupid things.

24. The outlaws did not set a specific day for the gunfight.

25. Ike and Tom rode into town on a wagon the previous day. Billy and Frank had their horses with them at the fight.

26. The Earps had already seen the Clantons and the McLaurys in front of the justice's office and at Spangenberg's gun shop.

27. He leaves out Billy Claiborne, and Wes Fuller and Billy Allen were on their way there.

28. Hardly. Ike wasn't even armed. The gunfight was more spontaneous than planned.

29. He's exaggerating again. A few people along the street did suspect something might happen, primarily because of Ike's threats.

30. By this time Wyatt and Morgan had already been involved in Ike's arrest and Doc had been up for at least an hour.

31. Sic throughout this article.

32. This is an old spelling of Mohammed.

33. Ike had hunted for the Earps that morning. When they left the corral, they went a few lots away from where the Earps were. Apparently they were waiting for Doc to return to Fly's Lodging House.

34. Only two horses were on the scene—Billy Clanton's and Frank's. They hadn't corralled them after their arrival.

35. When the shooting started, only Tom McLaury got behind a horse and some witnesses said he fired a pistol from behind the horse.

36. When Billy and Frank went for their pistols, so did Wyatt and Morgan. The first shots happened almost simultaneously.

37. Only about one half of the shots fired by the Earps and Holliday hit their target.

38. Tom was hit by twelve buckshot from Doc's shotgun blast four to six inches below his right arm. Also, the rear portion of his right arm was hit. Frank was hit twice—one inch to the left of his navel and right below his right ear, passing through the base of his brain. Billy was hit three times—two inches below his left nipple and into his lung, six inches to the right of his navel, and through his right arm two inches above the wrist. There may have been other unreported wounds.

39. Frank and Tom died within minutes. Billy died within the hour.

40. Morgan was seriously wounded in the back, Virgil received a painful wound in the calf of one of his legs, and Doc had a slight flesh wound.

41. Ike was unarmed. There was not much he could do, but escape.

42. The assassins were close associates of the Clantons and McLaurys and may have been hired by Will McLaury.

43. There were at least three assassins, possibly five—two may have been lookouts.

44. This was the Huachuca Water Company building.

45. At least three shotguns were used.

46. He did regain some use of his hand.

47. Bob Hatch, one of the owners of Campbell & Hatch's Billiard Parlor, where Morgan was shot.

48. Sherman McMaster and Turkey Creek Jack Johnson.

49. Wyatt insisted Spence wasn't involved in Morgan's death, but that Curly Bill, Johnny Ringo, Frank Stilwell, Hank Swilling, and Florentino Cruz were.

50. Spence had a wood camp, not a ranch.

51. This is another incidence of the offensive racial slurs that were common at the time. It seems amazing today that a respectable family magazine would print terms like this in their pages. *Human Life* was a popular Hearst publication.

52. The Earp party did not return to Tombstone.

53. Stilwell was killed two days before Cruz and Wyatt didn't go to Tucson looking for Stilwell, he was escorting Virgil and his wife, Allie.

54. Forty miles further west.

55. The Earp party did return to Tombstone after killing Stilwell. Then they went to Pete Spence's camp looking for him and finding Cruz.

56. Pima County Sheriff Bob Paul was Wyatt's friend and knew all about Behan's association with the cowboys. He would not have telegraphed Behan to arrest Wyatt unless he felt he had no choice or knew Wyatt was out of Behan's reach. When he arrived in Tombstone he refused to have anything to do with Behan or his posse.

57. Wyatt did not think Curly Bill shot Virgil and was not searching specifically for him at Iron Springs. Curly Bill and his men may have been there by coincidence or they might have gotten word that the Earp party was to meet someone there from the Vigilance Committee and then decided to set up the ambush.

58. Iron Springs in the Whetstone Mountains.

59. They did not return to town.

60. Spence did flee into Mexico, but eventually came back and ended up in the territorial prison at Yuma.

61. This and the rest of Bat's article are pretty accurate.

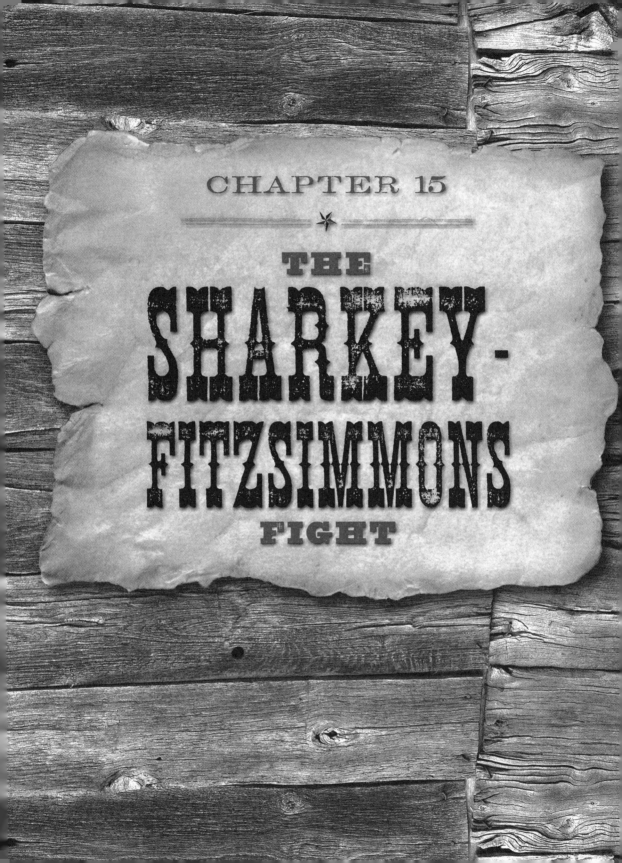

# CHAPTER 15

## THE SHARKEY-FITZSIMMONS FIGHT

For a number of years around the turn of the century, Wyatt was better known for his involvement in another controversial incident than for his part in the O.K. Corral shootout. This can be seen in how newspapers at the time referred to him, often not even mentioning the gunfight. For example, Portland's *Morning Oregonian* on April 22, 1899 had "Wyatt Earp, of Sharkey-Fitzsimmons-fight fame," while the *Seattle Post-Intelligencer* for July 22, 1900 said, "The one of the Earps best known in Seattle was Wyatt, who refereed the Fitzsimmons-Sharkey fight."

The fight in question was a major heavyweight prizefight between Robert "Ruby Bob" Fitzsimmons and Thomas "the Sailor" Sharkey. The event, billed as a world championship, took place on December 2, 1896 at the Mechanics' Pavilion in San Francisco and some say it may have been the most significant sporting event held on the West Coast during that entire century. It was also the first fight that women were allowed to attend, the first fight publicly attended by San Francisco's high society, and the first fight where the referee had to be disarmed before entering the ring.

Fitzsimmons was a 34-year-old Englishman who was considered to be the heavyweight champion, but only because a previous champion, James "Gentleman Jim" Corbett, refused to defend his title. Fitzsimmons had previously been the middleweight champion. He won this title in 1891 by knocking out Jack Dempsey, but had lost it in 1894.

Sharkey was a 23-year-old Irishman who, out of twenty-five fights, had twenty-one KOs, one win, two draws, and a no decision. One of the draws was with Jim Corbett. As many as 20,000 people attended the fight and thousands more were outside. The bookies were doing a booming business. At stake was a $10,000 winner-take-all purse and each man was determined to get it.

Up until noon on the day of the fight, the boxers' managers were unable to agree on a referee. Finally, the National Athletic Club appointed 48-year-old Wyatt Earp, who had been refereeing matches for twenty-eight years. Almost immediately after Wyatt was chosen, Martin Julian—Fitzsimmons' manager and brother-in-law—started hearing rumors that Wyatt was going to throw the fight in Sharkey's favor.[1] The fight went ahead anyway.

On several occasions Wyatt had to warn Fitzsimmons against delivering low blows. By the eighth round, Sharkey was taking a beating. Then, after a flurry of blows, Sharkey received a powerful body punch and dropped to the canvas clutching his groin. Wyatt stopped the fight and retreated to a corner of the ring to think for a few moments. He then declared a foul blow and awarded the fight to Sharkey. The crowd went wild and the headline on the front page of the next day's *San Francisco Examiner* read, "'Sharkey Wins by a Foul,' Said Referee Earp. Although Declared the Victor He Was Writhing on the Floor When the Decision Was Given in His Favor."

San Francisco's newspapers, which were already enmeshed in a press war, fought over this fight for weeks afterward, with Wyatt as the focal point. Wyatt received more publicity from this decision alone than all his previous publicity combined. As usual, much of it was bad. A few months previously, Wyatt had written three feature articles for the *San Francisco Examiner* on the gunfight, stagecoach robberies, and Bat Masterson, so the *Examiner* promptly jumped on his side, while the *San Francisco Call* suddenly became rabidly anti-Earp. The other two papers—the *Chronicle* and the *Bulletin*—fell somewhere in between. There were rumors the *Call*'s editor lost quite a bit of money on the fight, but, for whatever reason, the *Call* began publishing everything they could find to make Wyatt look bad, and they soon took to publishing rumors and even making up stories about Wyatt. These phony stories found their way into other papers across the nation and would plague him for years to come.

Wyatt, Bat, and Sharkey attended the Corbett-Fitzsimmons fight on March 19, 1897. This time is was Fitzsimmons who was getting the worst of it. Then, in the fourteenth round, Fitzsimmons delivered a body punch that knocked Corbett down. Corbett's seconds cried foul, but the referee kept counting as the champion lay writhing on the canvass. Fitzsimmons was proclaimed the winner and the indisputable heavyweight champion. He eventually lost the title, but went on to win a third title—that of light-heavyweight champion. His boxing career spanned a total of 30 years.

Sharkey never won a title, though he did have a fine career and he was eventually elected to the Boxing Hall of Fame. Sharkey and Fitzsimmons fought it out again four years after their San Francisco fight, but this time Sharkey was knocked out in the second round.

The day after the first Sharkey-Fitzsimmons fight, on the front page of the *San Francisco Examiner*—between Sharkey and Fitzsimmons's own accounts of the fight and other pro and con arguments over Wyatt's decision—Wyatt explained what had happened.

# WYATT EARP, WHOSE DECISION MEANT $10,000.

When I decided this contest in favor of Sharkey, I did so because I believed Fitzsimmons deliberately fouled him, and under the rules the Sailor was entitled to the decision. I would have been willing to allow half fouls, that is fouls that might be considered partly accidental—to pass by with only a reprimand, but in such a case as this I could only do my duty.

Julian approached me before the contest and said he had heard stories to the effect that I favored Sharkey. We talked a few moments and he went away apparently satisfied that everything was on the square.

Any talk to the effect that I was influenced in any way to decide wrongly against Fitzsimmons is rubbish. I saw Sharkey but once before in my life and that was when he boxed with Corbett. I had no reason to favor him. If I was to have allowed my feelings to govern me, my decision would have been the other way.

I am a pretty close observer and under most conditions I think I am cool. I went into the ring as referee to give a square decision, and so far as my conscience speaks I have done so. It made no difference to me who won, the victory should be to the best man. As I have already said, I met Sharkey only once before to-night, and that was when he fought Corbett. To-night I was standing in the enclosure near the ring when I met him again.

I have met Fitzsimmons several times; the first, I believe being four or five years ago, when one of the best friends I have in the country and one of the truest supporters Fitzsimmons ever had, Bat Masterson, introduced us. I am very sure that Bat Masterson has lost a great deal of money on this fight, but I have always been able to decide against my own money and my friends can stand the consequences of such a decision.

I feel that I did what was right and honorable and feeling so I care nothing for the opinion of anybody. I saw the foul blow struck as plainly as I see you, and that is all there is to the story. In the fourth or the fifth round I warned Fitzsimmons that he was fouling in the wrestling. In every clinch the tall man would force himself down upon Sharkey, who was fighting low, and attempt to smash him.

Fitzsimmons replied that he was not fighting foul. I answered that I wanted no more of it and demanded that he quit it and be square. I told him that I would warn Sharkey as I had warned him and that I would do something more than reprimand if the foul fighting continued.

There is one thing I regret. I should have given Sharkey the fight earlier in the contest. In the fourth round, I think it was, Fitz landed a left handed blow and returned with his elbow, cutting Sharkey's eyebrow open. The Sailor should have had the fight then.[2]

The foul blow of the right was seen plainly by me. Fitz smashed with his right on Sharkey's shoulder and then with an uppercut with the left he struck the Sailor below the belt. Sharkey was leaning over and the blow knocked him down. It was clearly a foul and before the Sailor moved I mentioned that the fight was over. The first blow had been weak and I believe the second was intended for an uppercut, but it struck foul. No man until now has ever questioned my honor. I have been in many places and in peculiar situations, but no one ever said, until to-night, that I was guilty of a dishonorable act. And I will repeat that I decided in all fairness and with a judgment that was as true as my eyesight. I saw the foul blow.

WYATT EARP.

Right after the fight, Wyatt went to Sharkey's room to check on the ailing boxer. A reporter for the *San Francisco Bulletin* was there and he reported the following on December 3, 1896:

The swollen groin satisfied Mr. Earp that he did not err in giving the prize to Sharkey. "It was the most deliberate foul I ever saw struck," said the referee. "Fitz hit him squarely below the belt. I can understand how many could not see where the blow landed. It was an upswoop, which to many not near the ring looked as if Fitzsimmons struck him in the stomach, when in reality it was clear below the belt. Of course Fitz was the favorite in the betting, and he carried more money. You know how it is at the racetrack when they tip over a favorite well played. Won't a roar go up to the clouds especially if the judges disqualify the favorite for fouling?"

On the morning of December 4, 1896, Wyatt and his lawyer appeared in police court to face the charge of carrying a concealed weapon. This stemmed from Wyatt's having to be disarmed before the fight. After obtaining a continuance, Wyatt had a short interview with a Bulletin reporter.

A quiet, determined-looking man is Wyatt Earp. Not the fierce desperado that many unjust rumors have pointed out, by any means. He looks peaceable enough, even kindly, though he has a steel blue eye that is the outward and visible sign of the inward and spiritual temperament of a man not to be trifled with. Tall, and of an athletic, agile build, he looks like a man who has been in training all his life. He is courteous, too. During his conversation with the Bulletin representative his hand did not wander once toward his hip pocket.

"I am asking for a continuance of this matter," he said, because I have not yet decided what I shall do. I want time to think it over.

"You see, I make no pretense that I did not have a gun. I had it all right, just here," slapping that hip pocket. "It was foolish of me to have it, of course. But I gave it up when called upon. It happened in this way. I am out at the races all day, and when the last race is run I have to cross over from the stables to the cars after everybody has gone, and I do not reach home sometimes until 8 or 9 o'clock. I never know whom I am going to meet, so I deem it right to protect myself.

"Now on the night of the fight I got in very late from the races, much later than I expected, and had to go straight out to Mechanics' Pavilion. If I had any place to leave my gun I'd have put it away, but I hadn't; so I just clambered up into the ring with it on. It was foolish of me, of course.

"But there is another consideration which makes me uncertain as to whether I should plead guilty and take my fine or whether I should demand a hearing. I'll decide by Tuesday. This is a new experience to me. I was never arrested like this before.

Earp was most unwilling to talk about the fight. "I've said enough, and have been reported to have said more than I have. My attorney, Mr. Kelly,[3] advises me that the less I say the better. So I'll await results.

> "FITZSIMMONS AND HIS manager filed a lawsuit claiming the fight was fixed and that they should receive the prize money. Wyatt, of course, featured prominently at the trial, but everyone seemed to have trouble with his unusual name. The *Chronicle* of December 10, 1896 explained, "Wyatt Earp is indignant about the manner in which the various parties to the present case are meddling up the correct pronunciation of his name every attorney and witness who has spoken in public so far has a novel notion of his own about the right way to handle them. The bailiff calls 'Wah Yah,' Colonel Kowalsky addresses the referee as 'Wat Yirrup,' while Witness Smith mentions him as 'White Hurp.' General Barnes with no regard whatsoever for the gentleman's feelings invariably refers to him as 'Wart Up.'"

Wyatt decided to plead not guilty, saying convicts all over the West would like to kill him on sight and so he had to be able to protect himself. After what happened to Virgil and Morgan, he must have been concerned that someday an Arizona outlaw might catch him off guard and try to plug him. But rather than dredge up his misunderstood deeds in Arizona, his lawyer probably thought it was best to generalize the threat. A judge could easily understand that a famous lawman might be a target for a wide variety of criminals. In the end, the judge decided Wyatt had committed a "technical violation" of the law and fined him fifty dollars.

Meanwhile, publicity was building and it didn't take long for Wyatt to get tired of it. Though he became reluctant to discuss the fight, the *Los Angeles Times* did quote him on December 5, 1896.

Wyatt Earp, the most talked of man of the hour, takes a philosophical view of the criticisms that are being heaped upon him for his decision on Wednesday night, and says that he will wait for time to set him right with the public.

"If I had any fears that I erred in my decision they would have disappeared when I saw Sharkey today,"[4] he said last night.

"Sharkey did not strike a foul blow, to my mind. At the break he struck Fitzsimmons as soon as his arm was free, but that is following Queensbury rules.[5] It is true that it was agreed that there was to be no fighting at the break, but my instructions from the club were not to be technical, but to give the audience a good fight for their money.

"I have one regret about the whole matter, and that is that I did not leave the ring when Julian objected to me. I thought of doing it, but it occurred to me that it would be "showing the yellow" to do that. I would be quitting under fire, and I made up my mind to stay until ordered off by the club. I am sorry that I acted as referee at all."

The only inconvenience Fitzsimmons is suffering as a result of his meeting with the sailor is a painful swelling of the joints of the hands.

"I have nothing more to say in explanation," he[6] said, "except that we for a certainty know what we only surmised yesterday, and that is that members of the National Club were in this deal with Lynch and Sharkey to rob us, and what is more, we are going to prove it in court.

"Had it not been that I was saving my hands as much as possible I would have put Sharkey out in the second round. His head is as hard as a bullet, and I must have landed on him there fully forty times."

Fitzsimmons did take his case to court and a hearing was held to look into Wyatt's decision and determine who should receive the $10,000. The court exonerated Wyatt and gave the purse to Sharkey.

Five years later, after returning from prospecting and running a saloon in Alaska, Wyatt was again interviewed by the *Los Angeles Times*. They printed this short article on December 12, 1901.

Wyatt Earp, the well known sporting authority, passed the day in Los Angeles with his wife. He has just returned from Nome, where he has mining properties sufficient to make him financially comfortable for the remainder of his life. He states that the inland prospects at Nome are proving rich and that practical miners, who apply themselves steadily, are taking out good money.

Mr. Earp has not retired from the world of sport. He states that he intends to enjoy the roped arena and other characteristic sports for some time yet, although the criticism he received from his decision in the Sharkey Fitzsimmons fight was unfair, he alleges.

"I easily can explain the attack of certain newspapers," said Mr. Earp. "I had been doing work for the Examiner for three months previous to the fight. At that time both the Call and Chronicle were bitterly fighting the Examiner, and when I refereed the mill, I was their chance to get back at their rival over me. However, a referee is always open to the attacks of newspapers, friends of either fighter and to incompetent sporting editors who have exalted opinions of themselves."

Mr. and Mrs. Earp will continue their journey south tomorrow and will return to Nome the coming season.

# References

1. This was not unusual. Before most fights in those days, rumors would circulate that the fight was fixed against the favorite.

2. According to Stuart Lake's notes, Wyatt said he talked to Sharkey about this but Sharkey told him not to stop the fight.

3. Frank Kelly.

4. After Sharkey was hit, he was unable to use his legs and when his seconds tried to stand him up, he passed out. He was unconscious when they removed him from the ring and spent several days in the hospital. The opposition said he was faking it and medical tests were inconclusive, but the Associated Press reported, "Sharkey recovered consciousness half an hour later. He was not very badly injured, although his groin was swollen."

5. Up until shortly before this fight, boxing was fought bareknuckle with few rules. Boxing was also illegal. The police and courts began to ignore it's illegality when boxing became a bit more civilized by adopting the Marquis of Queensbury rules. Boxers now wore gloves and were not allowed to strike below the belt. This was the most publicized fight up to that time to be held under the new rules.

6. Fitzsimmons.

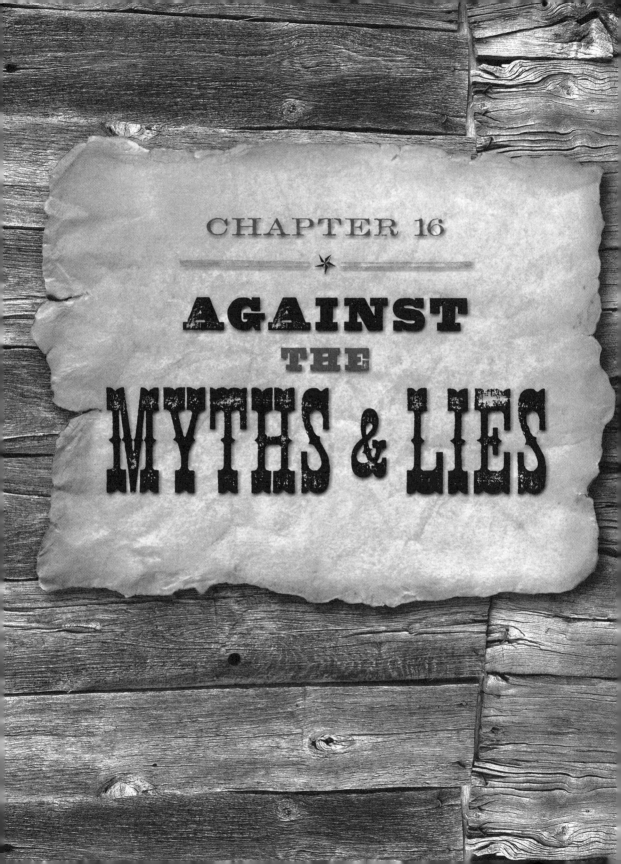

# CHAPTER 16

## AGAINST THE MYTHS & LIES

At this stage in his life Wyatt was frequently mentioned in newspaper articles, but not all of these notices were positive. He was frequently praised, but he could not keep up with the many distorted newspapers and magazine articles.

Around the turn of century, a number of particularly bad articles appeared—many of which originated with his Sharkey-Fitzsimmons decision. On August 16, 1903 the *New York Sun* published an article about a rowdy Wyatt being put in his place by a Canadian mountie. This incident was said to have occurred in Dawson in the Klondike, but Wyatt was never in Canada. The newspaper quoted an unnamed "San Francisco man," who described Wyatt, saying:

"…like Bat Masterson and a few other relics of the old days, he had been quite orderly and well behaved for some years.

"But when he got to Dawson he found a settlement like the places in which he made his reputation as a bad man many years ago. He found men carrying guns around in their belts and getting drunk and shooting people who happened to displease them, and it gave him the fever to get back into the game in which he was an adept in the days gone by.

"So Earp discarded his store clothes, got himself a flannel shirt, a pair of leather trousers and a sombrero, stuck a gun in his belt, loaded up on bad whiskey and went around the saloons and faro banks ballyragging everybody who would stand for his game, and taking a few shots at some men who resented it. There were a number of bad men in Dawson who were sufficiently awed by Earp's reputation to stand for him, and for a week he had things pretty much his own way.

> ☞ "IT DOES BEAT the band how the truth will be warped and misstated over a period of years."
> —*Wyatt Earp in a letter to William S. Hart, November 18, 1927*

"Well the fact that Earp was hitting it up got to the ears of a little five foot cockney member of the Canada mounted police, one of whose duties it was to see that Dawson behaved itself. Now, Earp didn't know much about the Canada mounted police and the manner of men who compose it.

"Therefore when he was interrupted in the gentle amusement of cleaning out a faro bank in Dawson one night by this little chap coming up to him with a request that he give him his gun, he opened his mouth and his eyes very wide, swore a mighty round of oaths and asked the little fellow in riding boots and cap if he wanted to visit Hades at once or wait a few hours.

"Earp was somewhat surprised when the little fellow simply smiled politely and said:

"'You must give me the gun or bury it sir,' and extended his hand for the weapon.

"Earp swore some more, but not quite so eloquently, for all the while the little man was smiling calmly in his face. Finally, Earp, clean flustered by the situation pulled his gun from his belt and fired it three times into the ceiling, whereupon the little man still smiling said:

"'Now you'll have to bury it or I'll have to take it away from you sir.'

"'Take my gun away from me!' roared Earp.

"'Exactly,' said the little man. 'Maybe you doubt I'll do it, sir?'

"The witnesses of this colloquy didn't know what to expect from Earp…However a crisis was averted by Earp's putting his gun back into his belt and starting to leave the place. Just as he got to the door the policeman walked over and tapped him on the shoulder.

"'I beg your pardon, sir,' he said, 'but if you come out with a gun in sight tomorrow, I shall have to take it away from you.'

"Earp turned purple with rage, but he had no nerve left when he confronted that politely smiling face. He roared a few oaths back at the amused crowd in the gambling house and then went to the Golden Lion saloon, where he took a few drinks and proceeded to tell what he would do the next day when the cockney tried to take his gun.

"'Why I'll blow him full of holes,' he said.

"'Yes,' said a listener, 'but when you put a hole in him you put a hole in the British Empire, which it will fill with two men. If you kill them, four will take their places. In the end, Earp, you will have the whole British Army here if necessary just to put you out. Better let him alone.'

"The next day, Earp, very sober and very thoughtful appeared on the streets of Dawson in the store clothes he came to town with."

Wyatt was not pleased when he read a version of this article with the headline "The Taming of Wyatt Earp, Bad Man of Other Days" in the *Los Angeles Herald*. He responded by writing a letter to the editor, which appeared in the issue of September 8, 1903.

It relates to an experience I was reported to have had in Dawson City, in which I was said to have attempted to "shoot up the town" and to have been subdued by one of the Canadian Mounted Police.

The falsity of the article is shown by the fact that I never was within 1000 miles of Dawson City.

I wish to say that neither I nor my brothers were ever "bad men," in the sense that term is used, nor did we ever indulge in the practice of "shooting up" towns. We have been officers of the law and have had our experiences in preserving the law, but we are not, and never have been professional bad men. In justice to me and my friends and relatives I would like to have you make this statement.

WYATT EARP.

The article also prompted a response from George Parsons, a fellow prospector and a friend of his from Tombstone and Nome, Alaska. Parsons' letter appeared in the *Herald* on September 9th.

As an old Tombstoner and one who knew the Earps in the stormy days of the early '80s, I wish, in simple justice to the family in general and Wyatt Earp in particular, to confirm his statement in yesterday's Herald that they were not "bad men" in the common acceptation of the term, but were ever ready to discharge their duty as officers of the law, and did it so effectively that they incurred the enmity of the rustlers and desperadoes congregated in that lively town and section of the country and were always on the side of law and order.

There was one exception. When their brother Morgan was assassinated, Virgil Earp shot and Wyatt Earp's life attempted, then they took the law into their own hands and did what most anyone would have done under the peculiar circumstances existing at the time, and what anyone reading the Virginian would consider their right to do.

I speak of a time I am familiar with for I lived in Tombstone during the entire stay of the Earps, chased Apaches with them, and have seen them, and particularly Wyatt Earp, defending and enforcing the law in the face of death. To call such men "bad men," when the better element was siding with and supporting them morally and financially, is to deal in terms misapplied; and I feel today as I felt in Nome, Alaska, where I saw Wyatt Earp, that if anybody was undeservedly illtreated[1] and particularly an old Tombstoner, he would find a champion in the same Wyatt Earp, who is older now but none the less gritty, I believe. I state this in justice to a much maligned man who, as a public character, was a benefit and a protection to the community he once lived in.

G. W. PARSONS

Of course, these letters had little effect when the story was appearing in newspapers across the country. One of Wyatt's friends, John Hays Hammond, even repeated the story in the March 1925 issue of *Scribner's* magazine.

Another story of this type was published three years earlier in the *San Francisco Call* on April 28, 1900. It claimed:

Wyatt Earp, gun-fighter and all around bad man was knocked down and out late Saturday night by Tom Mulqueen, the well-known racehorse man. The trouble…was precipitated by Earp. Both men had been drinking at the bar, when Earp brought up the subject of a recent scandal at the Tanforan track. He made several disparaging remarks about the jockey who was on very friendly terms with Mulqueen. When called down he became belligerently indignant and threatened to wipe the floor with the horse owner.

George Parsons.

Instantly Mulqueen grabbed him and after throwing him against the bar landed a blow on the gunfighter's face, knocking him out.

John Farley, the proprietor of the saloon, fearing serious trouble between the two men, managed to induce Mulqueen to leave the place. Earp, after recovering from the effects of the blow, was also lead from the saloon and placed aboard a passing street car. Earp was not armed at the time, having left his trusted "gun" with a friend shortly before the occurrence.

---

Wyatt was 52 at the time of this supposed brawl with the 56-year-old ex-boxer Mulqueen. Papers across the country reported the story.

A couple months after this, on July 14, 1900, an article out of San Francisco detailed how Wyatt had been shot in Nome. This, of course, never happened. The article also repeated the story of Wyatt being knocked out by Mulqueen.

About the same time another article came out of San Francisco supposedly on the death of Virgil in Willcox, Arizona. It was a crazy piece describing how the stage-robbing Earps fought a battle with the rustlers in the Bird Cage Theater in which twelve men were killed or wounded. The Earps then holed up in an adobe fortress at the edge of town, but Warren couldn't resist returning to a saloon to gamble and a rustler promptly shot him in the head. The Earps were run off to Gunnison, Colorado, where their sister eloped with Ike Clanton. The Earps chased Ike and his bride into a mine, but the miners prevented the Earps from killing him. Ike then proposed to fight a duel to settle the matter. In the duel, Ike killed Julian Earp.[2] The Earps left Ike and his wife alone for two years until Wyatt, Virgil, and Curly Bill finally went after him and killed him,[3] but Ike killed Curly Bill in the process. Virgil was then killed by cowboy John Boyett, leaving Wyatt as the last surviving Earp brother.

This story was reprinted in a Seattle newspaper and even in the November 1901 issue of *Munsey's Magazine*. It's said this story originated with a San Francisco sportswriter who lost money on the fight. He in turn got some of his muddled information from a *San Francisco Call* article that appeared shortly after the fight. This article

☞ "NOTORIETY HAS BEEN THE bane of my life. I detest it, and I never have put forth any effort to check the tales that have been published in recent years, of the exploits in which my brothers and I are supposed to have been the principal participants. Not one of them is correct. My friends have urged that I make this known on printed sheet. Perhaps I shall; it will correct many mythic tales."

—*Wyatt Earp in a letter to his friend, John Hays Hammond, May 21, 1925*[4]

was by former Tombstoner Charles H. Hopkins. The *Call* claimed Hopkins was a "distinguished journalist," though Tombstone records show he was a teamster who was arrested by Wyatt Earp for being drunk and disorderly.

Hopkins, in his article, said he joined Behan's posse during the Vendetta so he could write up the Earps' funeral. He also wrote, "All of this talk about Wyatt Earp being a brave man on the square makes me tired....Many incidents led a good many people to think that Earp was not so game as he might be, so one night a job was [fabricated] to test him. Just about dusk a crowd of men climbed to the flat roof of an adobe building, commenced firing at a general rate, and threw a dummy figure of a man over into the street. Earp was at the town pump, about 100 feet away, and saw it all. It looked like a case of real trouble, requiring the interference of the Marshal, but Earp disappeared and was not seen around his usual haunts until things quieted down."

While there were other articles of this type, the five articles mentioned here all originated in San Francisco and mention the Sharkey-Fitzsimmons fight. While Wyatt received bad publicity during his days in Tombstone, most of it was localized to Arizona. It was his involvement in the boxing match that took it to the national level, doing considerable damage to his reputation. All this began to swing to the other extreme in the late 1920s.

In early 1920s, Wyatt decided he needed a biography to set the record straight. At the time, he was in his 70s and living in poverty. He thought that if he could sell his story, he could at least leave some money to Sadie after he was gone. Unfortunately, he chose John Flood, an engineer, to write the book for him. The manuscript, which is absolutely dreadful, didn't sell.

Six months before his death, Stuart Lake approached him to write the biography that was later published as *Wyatt Earp, Frontier Marshal* (1931). Wyatt died after just a few interviews, so Lake was forced to rely heavily on other sources—not all of them accurate. But Lake was an excellent writer and his biography quickly became a bestseller. It was also the basis for the 1950s television series, *The Life and Legend of Wyatt Earp*, starring Hugh O'Brian, and for numerous Hollywood movies. Lake's book turned Wyatt into a legend. Then Hollywood took over and turned Wyatt into a mythical figure. In one way or another, Wyatt's life ended up influencing practically the entire Western genre.

# References

1. Sic.

2. There was no Julian Earp, but it is interesting that Fitzsimmons' manager and brother-in-law was named Martin Julian.

3. Ike was actually killed by a detective in 1887.

4. This was the same John Hays Hammond who wrote the 1925 *Scribner's* article on him.

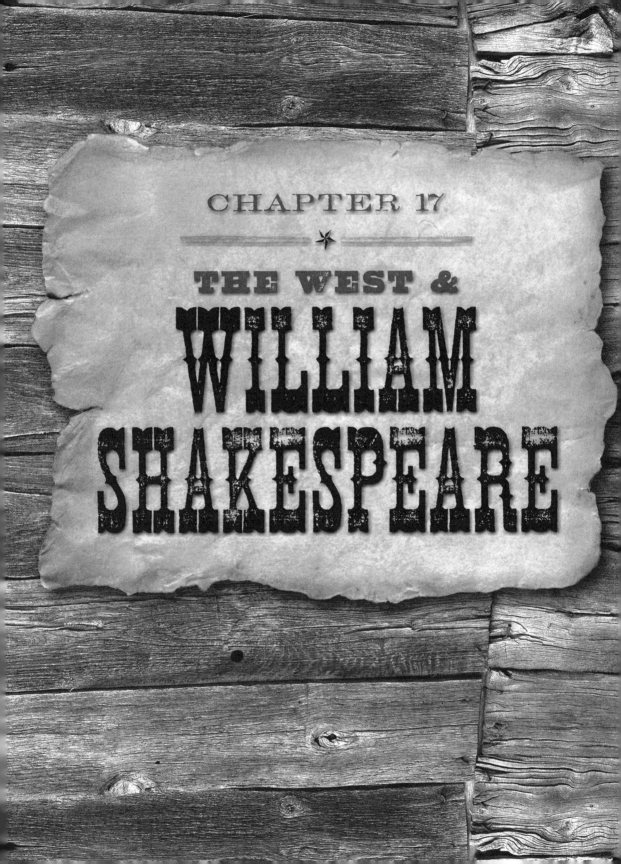

# CHAPTER 17

## THE WEST &

# WILLIAM SHAKESPEARE

n interesting article written by Adela Rogers St. Johns, a well-known author and journalist at that time, appeared in the May 22, 1960 issue of *The American Weekly*.[1] This was a small magazine from Tempe, Arizona, that went out of business in 1969. Whether she took notes at her meetings with Wyatt—perhaps she wrote an article on him at the time—or whether she wrote this from memory is unclear. Either way, she seems to have added some color to his quotations.

# I KNEW WYATT EARP

*It dates me—but I'm glad I had the privilege*

By Adela Rogers St. Johns

When I tell people that I knew Wyatt Earp—the man who has justly been called "the greatest gun fighting marshal of the Old West"—they look at me as though I'd claimed a personal acquaintance with Daniel Boone, seen Davy Crockett at the Alamo, and General Custer at the battle of Little Big Horn.

But I *did* know Wyatt Earp, whom I had supposed was dead until Mark Kelly, then sports editor of the Los Angeles Examiner, invited me to accompany him on a visit to the old gun fighter and his wife Josephine in their little frame house on the west side of Los Angeles.

I'll never forget the man who rose from his chair on the shaded porch to welcome us. He was straight as a pine tree, tall and magnificently built. I knew he was nearing 80, but in spite of his snow-white hair and moustache he did not seem, or look old. His greeting was warm and friendly but I stood still in awe. Somehow, like a mountain or a desert, he reduced you to size.

Inevitably the talk got around to the Battle of the O.K. Corral—probably the most celebrated gun fight in frontier history—in which Wyatt Earp. His brothers Virgil and Morgan, and a dentist named Doc Holliday, fought a pitched battle with five tough cattle rustling outlaws, killed three of them and put the other two in jail.

Both of Wyatt Earp's brothers were wounded but he came through unscathed.

"That fight didn't take but about 30 seconds," he said. "and it seems like, in my going on 80 years, we could find some other happenings to discuss."

He did, however, admit that "a good deal went on in them 30 seconds" in the streets of Tombstone, Arizona, on October 26, 1881. "The men we killed there had to be killed," he said. "They were bad, and if any part of the country lets itself be stampeded by bad men, it will infect the whole shebang before it's through."

As to gun fighting in general—and at the O.K. Corral in particular—he said, "A good gunman shouldn't figger to pull the trigger but once. If he does, it means he's in a hurry and the chances are he don't hit you. Any gunplay I ever happened to get mixed up with, the winner was always the man who stayed calm, kept his mouth shut and took his time."

"Seeing that the O.K. Corral fight took less than 30 seconds," I said timidly, "it doesn't seem to me there was much time to take."

"Young lady," said Wyatt Earp, "no matter whether it's 30 seconds, or three months, or three years, a man can take his time and be sure he sees what he is shooting at, so he has a reasonable chance of hitting it. Likewise, I was a United States Marshal,[2] so I was coming forward, and they was usually going back. You shoot straighter coming forward."

This was the first of many conversations I enjoyed in the little frame house where Wyatt Earp and his wife welcomed such friends as movie stars Bill Hart and Tom Mix, Jack Dempsey, Stuart Lake (who wrote *Wyatt Earp, Frontier Marshal*) and my sports editor friend, Mark Kelly.

Kelly, who knew Bat Masterson and Wild Bill Hickok, said they told him no one could dispute that Wyatt Earp was the greatest single gunfighter who ever lived and that no other man in the Old West was even a close second to him.

Wyatt Earp on the Colorado River in 1925.

He knew, as I came to know, the life story of the man who was famous in his day and who became a legend when he died—that he was born in Monmouth, Illinois, in 1848, and that, at the age of 16, he drove a wagon from Pella, Iowa, to California when his family moved West with other settlers, and was a stage driver and buffalo hunter before he became famous as a lawman.

On one of my visits to his house I found him reading a book. To my surprise, it was *Hamlet*. He told us that he and Tom Mix were reading Shakespeare for the first time.[3]

"Neither of us had much schooling," he said, "and I was just a boy along about the time my father pulled out West in a wagon train. We was short handed and on the way I had to stand my watch guarding the women and children and the wagons. We was in a couple of little fracases with the Sioux and I never seemed to relish going back to school.

"Tom Mix, he was fighting in the Boxer Rebellion when he wasn't but 15.[4] Both of us admired education and one day we got to wondering how Mr. Shakespeare would stand up if you could uncondition yourself to his reputation and renown. You always got to take into consideration that a man's reputation will most usually influence your judgment of him.

"How did it come out?" I asked.

"Well," he said, "you and Mark (Mark Kelly was with me at the time) being writers, know that a writer has got to make you believe him. Now Shakespeare never did make me believe that a man like he told me Othello was, would act that ornery, and strangle a nice little thing like his wife appeared to be, all on account of a handkerchief.

"There are more corpses in Hamlet than there was in the O.K. Corral, and with less reason We didn't kill none of the wrong men like Hamlet done to poor old Polonius . . . He was a talkative man and wouldn't have lasted long in Kansas.

"If he couldn't find anybody else to talk to, he talked to himself. A man talks himself into a spot which he had no more intention of doing than a prairie dog and then he's obliged to do things he don't wish to do."

Remembering that he had killed three of the men who shot his younger brother Morgan in the back, I said. "Wasn't Hamlet's honor involved in finding his father's murderer, as much as yours, in finding the men who killed your brother?"

After a pause he said, "It takes a resolute man not to make mistakes when he gets to acting as his own law." And then he said, "Morg could stand his own bad luck but he had an awful time standing the other fellow's. He was too truthful to be a good gambler, so after I quit as marshal I run up a nice little stake at faro bank, to give him a start in life. Last thing he said to me was that he expected to meet me again in heaven. I hope he's right."

I thought of that the day of Wyatt Earp's funeral in 1929—and I hoped so, too.

## References

1. Copyright © by Adela Rogers St. Johns, 1960. This article is reprinted with the kind permission of her granddaughter, Kris Wolf.

2. Deputy U.S. marshal.

3. It may have been Wyatt's friend, actor William S. Hart, who got him interested in Shakespeare. Before becoming famous for his cowboy roles, Hart was a Shakespearean actor.

4. Tom Mix (1880–1940) was actually 19 at the time of the Boxer Rebellion, which was in 1899 and 1900.

Wyatt Earp's funeral.

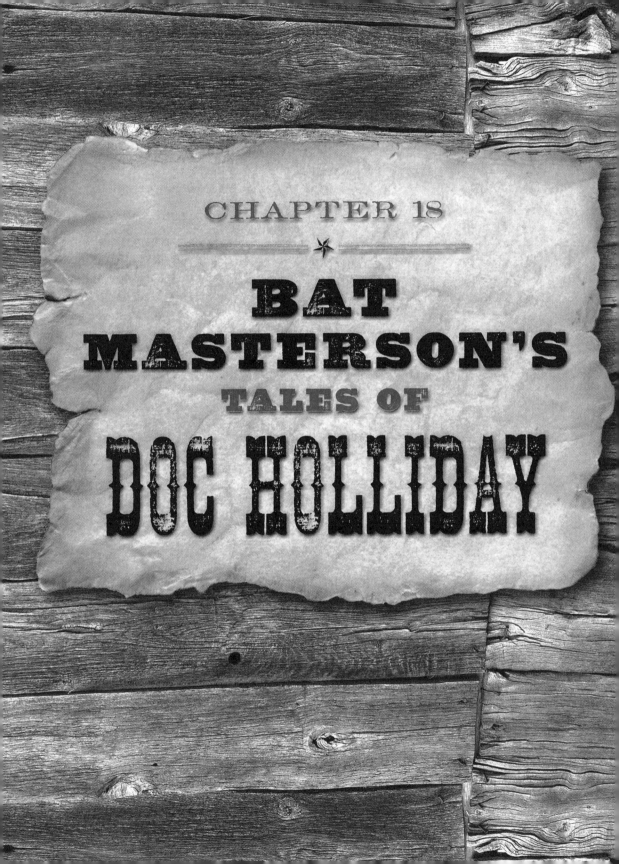

# CHAPTER 18

## BAT MASTERSON'S TALES OF DOC HOLLIDAY

oc Holliday was Wyatt's closest friend during his Tombstone days. Bat Masterson didn't think as highly of Doc, but he did occasionally help him for Wyatt's sake. Bat wrote about Doc for the fourth article in his gunfighter series for *Human Life* magazine. It appeared in the May 1907 issue.

# FAMOUS GUN FIGHTERS OF THE WESTERN FRONTIER

## Fourth Article. 'Doc' Holliday

### By W. B. (Bat) Masterson

EDITOR'S NOTE:—Mr. Masterson's previous articles, on Ben Thompson, Wyatt Earp, and Luke Short appeared in the January, February and April issues. He will, from month to month, tell the stories of other western characters, once famous among the hard riding, quick shooting chivalry of the plains.

Mr. Masterson himself has witnessed stirring times, and stood for years a central and commanding figure in a dangerous day that is gone. He has been buffalo hunter, Indian trader, and scout for Miles under the great Ben Clarke—in the Indian war of 1874. Later, Mr. Masterson was elected sheriff of Ford County, Kansas, with headquarters at Dodge City. Dodge then was reckoned the roughest camp on the border. That day is now past and Mr. Masterson is no longer a queller of "bad men," but a resident of New York and a contributor to the press. Also he is a warm personal friend to President Roosevelt, who caused him to be named a Deputy United States Marshal for the southern district of New York.

While he never did anything to entitle him to a statue in the Hall of Fame, Doc Holliday was nevertheless a most picturesque character on the western border in those days when the pistol instead of law courts determined issues. Holliday was a product of the state of Georgia, and a scion of a most respectable and prominent family.

He graduated as a dentist from one of the medical colleges of his native state[1] before he left it, but did not follow his profession very long after receiving his diploma. It was perhaps too respectable a calling for him.[2]

Holliday had a mean disposition and an ungovernable temper, and under the influence of liquor was a most dangerous man. In this respect he was very much like the big Missourian who had put in the day at a cross road groggery and, after getting pretty well filled up with bug juice of the Moonshine brand, concluded that it was about time for him to say something that would make an impression on his hearers; so he straightened up, threw out his chest and declared in a loud tone of voice, that he was "a bad man when he was drinking, and managed to keep pretty full all the time." So it was with Holliday.

☞ "DOC HOLLIDAY REMAINED a few days in Las Vegas [New Mexico] before taking his departure for Arizona, and I met him quite frequently and found him to be a very likeable fellow."

—*Miguel Antonio Otero, who later became governor of New Mexico*

## COULDN'T HAVE WHIPPED A BOY

Physically, Doc Holliday was a weakling who could not have whipped a healthy fifteen year old boy in a go as you please fist fight, and no one knew this better than himself, and the knowledge of this fact was perhaps why he was so ready to resort to a weapon of some kind whenever he got himself into difficulty. He was hot headed and impetuous and very much given to both drinking and quarrelling, and, among men who did not fear him, was very much disliked.

He possessed none of the qualities of leadership such as those that distinguished such men as H. P. Myton, Wyatt Earp, Billy Tilghman[3] and other famous western characters. Holliday seemed to be absolutely unable to keep out of trouble for any great length of time. He would no sooner be out of one scrape before he was in another, and the strange part of it is he was more often in the right than in the wrong, which has rarely ever been the case with a man who is continually getting himself into trouble.

The indiscriminate killing of some negroes in the little Georgia village in which he lived was what first caused him to leave his home.[4] The trouble came about in rather an unexpected manner one Sunday afternoon—unexpected so far at least as the negroes were concerned.

Near the little town in which Holliday was raised, there flowed a small river in which the white boys of the village, as well as the black ones, used to go swimming together. The white boys finally decided that the negroes would have to find a swimming place elsewhere, and notified them to that effect.[5] The negro boys were informed that in the future they would have to go further down the stream to do their swimming which they promptly refused to do and told the whites that if they didn't like existing conditions, that they themselves would have to hunt up a new swimming hole.

☞ "THE DOCTOR HAD just as lief [i.e. willingly] kill a man as not. All he looked for usually was to have the law on his side. I said to him one day: 'Doctor, don't your conscience ever trouble you?' 'No,' he replied, with that peculiar cough of his, 'I coughed that up with my lungs long ago.'"

—*Colonel John T. Deweese, one of Doc's lawyers, as quoted in the* Denver Republican, *December 25, 1887*

## SHOT A CROWD OF NEGROES

As might have been expected in those days in the South, the defiant attitude taken by the negroes in the matter caused the white boys to instantly go upon the war path.[6] They would have their order obeyed or know the reason why.

One beautiful Sunday afternoon, while an unusually large number of negroes were in swimming at the point in dispute, Holliday appeared on the river bank with a double barreled shot gun[7] in his hands, and, pointing it in the direction of the swimmers, ordered them from the river.

"Get out, and be quick about it," was his peremptory command. The negroes, as a matter of course, stampeded for the opposite shore, falling over each other in their efforts to get beyond the range of the shot gun. Holliday waited until he got a bunch of them together, and then turned loose with both barrels, killing two outright, and wounding several others.[8]

The shooting, as a matter of course, was entirely unjustifiable, as the negroes were on the run when killed; but the authorities evidently thought otherwise, for nothing was ever done about the matter. Holliday, afterwards in speaking about the occurrence, justified the deed on the broad grounds that the "niggers"[9] had to be disciplined, and he knew of no more effective way of doing it than with a shotgun.

His family however, thought it would be best for him to go away for a while and allow the thing to die out; so he accordingly pulled up stakes and went to Dallas, Texas, where he hung out his professional sign bearing the inscription, "J. H. Holliday, Dentist."

This was in the early seventies and at the time when Dallas was a typical frontier town in everything the term implied. A stranger in Dallas in those days could get anything he wanted from pitch and toss to manslaughter at any hour of the day or night, and that was exactly what suited the Georgia dentist.

Gambling was not only the principal and best paying industry of the town at the time, but it was also reckoned among its most respectable and, as the hectic Georgian had always shown a fondness for all things in which the elements of chance played an important part, his new environment furnished him with no cause for complaint. In a short time those who wished to consult professionally with the doctor, had to do so over a card table in some nearby gambling establishment, or not at all.

While Holliday never boasted about the killing of the negroes down in Georgia, he was nevertheless regarded by his new made Texas acquaintances who knew about the occurrence, as a man with a record; and a man with a record of having killed someone in those days, even though the victim was only a "nigger,"[10] was looked upon as something more than the ordinary mortal; wherefore the doctor on that account was given instant recognition by the higher circles of society in Dallas.

## A POKER GAME INCIDENT

If there was any one thing above another Holliday loved better than a session in a poker game, it was conflict, and, as Dallas was the home of conflict, the doctor was in his element. It was not a "nigger" that he shot this time, but a white man of some local prominence for which he had to emigrate to some more congenial place. He brought up next at Jacksboro, a small, out of the way place just west of the Fort Richardson Military Reservation, on the north western border of the state, where civilization was only in a formative stage.

The doctor had by this time heard much about the man killers who abode on the frontier, and regarded himself as well qualified to play a hand among the foremost of the guild. He was not long in Jacksboro before he was in another scrape. This time it was with a soldier who was stationed at the Fort, and who had been given permission to visit the town by his commanding officer.

The trouble was over a card game in which the soldier claimed he had been given the worst of it by the man from Georgia. This of course, necessitated the fighting Georgian taking another trip on the road, for he knew it would never do to let the soldiers at the Fort capture him, which they would be sure to try to do as soon as word reached them about the killing of their comrade.[11]

He therefore lost no time in getting out of town, and, seated on the hurricane deck of a Texas cayuse,[12] was well on his way to safety by the time the news of the homicide reached the Fort. It was a long and dangerous trip that he mapped out for himself on this occasion.

## HIS CAREER IN DENVER

From Jacksboro to Denver, Colorado, was fully eight hundred miles, and, as much of the route to be traversed through was the Texas Panhandle and No man's land, which was in those days alive with Indians none too friendly to the white man, and renegade Mexicans from New Mexico, the journey was a most perilous one to take; but the doughty doctor was equal to the task[13] and in due time reached Denver without either having lost his scalp, or his desire for more conflict.

This was in the summer of 1876 and while Denver was a much more important city than Dallas, its local government was conducted on very much the same principles. Like Dallas, everything went in Denver, and the doctor, after looking the situation over for a day or two, concluded that he had lost nothing by the change.[14]

☞ "Dr. Holliday and Mr. [Frank] Austin, a saloon-keeper, relieved the monotony of the noise of fire crackers by taking a couple of shots at each other yesterday afternoon. The cheerful note of the peaceful six-shooter is heard once more among us. Both shooters were arrested."

—Dallas Herald, *January 12, 1875*

☞ RIDGLEY TILDEN, WRITING for the *San Francisco Examiner*, on May 11, 1882 blamed the fight on Doc, saying, "Now comes Doc Holliday, as quarrelsome a man as God ever allowed to live on earth....Doc Holliday is responsible for all the killings, etc., in connection with what is known as the Earp-Clanton imbroglio in Arizona. He kicked up the fight, and Wyatt Earp and his brothers 'stood in' with him, on the score of gratitude. Everyone in Tombstone conversant with the circumstances deprecates the killing of the McLowerys and Clanton. It's produced a feud that has driven the Earps from Arizona and virtually made outlaws of them."

In all respects the Rocky Mountain town looked good to him, and as he had set out to build up a record for himself as a man killer, he did not purpose lying idle very long. While Denver, in many respects in those days was a rough and ready town, it nevertheless enforced to the very letter the ordinance against the carrying of fire arms, and Holliday, for the nonce becoming prudent, put his cannister aside, but straightway went and bought himself a murderous looking knife.

Thus heeled, he did not long delay in getting into action, and in so doing, carved up the face and neck of one Bud Ryan, a quiet and gentlemanly looking sport, in a frightful manner. Bud Ryan still lives in Denver, and carries around with him the marks of his run in with the fighting Holliday, more than thirty years ago.[15]

It was again the doctor's turn to take the road and escape from the scene of his recent malefaction, and this time he headed for Dodge City, Kansas.[16] It was there I first met him, although I had heard about his doings in Texas.

He was slim of build and sallow of complexion, standing about five feet ten inches, and weighing no more than 130 pounds. His eyes were of a pale blue and his moustache was thin and of a sandy hue. Dodge City was then very much like Dallas and Denver, only a little more so, and the doctor did not express regret at having come.

It was easily seen that he was not a healthy man for he not only looked the part, but he incessantly coughed it as well. During his year's stay at Dodge at that time, he did not have a quarrel with anyone, and, although regarded as a sort of grouch, he was not disliked by those with whom he had become acquainted. It was during this time that he also made the acquaintance of Wyatt Earp and they were always fast friends ever afterwards.

## HIS FRIENDSHIP WITH WYATT EARP

He went from Dodge to Trinidad, Colorado, where, within a week from the time he landed, he shot and seriously wounded a young sport by the name of Kid Colton, over a very trivial matter.[17] He was again forced to hunt the tall timber and managed to make his escape to Las Vegas, New Mexico, which was then something of a boom town, on account of the Santa Fe Railroad having just reached there.

Holliday remained around Las Vegas for some time, doing the best he could in a gambling way; then he had a quarrel with one of the town rounders by the name of Mike Gordon, whom he invited to step outside of the saloon in which they were quarrelling. No sooner had Gordon stepped from the door than Holliday shot him dead.[18] From Las Vegas to Dodge City across country, without following the traveled road, was about five hundred miles and this was the trip Holliday was again compelled to make on horseback, in order to get away from the authorities who were hot on his trail.[19]

He reached Dodge City safely and remained there until Wyatt Earp took him in his covered wagon to Arizona in the fall of 1880. Again he showed no disposition to quarrel or shoot while in Dodge, and many thought that much of the trouble he had been having in other places had been forced upon him, but I am satisfied that it was pretty much all of his own seeking. His whole heart and soul were wrapped up in Wyatt Earp and he was always ready to stake his life in defence of any cause in which Wyatt was interested. He aided the Earp brothers in their street fight in Tombstone, against the Clanton and McLowery[20] brothers, in which the latter two were killed, along with Billy Clanton.

It was Doc Holliday, who, along with Wyatt Earp, overtook and killed Frank Stillwell at the railroad station in Tucson for having participated in the murder of Morgan Earp in Tombstone. He was by Wyatt's side when he killed Curly Bill at the Whetstone Springs[21] outside of Tombstone. Damon did no more for Pythias than Holliday did for Wyatt Earp.

After Wyatt and his party had run down and killed nearly all their enemies in Arizona, Holliday returned to Denver, where he was arrested on an order from the Arizona authorities, charged with aiding in the killing of Frank Stillwell.

## Doc's Death Toll

☞ "The doctor [Holliday] was as mild mannered as Byron's 'Pirate' and perhaps he was not after all such a bad man. Local histories of him are very indefinite and unsatisfactory. Some people put him down as a killer of four men. Others, among them his most intimate friends, declare that 'he never killed mor'n two men.' The best authorities, however, say he had killed sixteen."

—Denver Republican, *December 25, 1887*

☞ "He is known to have killed at least eight men and is suspected of killing many more."

—Glenwood Post, *August 23, 1985*

☞ "Reports vary as to the number of men he actually killed, but he is variously said to have 'done in' from 12 to 36."

—Grand Junction Sentinel, *May 30, 1956*

☞ "His nerve and eye, victorious in more than thirty duels to the death, were the admiration and envy of all the fighters of the time."

—E. D. Cowen, Rocky Mountain News, *October 23, 1898*

☞ "That's Doc Holliday. He's killed thirty men in his day, and there's no telling when he'll turn himself loose again."

—*A man in Silverton, Colorado, quoted by the* New York Sun, *June 1886*

☞ "'How many lives has he [Doc] taken?'

"'That is a hard question to answer, but they approach close to fifty. While in Tucson he shot six men within two weeks, all of whom he killed without cause or reason. He was forced to leave there to avoid lynching.'"

—*A correspondent interviewing "Sheriff" Perry Mallen in the* Cincinnati Enquirer, *May 28, 1882*

☞ "The *Cincinnati Enquirer* of Sunday, which arrived here yesterday, contained over a column of twaddle devoted to this case. A biographical sketch of the principal [Doc] was included, in which it was made to appear that has in his time killed over fifty men, and that Jesse James is a saint compared with him. The article in question has caused much amusement among Holladay's [*sic*] friends."

—Pueblo Daily Chieftain, *June 1, 1882*

This happened in the spring of 1882. I was in Denver at the time, and managed to secure an audience with Governor Pitkin who, after listening to my statement in the matter, refused to honor the Arizona requisition for Holiday. I then had a complaint sworn out against Holliday, charging him with having committed a highway robbery[22] in Pueblo, Colorado, and had him taken from Denver to Pueblo, where he was put under a nominal bond and released from custody.

The charge of highway robbery made against Holliday, at this time, was nothing more than a subterfuge on my part to prevent him from being taken out of the state by the Arizona authorities, after Governor Pitkin went out of office, but the Colorado authorities did not know it at the time. Holliday always managed to have his case put off whenever it would come up for trial, and, by furnishing a new bond, in every instance would be released again.[23]

When he died at Glenwood Springs a few years afterwards,[24] he was still under bond to answer to the charge of highway robbery I had caused a certain person to prefer against him.

Doc Holliday, whose right name was John H. Holliday, lived during his stormy career in three states of the Union besides the one in which he was born, and in two territories; namely Texas, Colorado and Kansas, and in the territories of New Mexico and Arizona. Besides the killing of the negroes in the river in his home town, he shot a man in Dallas, Texas, and killed another in Jacksboro. He stabbed Bud Ryan in a frightful manner in Denver, Colorado, and shot another in Trinidad in the same state. He killed a man in Las Vegas, New Mexico, and was directly connected with several killings in Arizona. Kansas, it will be observed, was the only state in which he lived, in which he failed to either slay or bodily wound some person. The question as to the extent in which he was justified in doing as he did, is of course open to debate. I have always believed that much of Holliday's trouble was caused by drink and for that reason held him to blame in many instances. While I assisted him substantially on several occasions, it was not because I liked him any too well, but on account of my friendship for Wyatt Earp, who did.

Holliday had few real friends anywhere in the West. He was selfish and had a perverse nature—traits not calculated to make a man popular in the early days on the frontier.

In 1910 Bat summarized much of this in an interview for the *New York Herald*. He said:

"Speaking of picturesque characters, I guess Doc Holliday stand in that category. I never liked him and few persons did. He had a mean disposition and differed from most of the big gun fighters in that he would seek a fight. He was a consumptive and physically weak, which probably had something to do with his unfortunate disposition. He was of a fine Georgia family and was educated as a dentist. He went West after shooting down some defenseless negro boys in a quarrel as to who should occupy a certain swimming hole. He made Dallas in the early seventies, and hung out his shingle. 'J. H. Holliday, Dentist,' but he soon quit that for gambling. His shooting of the negroes became known, and so he got a reputation as a bad man from the start and associated on equal terms with men of more notable record.

"He finally killed a man in Jacksboro and fled. Then he killed a soldier, and to avoid being caught by the military authorities made a desperate flight to Denver, across 800 miles of waterless, Indian infested desert. He made Denver in '76. The law forbade him to carry a gun there, so he slipped a knife into his bootleg and presently carved up the face of one Bud Ryan, who bears the marks to this day. He fled then to Dodge City, where I first met him. He kept out of trouble in Dodge somehow but presently wandered to Trinidad, Colo., where the first thing he did was to shoot and serious wound Kid Colton. Then he escaped to Las Vegas, a boom town in New Mexico, where he disagreed with Mike Gordon and shot him dead in a doorway. Again he lit out 500 miles across country to Dodge City. He went to Arizona with Wyatt to Earp in 1880 and took part in the famous battles of the Earp brothers in and around Tombstone. He died of consumption in Glenwood Springs."

# References

1. He graduated with honors in 1872 from the Pennsylvania College of Dental Surgery, which was later absorbed by the University of Pennsylvania. His graduate thesis was titled *Diseases of the Teeth*.

2. It's more likely the coughing caused by his tuberculosis kept potential patients away.

3. Bill Tilghman was a lawman for 46 years and was a close friend of Bat's. Bat met him right after the Battle of Adobe Walls.

4. There are a number of versions of this story but so far no documentation has been found to confirm them.

5. Other versions of this story say the place where this happened was owned by William and Thomas McKey—Doc's uncles. Since they bought the river property in February 1872, the incident probably occurred after that date. Most of Doc's biographers place the date between 1866 and 1870—before Doc went to dental school. Some accounts say these were soldiers from the nearby Negro federal garrison. If this is correct, the incident would have had to have occurred before 1867, as there were no troops there after that date.

6. The Holliday family says Doc was riding in a buggy with his uncle, Tom McKey, when he spotted the African Americans.

7. The gun that Holliday family tradition says was used by Doc in this incident is a Colt's 1851 Navy revolver.

8. Some say a young boy was killed, while others say fourteen died. Tom McKey's daughter said, "Papa told me Doc shot over their heads. They rode up on the Negroes in swimming in a part of the Withlacoochee River that Doc and his friends had cleared out to be used as their swimming hole. The presence of the Negroes in their swimming hole enraged Doc, and he drew his pistol—shooting over their heads to scare them off. Papa said, 'Shot over their heads.'" This is more likely, otherwise it would be easier to find record of the incident.

9. This is another example of the offensive racial terms commonly used at that time.

10. Another offensive racial slur that you won't see in national magazines today.

11. There's no confirmation of Doc killing a soldier in Jacksboro, Texas.

12. Cayuse: an Indian pony.

13. Not bloody likely, especially for a sick man.

14. Doc was in Denver in 1875 and 1876.

15. The earliest known version of the Doc-Ryan story is in an article that appeared in the *Denver Republican* on December 25, 1887, shortly after Doc's death headlined "Holliday's Trail of Blood." This is one of those articles that is so chock full of errors that it's difficult to find anything correct in it.

According to this article, when Doc decided to winter in Denver in 1876, he decided to go by an alias since the city was full of federal authorities, but he was soon found out. They said, "The Doc had taken the name of Tom Mackey [his favorite uncle's name was Tom McKey (pronounced "Mac´-ey), so he probably did use this alias]. He was a quiet, modest man, with a smile that was childlike and bland; he was generally regarded as very inoffensive, but one night he electrified the town by nearly cutting off the head of Budd Ryan, a well-known Denver gambler. 'Doc' Holliday, alias Tom Mackey, was a little better known in Denver after that." Their source for this story was none other than Bat himself.

Bat seems to have confused the story of the stabbing of Ed Bailey, which supposedly happened in Fort Griffin, Texas, with another knife incident that Doc had no part of. On June 22, 1887, the *Denver Republican* reported, "'Kid' Ryan, a waiter bearing a hard reputation, was arrested last evening by Officer Bohanna. Ryan early in the evening was drinking in Moses' Home, a low saloon located at No. 487 1/2 Larimer St. During the evening Jack Brogan entered the saloon and accidentally brushed against Ryan. This enraged him and hastily drawing a pocket knife he made a lunge at Brogan. The knife struck him in the neck and inflicted a deep gash. The wound bled profusely but it is not a dangerous one. Had Ryan used a larger knife the chances are that Brogan's throat would have been cut. The police were loud in their denunciation of Moses' Home. They characterize it as a resort of the lowest type, where tramps, holdups and other evil characters resort."

16. It's known Doc was in Dodge City in June of 1878 and from then on into early 1879.

17. This would be in early 1879, but again, there's no confirmation of this story. By March he was in Las Vegas, where he opened a saloon on Centre Street.

18. Mike Gordon became involved with a girl who worked in Doc's saloon and tried to get her to quit her job, but she refused. On July 19, 1879, Gordon fired two shots into Doc's place from the street. Doc promptly stepped out and downed him with one shot. He died the next day.

19. Doc did not flee Las Vegas.

20. Sic.

21. Iron Springs in the Whetstone Mountains.

22. The charge was that he conned someone out of $100 or $150 (depending on which newspaper report you believe), not highway robbery.

23. Apparently this ploy was Doc's idea. He had been accused of being a con man before and it was decided to turn that to his advantage. The ploy worked, but it also enhanced his reputation of being a con artist.

24. November 8, 1887.

# CHAPTER 19

★

# DOC HOLLIDAY
## ON HIS
# ARREST
# FOR MURDER

ess than a month after the Earp party left Arizona, Doc was arrested in Denver. This arrest sparked around fifty articles in Colorado newspapers over the next couple of months. Suddenly they were all debating whether Doc was on the side of law and order, or whether he was a notorious outlaw. There was also considerable discussion over what happened in Tombstone.

Throughout all this, Doc was fighting for his life. He knew if he was extradited back to Arizona, it was curtains for him.

Doc was wanted in Tombstone for the murder of Florentino Cruz, but Sheriff Bob Paul got to Denver first with the warrant for Frank Stilwell's murder.

Bat Masterson was in Denver when Doc was arrested and Bat quickly rounded up a lawyer to prevent Doc's extradition.

Doc was arrested on May 15, 1882[1]—and the next day most of the papers crucified him. Things were looking pretty bleak. Below is an example of how Doc was being represented in the press. This is from Denver's *Rocky Mountain News* for May 16, 1882.

## DOC. HOLLADAY,[2] LEADER OF THE EARPS, CLEVERLY CAPTURED LAST NIGHT IN THIS CITY.

A highly important arrest was made in Denver last night in the person of the notorious Doc. Holladay, leader of the infamous Earp gang of thugs, murderers and desperadoes, who have made their headquarters in Arizona and who have committed murders by the dozen. The arrest was made by Sheriff Perry Mallon,[3] who has been on the track of Doc since the desperate fight had with the gang by the Sheriff's force of Tucson, Arizona, six weeks ago, in which Sheriff Stillwell was killed in an attempt of the gang to murder Charley, a brother of Deputy Sheriff Clintry, murdered by one of the Earps in a billiard hall at Tombstone a few weeks ago. In the arrest he was assisted by Deputy Sheriff Fenton[4] and Barney Cutler. The arrest was made about 8 o'clock last evening at the corner of Sixteenth and Lawrence streets. Holladay was accompanied by two gamblers, who had come with him from Pueblo to attend the races. The officers knowing the desperate character of their man, covered him at once, when he threw up his hands and allowed himself to be conducted quietly to the jail.

Sheriff Mallon deserves great credit for the persistence with which he followed up his man. He met him in Pueblo but did not dare undertake the arrest there and waited until he came here. Holladay, while in Pueblo went armed to the teeth, but here put on the ways of civilization, laying away the fire arms with which he had been accoutred.[5] The total amount of reward for the capture of Holliday is in the neighborhood of $5,000.[6] He will be taken back to Tombstone, but it is feared that he will be hanged before he reaches there.

☞ ACCORDING TO PATRICIA JAHNS' *The Frontier World of Doc Holliday* (1957), Doc's motto was "Man cannot do what he wants to do in this world, but only that which will benefit him." Ironically, Doc spent much of his life proving this wrong.
—*Fred Dodge in his journal, Under Cover for Wells Fargo (1969)*

Fortunately, one reporter was able to talk briefly with Doc and then with Bat Masterson to get the other side of the story. This article appeared in the *Denver Tribune*, also on May 16th.

# CAPTURE IN DENVER OF "DOC." HOLLIDAY, ALLEGED TO BE A DESPERADO AND MURDERER.

## Marshal Masterson, of Trinidad, Says He is a United States Marshal and All Right

### Suspicion That the Arrest Was a Plan to Have the Man Murdered by Cow Boys

### Statement of the Man Who Smiles

At about 8:30 o'clock last night persons passing along the sidewalk on Fifteenth street, in the immediate vicinity of the Sheriff's building, might have seen a thin, spare man, with a blond mustache and a piercing eye, which glanced covertly and suspiciously from under the brim of a black slouch hat, passing quietly along the street. The stranger glanced restlessly from side to side without turning his head as if he feared the approach of some unknown enemy. Had it not been for this, which would have created the suspicion in the mind of an acute observer that he had committed some great crime, ordinary suspicion of evil would have been averted by the man's meek appearance and quiet demeanor. The stranger's hair was slightly streaked with gray, his clothes were custom made and such as are worn in civilized communities, and altogether there was nothing to denote that he was the desperate, blood thirsty and notorious murderer, stage robber and villain which he was soon afterward represented to be. The street at the point indicated is brilliantly lighted with electric lights at both ends of the block and all that passed could be as readily seen as in broad day light. But few people were passing at the time and the streets were momentarily deserted[7] when suddenly a man stepped from the deep shadow which is thrown by the electric light, and is seen in every place where its rays cannot penetrate, and accosted the first stranger. He accosted him in the most summary manner. His manner of salutation was to drop two six shooters full into the face of the spare, quiet pedestrian and halt him with the words—more suited to the highway than to the smooth pavements and surroundings of a brilliantly lighted street—

"Throw up your hands!"

A muttered imprecation and the words heard only indistinctly, "Doc Holliday, I have you now," were all that gave indication of the first stranger's crime or the need for this summary arrest. As the man with the pistols spoke his throat seemed to expand, his veins swelled, his chest heaved and it was evident he was straining every nerve to hold himself in check and keep from killing his victim.

## A TWO-SIDED STORY

The two men, accompanied by Deputies Linton and Barney Cutler, hurried into the Sheriff's office, where another exciting scene occurred. It was almost impossible to tell what the prisoner was charged with, and the reticence of the Sheriff, together with the prisoner's own cool and rather intrepid actions, only added to the interest of the affair.

It was afterwards learned, however, that the prisoner's name was John H., alias Doc, Holliday, a man very much hated in Arizona by the cowboys, and who was recently compelled to leave there through fear of being assassinated, as two of his friends and brother officers have been. The man who arrested him on the street gave his name as Perry Mallan and claimed to be a Deputy Sheriff from Los Angeles, California. To the officers here he gave Doc Holliday the record which the cow boys give him in the South, charging him with every conceivable crime and exhibiting telegrams ordering Holliday's arrest as an accessory in the murder of Frank Stillwell[8] in Tucson, the murder of a railroad conductor on the Southern Pacific road,[9] the murder of a ranchman named Clanton near Tombstone, and attempted murder of his brother, the murder of Curly Bill, the noted cow-boy,[10] and half a dozen other crimes. Just what part Holliday had in these affairs is not known. He is represented by one side as a desperado and on the other side a well known officer[11] told a reporter last night that Holliday had been a United States Marshal in the employ of the government for years and stood well wherever he was known.[12] The record of Holliday, as given by his enemies, however, has attained wide celebrity and this was what Mallan claimed for him last night.

### "HE KILLED MY PARTNER"

Although charged with these various crimes, the one for which Holliday was followed so closely occurred over seven years ago. The manner of his arrest reads more like the story of a mining camp than a tale of Denver in her metropolitan splendor and all the circumstances are tinged with the romance of a past and bygone day.

Following close upon the capture a Tribune reporter was in the Sheriff's office, where a curious scene was witnessed.

Behind the railing and partially screened by the desk stood a man demanding to know why he had been arrested. Deputy Linton was telephoning frantically for a hack. Just on the other side of the desk, from Holliday, stood a young, thick set man, with a short cropped reddish mustache, his foot resting on the seat of a chair. A second glance showed that he held a revolver partially concealed behind his back.

"Oh you can drop that," said the other man, who proved to be Holliday. "Nobody is going to try to get away from you. I have no weapons."

Hot words passed between the two. Mallan, who held the weapon, was excited, but Holliday was cool, though with that coolness which knows that it is its only salvation, for he evidently feared that Mallan might kill him at any moment. A crowd of rough looking men, strangers to Holliday and most of those present, filed into the room. To the reporter, who did not know the circumstances of the case, it looked as if a murder or lynching was imminent.

## A SENSATIONAL SCENE

"No, you won't get away from me again," exclaimed Mallan, still holding his pistol in his hand. "You killed my partner, you bloodthirsty coward, and I would have taken you in Pueblo if the men I had with me had stood by me."

"I did not come here to be abused," said Holliday, looking toward the Sheriff[13] for protection.

Just then a crowd of rough, ill favored fellows filed into the Sheriff's office. To them Holliday appealed, saying he wanted to make a statement.

"This is not a court or jury," said Deputy Linton.

"But I want to set myself right," said the prisoner.

"Is it customary in this country to deny a citizen the right of speech? Is it right? Is it justice?"

No answer.

It was evident that the whole spirit of the Sheriffs[14] was with Mallan, and as he still grasped his revolver he held the winning hand.

The little group which Holliday addressed appeared, several of them at least, to be strangers in Denver. One or two were citizens who happened in through curiosity, but there were several suspicious faces in the group.

John Hebry 'Doc' Holliday,
taken by C. S. Fly in 1881.

"I can show who that man is"—said Holliday, vehemently, like a man at bay, but a threatening movement from the man with a pistol checked his speech for a moment. 'I can prove that he is not the Sheriff, and, in fact, no officer of Cochise County,[15] he continued boldly.[16] I can show you his reason for bringing me here; I can show, [17]—but Mallan and the Deputy Sheriff both cut short his speech. He desired to make a statement, but they said it was no place for it.

Mallan (if that be his name) stormed and threatened and fingered his pistol until he finally returned it to his pocket.

He talked about "his partner" killed by the blood thirsty Holliday, and said he would show him no quarter even as he (Holliday) had shown his victims no quarter.

The prisoner was taken to a hack and hurried to the county jail. Before going Holliday mentioned the names of several men he knew in the city, and. among others said that his friend Bob[18] Masterson, Marshal of Trinidad, Colorado, had come up with him.

"Can I come with you—I am a reporter," said The Tribune man collaring the hack at the foot of the stairs.

"Come on; you are just the man I want to see," exclaimed Holliday eagerly.

### AT THE JAIL

However, Holliday had evidently repented of the statement he was so anxious to make. He made no further charges against the man Mallan, only saying that he first wanted to see his friend Masterson and an attorney.

Up to this time the names of neither prisoner nor debtor had been mentioned. The prisoner gave the name of John H. Holliday. He refused to say who Mallan was, only reiterating that he was no officer of Cochise County, Arizona. He said that Mallan came to him in Tom Kemp's variety theater, Pueblo, a few days ago and claimed to be his friend, telling him that the Stillwells[19] were on his track to kill him and that he wanted to warn him.

This is probably the fact and was the circumstance referred to with so much unction by Mallan when he said he would have arrested Holliday before had his friends stood by him, etc.

As Holliday was hurriedly pushed into a cell the reporter heard Mallan address him as "Doc" and then for the first time came the remembrance of who Doc Holliday was. The reporter had heard of Holliday only from the cowboy standpoint and had supposed he was a very hard and desperate man. He did not look so, but such was the record he had been given. While riding back in the hack the subject was more fully discussed and then it was first learned that Mallan had given the estimation of Holliday already described. This was what had confirmed the Sheriffs in the belief that they had such an important prisoner. Mallan further said that Holliday had killed his partner, Harry White, seven years ago and that he was following him at his own expense for revenge. Holliday's history was further given as a partner of the notorious "Off Wheeler" and "Six shooter Smith,"[20] the latter of whom was killed about six weeks ago.

## A MAN WHO SHOOTS AND SMILES

Coming down town the reporter met Mr. Bob Masterson, Marshal of Trinidad, Colorado, and known as the "man who smiles." The New York Sun once wrote him up for this characteristic. He is said to have killed twenty one men[21] in the discharge of his duty each time so politely and with such a pleasant smile on his face that it was almost a pleasure to die at his hands. Bob is a gentleman, every inch of him, and no man stands higher where he is known. He was the man whom Holliday had called for on leaving the jail.

Being asked about the arrest, Masterson, who was even then with Mr. Frank Naylor[22] on his way to get a writ of habeas corpus for Holliday, gave an entirely different account of the affair. He had just heard of the arrest. To tell the story would require a review of the cowboy troubles in Arizona. Masterson said that Holliday was a responsible man, a Deputy United States Marshal, and for a time Deputy Marshal of Tombstone,[23] and that the cowboys only wanted to assassinate him as they had Virg and Morgan Earp.[24] It was feared that he would be taken from the jail last night and murdered. This accounted, then, for Holliday's strictures against Mallan (?) which he did not dare to express. If, as was suspected, Mallan was a cowboy playing the detective, Holliday feared to say so for fear of being shot down in the Sheriff's office. The case is a peculiar and sensational one throughout. Holliday, in company with the City Marshal, Virg Earp, and his brothers, Wyatt and Morgan Earp, was in the fight in Tombstone last fall, in which Bill Clanton and Frank and Tom McLowry were killed. It was feared last night that Mallan was no other than Sim Clanton,[25] a brother of the dead man, and that the arrest of Holliday was only a scheme to get him in their power and murder him. All the other men alleged to have been killed by Holliday are said to be notorious desperadoes.

At 3:30 o'clock this morning a writ of habeas corpus signed by Judge Elliott was served upon Sheriff Spangler, ordering him to hold the prisoner until he could be brought before the Court this morning."

---

This article began to turn things around for Doc, and the other papers began to look at Mallen's story more closely. Public opinion began to swing in Doc's favor.

# References

1. He had arrived the previous day to see the horse races at the Denver Fair Grounds on the 16th. He didn't get to see the races.

2. Sic throughout this article.

3. This should be "Mallen" throughout this article.

4. Charles T. Linton.

5. Sic.

6. Mallen was guessing. Sheriff Behan offered $500 and the Cochise County commissioners offered $1,000. One of the commissioners was none other than Milt Joyce, an ardent rustler supporter who was shot in the hand by Holliday. There was no reward offered in Pima County where Bob Paul was sheriff.

7. The *Denver Republican* of the same date said, "Such proceedings on a crowded street attracted the attention of many people, who were not a little surprised, to say the least, and the spectacle of a man being 'held up' on one of the most crowded thoroughfares of a city like Denver."

8. Sic throughout this article.

9. The *Denver Republican* of the same date quotes Mallen as saying, "I have also the evidence that he shot and killed Conductor Clantry, on the Atlantic & Pacific railway, about two months ago."

10. The outlaws denied Curly Bill had been killed, but here Doc was being arrested for his murder. Of course, Curly Bill wasn't murdered, he was killed while ambushing the Earp party.

11. This was Bat Masterson, who is quoted later in the article.

12. A big exaggeration. In January 1882, after Virgil was ambushed and Wyatt appointed deputy U.S. Marshal, Wyatt was authorized to form a posse and pick some deputies to assist him. He chose Doc, Warren, Sherm McMaster, and Turkey Creek Jack Johnson. This made Doc a deputy to a deputy U.S. marshal. Previous to this he rode on some posses with Wyatt and Virgil.

13. Sheriff Michael Spangler.

14. Sic.

15. The closing quotation marks are missing here.

16. The beginning quotation marks are missing.

17. Quotation marks are again missing.

18. It should be "Bat" throughout this article.

19. Stilwells.

20. Six-Shooter Bill Smith was a New Mexican gunman who is said to have enjoyed wounding people. Jeff J. Harlin, a.k.a. "Off Wheeler," terrorized towns in Colorado, Texas and New Mexico. This was after he was sent to the penitentiary for seven years in 1873 for rape "on a moving freight train." In 1881, Bat Masterson and George Goodell arrested him and his men—seven in all—in Trindad, but the undersheriff let them escape.

21. The *Denver Republican* talked to Bat about the *Sun* article and on May 19, 1882, they reported:

    Masterson is one of the most noted characters of the West, about whom many romantic stories are told. It has been said of him that he has killed twenty-seven men, but Masterson says this is not so and explains the story by saying that one night he was occupying a box in a theater in a mining town in company with an army officer. In the theater at the time was a correspondent of the *New York Sun*, who, like all tenderfeet, desired to converse upon the fascinating topic of "bad men." The army officer perceiving the gullibility of the correspondent pointed to Masterson and said: "Do you see that man?"

    "Yes," replied the correspondent.

    "Well," said the officer, "he has killed twenty-seven men, one for each year of his life." The officer then proceeded to relate in detail each and every one of these killings in a bloodthirsty manner, and the correspondent published nearly two columns of it. The article was copied all over the country, and Masterson received a great deal of notoriety; but while this is a very pleasant little story and a fiction it does not much exceed the real facts in the case.

    This incident occurred in Gunnison, Colorado, in the summer of 1881 and the story was published a few weeks later. The Army surgeon was Dr. Cockrell and the correspondent was the *Sun*'s managing editor Bill Young. Bat was not present at the time, the man Dr. Cockrell pointed to was someone else who was "grinning like a monkey." He just told Young that it was Masterson.

22. A lawyer.

23. If Bat actually said this, he was sure trying to make Doc sound good. Virgil said he swore Doc in to assist him before confronting the Clantons and McLaurys, but at the time he probably didn't bother with such formalities and just said this to cover himself and Doc at the Earp examination.

24. Of course, Virgil wasn't assassinated.

25. Phineas "Phin" Clanton. Apparently, Mallan had no connection with anyone in Tombstone. He arrested Doc primarily for reward money and the notoriety.

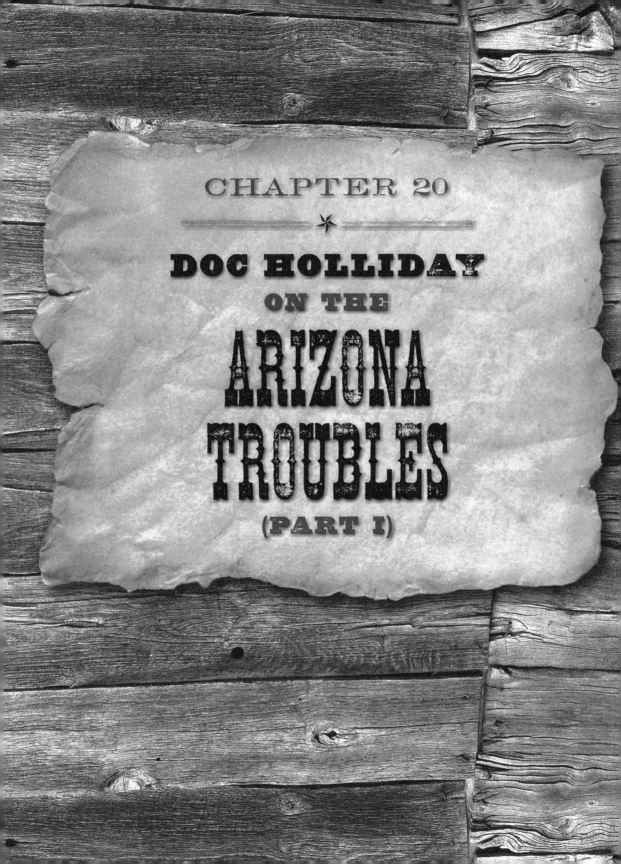

# CHAPTER 20

✶

## DOC HOLLIDAY

### ON THE

# ARIZONA
# TROUBLES

### (PART I)

The day the article on Doc's arrest appeared, the *Denver Tribune* reporter interviewed Bat and Doc again. While he included what Doc said in this next article, unfortunately he didn't quote him directly. This article appeared on May 17, 1882.

# CAPERS OF COWBOYS

### Additional Facts in Regard to the Arrest of "Doc" Holliday by Perry Mallan[1]

---

### "Doc" Thinks the Latter is Some Crank Trying to do the Great Detective Act

---

### A Short Resume of the History of the Cowboy Troubles in the South

---

Strictures by Bat Masterson and Holliday

---

At an early hour yesterday a writ of habeas corpus was served upon Sheriff Spangler ordering him to appear in court and show by what authority he kept the man, J. H. Holliday or "Doc" Holliday, in prison. Holliday is the man who was suddenly halted by a brace of six-shooters on Monday night, and with the assistance of two Deputy Sheriffs placed under arrest by a man who gave his name as Perry Mallan and said he was a Deputy Sheriff from Los Angeles, California. The circumstances of the arrest and the fact of the suing out of a writ of habeas corpus have already been fully detailed in The Tribune.

On examination, however, the story loses nothing of its interest and the conflicting statements of the two men, prisoner and captor are still more apparent. Sheriff Spangler has three days in which to make answer to the writ and during that time will keep the man in the county jail. This suits his friends here, as they say that their only fear is that the arrest is a strategem[2] adopted by the cowboys or their adherents to get Halliday[3] in their power and assassinate him. Marshal Bat Masterson, of Trinidad, and several reputable citizens here know Holliday well and say that the only trouble he ever had with the cowboys in Arizona were those which they brought on themselves and that Holliday's efforts to exterminate the band, together with the Earp boys, of Tombstone, were in the interests of law and order. For the killing he was arrested and completely

## EXONERATED BY THE GOVERNOR OF ARIZONA

and the Tombstone justice before whom the case came up. Marshal Masterson said yesterday.

☞ "CONCERNING OUR FIGHTS between the cowboys and myself and brothers, it has been stated over and over again that there was an old feud between us and some of our enemies, and that we were fighting only to revenge personal wrongs and gratify personal hatred. And such statements are false. We went into Tombstone to do our duty as officers. To do that we were put in conflict with a band of desperadoes, and it resolved itself into a question of which side could first drive the other out of the country, or kill them in it."

—*Virgil Earp in an interview with the San Francisco Examiner, May 27, 1882*

"The Earp brothers, under the administration of Virg Earp, Marshal of Tombstone, first undertook the suppression of lawlessness in Arizona, and for this they have been followed and assassinated or forced to leave the country. They are still followed and hated by the cowboys, rangers, desperados and stage robbers, who have terrorized Arizona, and who still are the scourge and terror of that unhappy Territory.[4] Holliday was notoriously in the fight in Tombstone between the Earp brothers and himself on one side and the Clantons and McLowreys[5] on the other. There were twelve men in the fight.[6] The two McLowrey boys and Bill Clanton were killed and several others mortally wounded. It was Holliday, then appointed Deputy Marshal of the town, who did such execution in the fight. He was armed with a shot-gun, and shot to kill. He traces all his troubles to this fight. It may be stated that these gangs of stage robbers, horse thieves and desperados are often alluded to as cowboys, although about the only cattle they are ever known to drive are those they steal."

That there have been two rival factions in Arizona, each of which calls the others cutthroats and desperados, is well known. It has been a country of lawlessness, where the passions of men ran wild and the ready pistol was the surest friend. But perhaps the statement of Doc Holliday himself, as given in the jail yesterday, will best set forth this state of facts, or at least

## HIS SIDE OF THE STORY.

He says that the entire difficulty arose financially from political differences. Cochise county, of which Tombstone is the county seat, was created while General Fremont was the Governor of the territory. The Governor had the appointment of the county officials. Wyatt Earp, who at that time kept a large saloon in Tombstone, was an applicant for the appointment of Sheriff. J. H. Behan was also an applicant. The Governor appointed Behan. Other private differences grew up between the two men. Behan did not keep his compact to appoint Earp under Sheriff. Earp became an active partisan of the United States Marshal, in his efforts to suppress lawlessness, while Behan took the side of the cowboys, who were responsible for the majority of the acts of lawlessness which have made the very name of Arizona a terror. The "Curly Bill" mentioned by Mallon was a most notorious character, and was wanted by the United States for a number of outrages, among which were the killing of the Marshal of El Paso and the shooting of Lieutenant Butler, a son of General B. F. Butler, during an attempted robbery of a stage coach.[7]

The Marshall,[8] the Earp boys and their adherents determined to rout out the cowboys. Troubles grew until the fight on the street, already described, took place. The respectable portion of the community were with them, but they could not maintain themselves against a horde, and the Earps and Holliday left to avoid being assassinated.

The Tombstone Epitaph was bold and outspoken in its denunciation of the Sheriff and his adherents, but the cowboys threatened to kill C. D. Reppy, the editor of the paper, and attempted to assassinate William Clum,[9] the President of the Epitaph company, by attacking the stage in which he was a passenger.

This statement is corroborated by a letter from C. D. Reppy to his brother, Mr. George Reppy, of this city.

Mr. Holliday says of Mallan,[10] who arrested him with such a flourish of trumpets, that he

## THINKS HE IS SOME CRANK

who thought he could win notoriety as a great detective by taking him into custody. Mallan had a little silver-mounted revolver such as a cow boy would disdain to carry. The manner in which he handled his pistol showed that he was afraid it would go off every moment, and that he was more frightened than Holliday was evident. It looked like the affectation of a tyro[11] to hold a pistol on a defenseless and unarmed man as Mallan did in the Sheriff's office. Holliday has not been in hiding nor has he disguised his name or features. He made himself known in Trinidad to Marshal Masterson at once. He was in Pueblo for a week before he came here and was intimate with Constable Pat Desmond and the City officials appearing desirous of making their acquaintance at once. In Denver he walks quietly about and his presence was known to General D. J. Cook and many well-known persons. The stories that have been told of "Doc." Holliday are wide-spread, and arise from his troubles with the cowboys in Arizona. To many he has the reputation of being a hard man, a dime-novel character, a sort of red terror of the border, and he thinks that Mallan has learned what he knows of Arizona and of him from what he has read of these wild tales and started out to do something wonderful on his own hook. Holliday does not think Mallan was ever a cowboy or in the habit of handling a pistol. Mallan, it will be remembered, charges that Holliday

## KILLED HIS PARTNER

Harry White, in a gambling room in St. George, Utah, seven years ago. Holliday and his friends say he was never in Utah in his life. The story of Mallan, already described in The Tribune, is a very sensational one, and, in fact, too highly colored throughout to bear the impress of truth.

Doc Holliday, according to Mallan's account, has killed, in all, twenty-five men. The story of the manner in which he has followed this desperado (?) from place to place is thrilling in the extreme.

If, as was at first suspected, Mallan was getting Holliday in his power, Holliday will not state. He would probably know any remaining member of the Clanton family, but politic reasons might lead him to conceal his sentiment for the present. On the night of his capture he declared that he knew and could tell something of his captor.[12]

Holliday will be held until he appears in court under the writ of habeas corpus already served on the Sheriff.

# References

1. Mallen's name is wrongly spelled "Mallan" and "Mallon" throughout this article.

2. Sic.

3. Sic.

4. This is an exaggeration. The Earps had severely damaged the power of the outlaws, plus the outlaws had killed off many of their own number fighting amongst themselves. The citizen's vigilante group also kept the few remaining outlaws from getting too far out of line while they were in town.

5. Sic throughout this article.

6. More exaggerations.

7. This is all a bunch of hooey.

8. Sic.

9. John P. Clum, who was also Tombstone's mayor and postmaster.

10. Sic throughout this article.

11. Tyro: a beginner.

12. Another article says that Doc was referring to papers and documents he was carrying with him, but doesn't say what they were.

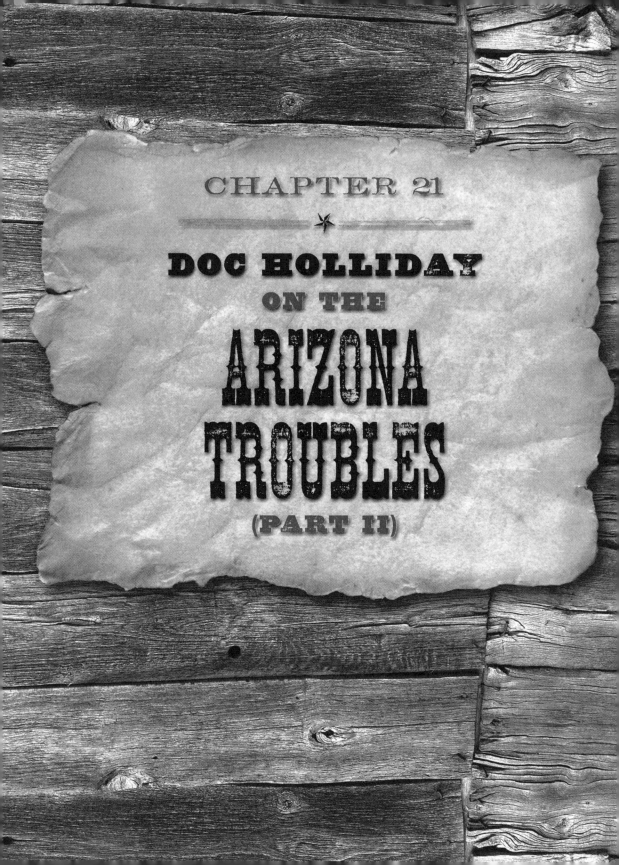

# CHAPTER 21

## DOC HOLLIDAY
### ON THE
# ARIZONA TROUBLES
## (PART II)

As public opinion continued to swing in Doc's favor, another newspaper, the *Denver Republican*, interviewed Doc to get his account of the O.K. Corral gunfight. They published his account on May 22, 1882.

# AWFUL ARIZONA

### Doc. Holladay[1] Tells the Story of the Country of Rustlers and Killers

---

### He Predicts That He Will Be Killed Should He Be Taken Back to Tombstone

---

### And Says He Would Rather Be Shot Down Here Than Murdered There

---

### Death By the Hands of An Officer Preferable to Hanging By Thieves.

---

A Republican reporter paid the noted Doc. Holladay a Sunday visit yesterday for a quiet little chat on the situation from his standpoint. Holladay has a big reputation as a fighter, and has probably put more "rustlers" and cow-boys under the sod than any one man in the West. He had been the terror of the lawless element in Arizona, and with the Earpps[2] was the only man brave enough to face the blood-thirsty crowd, which has made the name of Arizona a stench in the nostrils of decent men. The visitor was very much surprised at Holladay's appearance, which is as different as could be from the generally conceived idea of a killer. Holladay is a slender man, not more than five feet six inches tall[3] and would weigh perhaps 150 pounds. His face is thin and his hair sprinkled heavily with gray. His features are well formed and there is nothing remarkable in them save a well defined look of determination from his eyes, which the veriest

"THE COW-BOYS HAVE all left Tombstone, and it is thought that they have gone out in order to intercept Sheriff Paul as he returns from Denver with Doc Holliday, and assassinate his prisoner. They have threatened that Holliday will never again enter Tombstone alive."

—*New Mexico's* New Southwest & Grant County Herald, *May 27, 1882*

amateur in physiognomy could hardly mistake. His hands are small and soft like a woman's, but the work they have done is anything but womanly. The slender forefinger which has dealt the cards has dealt death to many a rustler with equal skill and quickness, and the slender wrist has proved its

## MUSCLES OF STEEL

in many a deadly encounter, when a quick motion of a six shooter meant everything. Holladay was dressed neatly in black, with a colored linen shirt. The first thing noticeable about him in opening the conversation was his soft voice and modest manners. He explained the case as follows:

"The men known as cowboys are not really cowboys. In the early days the real cowboys, who were wild and reckless, gained a great deal of notoriety. After they passed out their places were taken by a gang of murderers, stage robbers, and thieves, who were refugees from justice from the Eastern States. The proper name for them is Rustlers. They ran the country down there and so terrorized the country that no man dared say anything against them. Trouble first arose with them by killing of Marshal White by Curly Bill. Marshal White fell into my arms when he was shot and I arrested Curly Bill.[4] The trouble then is familiar to all."

"Do you apprehend trouble when you are taken back?" asked the visitor.

Holladay paused for a minute and gazed earnestly out of the window of Jailer Lambert's room

## INTO THE RAIN

outside and then said slowly, "If I am taken back to Arizona, that is the last of Holladay." After a pause he explained this by saying, "We hunted the rustlers, and they all hate us. John Behan, Sheriff of Cochise county, is one of the gang, and a deadly enemy of mine, who would give any money to have me killed. It is almost certain that he instigated the assassination of Morgan Earpp.[5] Should he get me in his power my life would not be worth much."

"But Sheriff Paul, of Tucson, will take you to that place, will he not?"

"Yes, and there lies my only chance for safety. I would never go to Tombstone. I'd make an attempt to escape right outside this jail and get killed by a decent man. I would rather do that than be hung by those robbers there."

"Cannot Paul protect you?"

## "I'M AFRAID NOT.

He is a good man, but I am afraid he cannot protect me. The jail is a little tumble down affair, which a few men can push over, and a few cans of oil thrown upon it would cause it to burn up in a flash, and either burn a prisoner to death or drive him out to be shot down. That will be my fate."[6]

"Haven't you friends who would rally to your assistance?"

"Yes, the respectable element will stand by me, but they are all intimidated and unorganized. They will never do anything until some respectable citizen is shot down, when[7] the people will rise and clean them out, as they did at Fort Griffin, where twenty four men were hung on one tree when I was there.[8] The Tombstone Rustlers are part of the Fort Griffin gang."

"You are charged with killing Frank Stillwell.[9] What do you know about that affair?"

"I know that Stillwell was

## A STAGE ROBBER,

and one of Morgan Earpp's assassins, and that he was killed near Tucson, but I do not know that I am in any way responsible for his death. I know that he robbed a stage, from the fact that he gave the money to a friend of mine to keep, and I know that he helped in the assassination of Morgan Earpp, as he was seen running from the spot

## THE HOLLIDAY-RINGO CONFRONTATION

☞ "EVERYBODY LOOKED FOR a fight every time Ringo came to town. He was plainly spoiling for a fight. He'd swagger up and down Allen Street, looking mighty hostile with his big, ivory-handled guns buckled around him. Or in cold weather, he wore a great shaggy buffalo-skin overcoat, a six-shooter, of course, in each pocket. Then he looked like a giant. If he saw the Earps standing on the corner, he made it a point to walk past them and stare them in the eye. Or he would stroll into the Oriental, the Earp hang-out, and take a drink as cool as you please with the place full of Earp men and maybe one or two of the Earps talking with Doc Holliday at the other end of the bar. It was fine, impressive swashbuckling, and the way everybody figured it was that Ringo was willing to get killed for the privilege of taking one or two of the Earps with him. His chances in a single-handed fight against the Earps would have been about the same a jackrabbit would have in a pack of lobo wolves."

*—William Lutley as quoted in Walter Noble Burns's* Tombstone *(1927).*

☞ "MUCH BLOOD IN THE air this afternoon. Ringo and Doc Holliday came nearly having it with pistols...Bad time expected with the cowboy leader and D.[oc] H.[olliday]. I passed both not knowing blood was up. One with hand in breast pocket and the other probably ready. Earps [probably Wyatt and Morgan] just beyond. Crowded street and looked like another battle. Police vigilant for once and both disarmed."

*—George Parsons in his journal, January 17, 1882*

☞ "A DIFFICULTY OCCURRED yesterday afternoon in front of the Occidental Saloon, Allen street, between John Ringo and Doc Holliday, that very nearly terminated in bloodshed. The parties had been on bad terms for some time past, and meeting yesterday morning words were exchanged and both parties stepped back, placing their hands on their weapons with the intention of drawing and using them. Fortunately chief of police Flynn was at hand and placed both parties under arrest. They were taken to Judge Wallace's court and fined $32 each for carrying deadly weapons."

*—Tucson Weekly Citizen, January 22, 1882*

by several responsible citizens. Pete Spence was with him, and I am morally certain that Sheriff Behan investigated[10] the assassination. He did it for two reasons. One was that he was the officer elected by the Rustlers[11] and the other was that he was afraid of and hated Morgan Earpp, who had quarreled with and insulted him several times. He feared Earpp and had every inducement to kill him. A word further about this man Behan. I have known him a long time. He first ran against me when I was running a faro bank, when he is

## IN THEIR POWER,

and must do as they say. This is shown by the fact that he has five Rustlers under him as deputies. One of these men is John Ringo, who jumped on the stage of the variety theater in Tombstone one night about three weeks ago, and took all the jewels from the proprietor's wife in full view of the audience. These are the men who want me and that is the kind of country I am going back to for my health."

☞ "IT IS ESTABLISHED that in the course of the Earp-Clanton feud Doc Holliday came within a skinny cat's whisker of losing his life at least nine different times. Of these, four involved efforts to have him swing, while the remaining five entailed gun-play or ambush."

—*John Myers Myers*, Doc Holliday (*1955*)

"It's a nice, sociable country, I must admit," responded the visitor, who ran over mentally all the terrible outrages which had been committed of late by the noted Rustlers, including a train robbery or two and several stage robberies. Holladay, in response to a question, then turned his attention to Mallon,[12] the officer who followed him and caused his arrest here.

"The first time I met him," said Holladay, "was in Pueblo just before I came to Denver. He approached me in a variety theater and introducing himself said he wanted to do me a favor in return for saving his life in Santa Fe once. I told him I would be very thankful for any favor he wanted to show me, but he must be mistaken about my saving his life in Santa Fe, as I had never been there. He did not reply to this, but told me that he had just come up on the train with Josh Stillwell, a brother of Frank Stillwell,[13] whom I was supposed to have killed, and that he

## THREATENED TO SHOOT

me on sight. I thanked him for his information, and replied, 'If you give me away I will kill you.' I told him I wasn't traveling around the country giving people away, and he left me. I met him in a saloon a few days afterwards, and asked the barkeeper who he was. He told me that Mallon represented that he was a ranchman, who had sold out in the lower country, and was looking for a location, upon the strength of which he

Johnny Ringo.

borrowed $8 at one time, and $2 at another. I met the barkeeper several times afterwards, and he told me that the money had never been paid. I then considered that there was no truth in his story which he had told me. The next time I saw him was in Denver, when he dropped his guns on me and caused my arrest. Paul does not know him, and I believe he is a crank. He acted like one at Pueblo, when he took down his clothes and showed a mark which he said was a bullet wound, but which was the mark of disease. I laughed in his face, the thing being so funny I couldn't help it. One thing which Mallen tells gives him away bad. He said in your paper that he was standing alongside Curly Bill when the latter was killed. The facts are these: We were out one day after a party of outlaws, and about 3 o'clock on a warm day after a long and dry ride from the San Pedro river, we approached a spring which was situated in a hollow. As we did so

## EIGHT RUSTLERS ROSE UP

from behind the bank and poured from thirty five to forty shots into us. Our escape was miraculous. The shots cut our clothes and saddles and killed one horse, but did not hit us. I think we would have all been killed if God Almighty wasn't on our side. Wyatt Earpp turned loose with a shot-gun and killed Curley Bill. The eight men in the gang which attacked us were all outlaws, for each of whom a big reward has been offered.[14] They were such men as Curley Bill, Pete Spencer, and Pony Deal, all of them wanted by the authorities and Wells, Fargo & Co. Pony Deal, I am told, was killed a few days ago on the railroad by soldiers. If Mallon was alongside of Curley Bill when he was killed, he was with one of the worst gangs of murderers and robbers in the country."

"Where are the Earpps?"

"In Colorado, over in the Gunnison, I believe."

"Didn't you have a quarrel with them in Pueblo[15] a few weeks ago?"

"We had a little misunderstanding, but it didn't amount to much."

"Would they help you now?"

"Yes, all they could; but they are wanted themselves, and of course couldn't go back with me without putting themselves in danger, without doing me any good."

Holladay in conclusion said that

## MALLON'S CLAIM

that he, Holladay had killed his partner in Utah, was false, as at the very time Mallan claims the killing was done, the speaker was here in Denver dealing for Charley Foster, in Babbitt's house, where Ed.[16] Chase is now located. Holladay further says he was never in Utah. After leaving Denver he went to Dodge City, Kansas, where he staid some time, going to Arizona from there. In going back he said he would be safe until he reached a point below Albuquerque and that it would not be healthy for Mallon to go on the same train.

The arrest of Holladay has caused

## A GREAT STIR

in Arizona. The Tombstone *Epitaph* says:

The Tucson *Citizen* is giving most of its time to abuse the Arizona Cowboy. As we are not familiar with the breed we are unable to determine whether or not the *Citizen* is interesting the public by the devotion of so much brain in their direction. There is one fact intensely evident even to the casual observer—that since the Earps who seem to be pets of the *Citizen* left the country, perfect peace has reigned in this section. The *Epitaph* only maintains that there is no difference between a murderous cowboy and a murderous United States Marshal, in fact, does not propose to defend crimes, fraud or corruption, whoever may commit it. Further, we are of the opinion that the people of Tucson are not in accord with the *Citizen* in the advocacy of men who have proved themselves assassins, murderers and thieves.

This position of the *Epitaph*, however, will not carry much weight in the light of recent events. Under the former management it was bitterly opposed to the Rustler element and a friend of the Earpps, but one fine day the Rustlers fired some fifty shots through a stage coach, in which Crumb,[17] the proprietor of the paper, was riding, and he experienced

# A CHANGE OF HEART

immediately. Soon after this Charley Reppy, the editor, was run out of the country, and under these cheerful influences the policy and tone of the paper was changed. All the other papers in the Territory seem to be friends to the Earpp's. The *Epitaph*, in an editorial, says:

> "THE VILLAIN OF THE first act becomes the hero in the second and the avenger and detective in one, the man who has devoted his life to his dead comrade, and has been shot so often that he has trouble in retaining his food, proves to be a petty swindler."
> —Denver Republican, *June 2, 1882*

We learn by the Tucson *Star* that Sheriff Paul of Pima was astonished at finding that Sheriff Behan, of Cochise, had applied for a requisition from the Governor to take the Earps.[18] As the arrest of the latter was due to Behan's exertion entirely, there is no merit in Paul's surprise, except that he is sorry for the Earps. Did Paul offer any reward for their capture? Did he do anything, in fact? It is somewhat singular, also, that it never struck the Sheriff of Pima county to apply for a requisition until the Sheriff of Cochise county had telegraphed for one. We have half an idea that S. Byers[19] of Gunnison, is a fraud and a delusion, from the fact that he telegraphed yesterday to Chief of Police Neagle,[20] making inquires as to the character of the Earps. Gunnison is 275 miles from Denver, and the Earps, according to a telegram received late yesterday, are still in jail in Denver.[21] If Paul had a dispatch from Gunnison, why did he wait until Behan took action before he gave the information to the Governor. It looks as though the *Star* has been given an emetic. Otherwise it would publish Paul's telegraphic correspondence.

In the issue of last Wednesday the same paper has a long editorial denouncing Governor Tritle in

## THE FOLLOWING ARTICLE:

"Ever since the Earps and Holladay left here, and warrants had been issued for their arrest, Sheriff Behan has spared neither trouble nor expense to effect their capture. The

executive officers of every county in the western portion of the country had been communicated with; descriptions of the fleeing desperadoes were sent, rewards offered,
and every inducement to bring the criminals under the influence of law, put forth. Some
days ago the Sheriff received information that the outlaws were heading for Colorado,
and immediately put himself in communication with the Sheriff of Arapahoe county,
the political division of which Denver is the chief city. Yesterday Mr. Behan received a
dispatch from Mr. Spangler, Sheriff of Arapahoe county, stating that he had the culprits.
The following is a copy of the dispatch:

"Denver—Have your men in jail.[22] Let me know what to do."

Mr. Behan immediately telegraphed to hold the prisoners securely, and soon as he
could secure the necessary requisition papers he would start for them. Later in the day
the following dispatches were received:

Denver—"Habeas corpus served. Can hold them three days. Can you get here in
time with papers and reward. Answer quick, specifying crime, so we can hold them."
M. Spangler,

SHERIFF

Denver—"Have arrested Doc. Holladay. The Earpps are here. As soon as you come
will take them. Answer.

SHERIFF

To all of these dispatches Sheriff Behan sent prompt answers, warning the Denver
authorities to be careful of the prisoners, and he would start for them immediately. The
Sheriff then made application to Governor Tritle for requisition on Governor Pitkin, of
Colorado, for the prisoners, to which he received the following reply:

Tucson, May 16, 1882

J. H. Behan, Sheriff:
Cannot issue requisition until indictment and warrant are presented to me. Am

ready to issue requisition at once. District Attorney absent at Benson. Have not at present the proper papers. When it is issued, the requisition must go to Prescott for the Territorial seal.

F.A. TRITLE

Sheriff Behan again telegraphed the Governor, urging haste, and calling attention to the importance of the case. In reply he received the following dispatch:

John H. Behan, Sheriff:

Mr. Horton, acting for District Attorney, asks for the requisition in the name of Sheriff Paul.

F.A. TRITLE

Later in the day the following dispatch was received from the Assistant District Attorney of Pima county:

John H. Behan:

Farley not here. Paul has made application for a requisition, and will leave tomorrow morning for Denver..

W.B. HORTON

Thus it can be seen that Governor Tritle is conniving with Sheriff Paul, so that the latter can claim the prisoners. The friendship of Paul for the Earps is notorious, and it is a well known fact that he has made no effort to effect their capture.[23] On the other hand, Sheriff Behan left no stone unturned to effect their capture. He has offered large rewards and went to much personal expense to bring the outlaws within range of justice. The opinion is advanced by a great many that the action of the Governor has not been fair to Behan, and that he has favored Paul for political or individual reasons.

Late last evening this office received the following dispatch from John M. Barret, managing editor of the Tucson *Star*:

"Governor issued requisition. Sheriff Paul starts to Denver at once."

To-day in the District court of Arapahoe county the writ of habeas corpus will come up. The requisition will arrive to-day. As it is pretty well assured that Holladay will be killed if taken back, the case will be thoroughly investigated before a requisition will be allowed.

Under closer scrutiny, Perry Mallen's story began to fall apart and he was forced to admit what he said about Holliday killing his partner in Utah was a lie. Doubt was also cast on his assertion that he was a Los Angeles sheriff. In the meantime, he almost tried to arrest someone who looked like Wyatt. It was then revealed he had swindled several people and he quickly left Denver. On June 6th, the *Pueblo Daily Chieftain* reported, "Word was received yesterday that Perry Mallen had been captured in Pittsburg [sic], Pa., and would be held there until a requisition from the governor arrived."

On May 24, 1882 the court finally heard Doc's habeas corpus case and decided Sheriff Spangler had no evidence that Doc had committed any crime to justify his arrest. As soon as he was released, Deputy Linton arrested him on Sheriff Paul's warrant and Doc's lawyers filed another habeas corpus.

Immediately after Doc's first arrest, Bat Masterson had arranged for someone to make a phony accusation that Doc had swindled either $150 or $100 out of a man in Pueblo, Colorado. Bat's ploy worked. Colorado's Governor Pitkin decided it was customary for a person to be tried for all offenses committed within the state before they're handed over to another state or territory. He also decided there were technical problems with the Arizona governor's requisition and Holliday's indictment.[24] Holliday was released again and re-arrested on the larceny charge. He went to trial in Pueblo in July 1882 and pled guilty. He probably received a fine and was released.

# References

1. Sic throughout this article.

2. Sic throughout this article.

3. Wyatt said Doc was 5' 10". Wyatt was 6'.

4. Doc is here taking credit for what Wyatt did, but this is not idle boasting to impress people. Doc was trying to avoid a noose. With all the lies the opposition was telling about him, perhaps it's understandable he would try to present himself in the best light possible. He probably also knew that Wyatt wouldn't mind him taking credit for something Wyatt had done if it would help save his skin.

5. It's doubtful Sheriff Behan was involved in this.

6. The power of the outlaws had largely been broken, but there were still a few around, along with many of their friends and sympathizers. The chance that Doc would be lynched was pretty slim, and it decreased as the case got more notoriety, but there was a good chance he could be assassinated or be given a kangaroo trial and then hung.

7. Sic, then.

8. I haven't been able to find any evidence that this happened in Fort Griffin, Texas.

9. Sic throughout this article.

10. This should probably be "instigated."

11. This does not seem to be true. Behan was sheriff for about a year and a half. He was initially appointed to the office and apparently never ran for the position in any election. Even if he had, the rustler vote was negligible, since only about half a dozen rustlers and ranchers registered to vote. It's also unlikely they would have made another attempt at voter fraud like that of the 1880 Shibell-Paul sheriff election.

12. Mallen's name is spelled both "Mallon" and "Mallen" in this article.

13. Two of Frank Stilwell's brothers were Reuben "Rube" Stilwell and "Comanche Jack" Stilwell, who was a well-known Texas scout, Indian fighter and later a lawman. About the time the Earp party left Arizona for New Mexico, Jack Stilwell arrived in Tombstone and took a posse out to search for them. This posse included Ike, Ringo, Spence and about thirty others.

14. This was probably not true.

15. In Albuquerque.

16. Sic.

17. John P. Clum. Actually between 15 and 25 shots were fired and these were primarily at the horses in the hope that killing one would stop the stage. The stagerobbers probably got this idea from Holliday. When Doc was accused of the attempted robber of the Benson stage, he replied, "If I had pulled that job, I'd have got the eighty thousand. Whoever shot Philpott was a rank amateur. If he had downed a horse, he'd have got the bullion." This time that's what the stagerobbers tried to do, but it wasn't as easy as it sounded.

18. They mistakenly thought the Earps had been arrested with Holliday.

19. Gunnison marshal Sid Byers.

20. Tombstone marshal Dave Neagle.

21. Byers wasn't a fraud. The Earps were in Gunnison. It was Sheriff Spangler's telegrams to Behan that were wrong.

22. It's strange Sheriff Spangler would say Doc and the Earps were in jail. Mallen must have had something to do with this.

23. Paul was a close friend of Wyatt's, but his comments to the newspapers at this time sound like he seriously wanted to bring Holliday and the Earps back to Tucson for trial. He may have been misquoted, but it's more likely all this was just a smoke screen. In 1898 he wrote a letter to the *Tucson Citizen* defending the Earps.

24. It took quite a bit of wheeling and dealing to get Pitkin to go along with this. As a politician, he could not afford to appear like he was helping someone who many people thought was as bad as Jesse James. Bat was able to recruit many impressive people to take Doc's side. This included E. D. Cowen of the *Denver Tribune*; General Dave Cook, who was Colorado's leading crime fighter; Wyatt's friend, Senator Horace Tabor; and probably Wells, Fargo & Company. In addition, W. S. Deckard, one of Doc's lawyers no doubt pulled some strings. At this time, this former federal judge was the dean of Denver's bar. Much of this effort was to save Wyatt, as he would have been the next to go if Doc was extradicted.

# CHAPTER 22

✷

## DOC HOLLIDAY

### EXPLAINS

# WHY HE SHOT BILLY ALLEN

Just two years after Doc's arrest in Denver, he was once again the center of controversy—this time for shooting Billy Allen. This incident raises some interesting questions. Could this be the same Billy Allen who was on his way to the site of the O.K. Corral gunfight and had almost arrived there when the shooting started and who may have taken a shot at the Earps from around the corner of Fly's? The same Billy Allen who, along with Ike Clanton and C. H. Light, had posted bail for Stilwell and Spence in the September 1881 stage robbery? It's difficult to tell. The Billy Allen here is said to be a policeman, but then the same was said of many of the outlaws.

When the Billy Allen in Tombstone testified at the Earp examination, the defense attorney asked him if he'd been indicted for larceny in Colorado under another name before coming to Tombstone, but the court ruled the question was irrelevant and he didn't have to answer it.

The Allen that Doc shot claimed his fight with Doc was over five dollars, but Doc said it was part of the Earp-outlaw conflict. Doc admitted he owed Allen five dollars, but why would he borrow money from an enemy? Could this have been a ploy by Allen to give himself an excuse to pick a fight so he could legally shoot Doc?

To make things even more interesting, Wyatt and Doc's old enemy Johnny Tyler is also on the scene and was a friend of Allen's. It will be remembered that Stuart Lake told how Wyatt had dragged Tyler out of the Oriental Saloon by his ear while Doc held a gun on Tyler's friends. Soon after that, Doc and Tyler had another confrontation in the Oriental that apparently resulted in Tyler's departure from Tombstone.

Additional research may turn up some answers and clarify the situation. In the meantime, here is an article on the shooting from the *Leadville Daily Democrat* on August 20, 1884, in which Doc explains what happened.

# HOLLIDAY SHOOTS

### The Event the Sports Have Been
### Anxiously Looking Forward to

---

### WILL ALLEN THE VICTIM OF HIS BALL

---

### A Killing Barely Averted
### Exciting Records of Both Men

---

The trite old saying that misfortunes never come singly can be aired again. The shooting by Jack Dougan was still the talk of the town, when at a little after 5 o'clock last evening William Allen an ex policeman and one of the best known of the old timers, was seriously wounded in a sensational scrimmage by "Doc" Holliday, a man who enjoys the reputation of being one of the most desperate and determined in the west, who has been the subject of more than one fancy writer of the day, and whose prowess is sustained by a long and bloody record.

It is probable that the true inside history of the shooting will never be told. For some days past it has been a matter of current information that there was apt to be trouble between the two men. Holliday claimed that there was a certain clique of gamblers and hard men who had sworn to take his life. The feud dated back into the

## TROUBULOUS DAYS

in Arizona in 1881, when several of the element here were residents of Tombstone. Several tragedies ensued and two factions were formed. Holliday, accused of murder, fled the territory to meet some of the ringleaders among his enemies here. John Tyler, a well known gambler employed dealing faro bank at the Monarch saloon, was one of them, and Tom Duncan, of the same place, another. On one occasion Tyler and Holliday made arrangements to fight a duel at Tombstone. Naturally their feeling were bitter here. Holliday, weak, out of health, spirits and money, slowly dying of a bullet that had pierced his lungs,[1] considered that he was imposed on, and several times notified the police that there was a plot on foot to kill him.

☞ "HOLLIDAY IS ONE OF the best boys that ever lived, if he is let alone, but you mustn't impose on him or you will smell gunpowder burning."

*—Lee Smith interviewed in the* Atlanta Post-Appeal, *July 8, 1882*

About three weeks ago words passed between he and the clique, at Hyman's bar, and several of them called on him to "pull his gun." He said he had none, and as he passed out was

## CALLED FILTHY NAMES.

This rankled. Next day he told the writer, tears of rage coming to his eyes as he talked, that they were insulting and humiliating him because they knew he could not retaliate.

"If I should kill some one here," he said, "no matter if I were acquitted the governor would be sure to turn me over to the Arizona authorities, and I would stand no show for life there at all. I am afraid to defend myself and these cowards kick me because they know I am down. I haven't a cent, have few friends and they will murder me yet before they are done."

This was probably his true feelings on the subject. He was searched several times for a gun but none was ever found. He was afraid to carry one for fear of being fined. He regarded Allen, who tended bar at the Monarch Saloon, as one of his enemies. Allen, however, told another story about the matter. He said that Holliday owed him $5, borrowed two months ago, and had persistently refused to pay it. He

Doc Holliday.

## SEVERAL TIMES DUNNED HIM

in the presence of a crowd, and Holliday promised to pay when a friend came in from Sowbelly gulch. Allen told him he would give him until noon Tuesday too pay it. What he would do in case of default, is a matter of dispute. Holliday and his friends say that Allen said he would "do him up," if the money was not forthcoming, but Allen says he simply said he would whip him.

Yesterday morning some of Holliday's friends went over to his room in the Star block and told him that Allen was looking for him with a gun. At about noon Holliday came over to Hyman's saloon, which he made a loafing place,[2] and said tersely to Mr. Hyman:

"The times's[3] up."

Mr Hyman had no idea what he meant and walked away. Soon after, Holliday upon the advise[4] of his friends went back to his room and remained there until nearly 5 o'clock. Then he sent over his pistol, a large single action Colt's 41,[5] by a friend who put it behind the end of the bar at Hyman's, shortly coming over himself and taking a stand close to it by the cigar lighter. Allen

## SAW HIM COMING

and started for the place. When he saw him he was behind the bar of the Monarch, where he was at work, and as he was putting on his coat Mr. Allen, one of the proprietors, told him that Holliday was in Hyman's and he had better not go.[6] He replied he wasn't going to have any trouble and started out. A dozen people on the sidewalk saw all these preliminaries and knew that a tragedy was to follow.

As Allen stepped across the threshold Holliday suddenly elevated his pistol and fired. The ball struck him below the muscle of the right arm, passing through the arm, emerging near the shoulder and shattering the upper light of the folding door. Allen at once fell, uttering a loud scream, and Holliday, rushing behind the cigar case, leaned over it and fired again. The bullet missed the prostrate man's head by a hair's breadth and buried itself in the door sill. At this juncture Henry Kellerman, one of the bartenders, rushed forward and seized the weapon. His courage undoubtedly

## PREVENTED A KILLING.

Almost at the same moment Captain Ed.[7] Bradbury, who was just outside, ran in and disarmed Holliday. Friends of Allen at once grouped about him and he was taken in a hack to his home on East Fifth street by Mr. Allen,[8] his employer. Holliday was hurried to jail and put at once behind bars. A DEMOCRAT reporter was soon after on the scene and interviewed him at once. He was perfectly cool and collected, and as to the question, what it was about, said: "It was not about the $5. That was taken as a pretext. It is the old trouble, and Allen was picked out as the man to kill me."

"Please describe the shooting to me?"

"Well, Allen had told me he intended to do me up this evening. I was standing behind the counter when he came in and saw that he had both hands in his pocket and that the handle of a pistol protruded from one of them. Of course I couldn't let him murder me so I fired."

"What has Allen got particularly against you?"

"He is the

TOOL OF THE GANG."

"How do you account for no pistol being found on him?"

"Was there none found?"

"No."

"His friends spirited it away—that's all."

"How about your trouble in Arizona?"

"I lived there for three years, was part of the time a peace officer, and all I ever did was forced on me and I was tried for and honorably acquitted of. There are people in town who desire to murder me for notoriety. They know I am helpless and have spread the report that I am a bad man, to protect themselves when they do the work. I defy anyone to say they ever saw me conduct myself in any other way than as a gentleman should."

At this juncture Holliday was assigned to a cell, and the interview necessarily closed.

Meantime a reporter called at Mr. Allen's house above the Fifth street skating rink. The physicians were examining his wound and found it to be quite serious, as the large artery had been cut and it had

## BLED INTERNALLY

until the member was swollen frightfully. They had determined to cut open the flesh and find and tie the ends of the artery, and while the instruments were being sent for the reporter opened the conversation.

"What was this about, Mr. Allen?"

"It was over $5 Holliday borrowed of me and never returned."

"Did you tell him that if he didn't pay it to day you would "do"[9] him?"

"I told him that if he didn't pay it by this noon I would go for him."

"What did you mean by that?"

"Why, that I would whip him. He has been blowing around that he has killed several men, but he couldn't scare me."

"Tell me about the shooting."

"I walked in Hyman's to look at the games in the rear. I have a habit of doing that. As I entered some one knocked me down and fired at the same instant. I did not see Holliday until he went to fire the second shot."

"Did some one tell you

## NOT TO GO IN?"

"Yes something was said about it,"

"Did you have a weapon?"

"Nothing; not even a pen knife."

Mr. Allen and "Cal," the old stage driver, who first lifted Allen, say he had no pistol. Holliday's friends on the other hand, are loud in their statements that at the right time they can produce two men who saw a gun taken off of his person.

As to threats there are several versions. Ed Doude, of Red Cliff, stated to a DEMOCRAT reporter that a few days ago he heard Allen threaten Holliday and use very profane language to him.

Pat Sweeny said: "I heard Allen say yesterday that if Holliday didn't pay up today he would hurt him, take his guns away from him and pawn them. He also said he would 'do' him."

Pat Lorden, better known as "Blackie," employed at Hyman's corroborated Sweeny's statement.

The most important witness perhaps is Frank Lowmaster, very well known here, and one of Hyman's bartenders. He said: "A few days ago Billy Allen told me that he had that forenoon told Holliday if he didn't pay him Tuesday he would

## START HUNTING FOR HIM."

"I didn't say anything, but I know that this story was repeated to Holliday and that he expected a shooting."

Mr. Allen's friends state emphatically that he never made any threats. At 7 o'clock last evening the cut artery in Allen's arm was tied and he was resting easily.

## THE MAN

Doc Holliday, whose real name is John H. Holliday, was born at Griffin Georgia forty two years ago.[10] He was educated at Philadelphia, graduated with high honors and chose dentistry for a profession.[11] He practiced it for a while, but his health being delicate he came west to Arizona. There, by one of those singular transformations that nobody can understand, he became widely known as a desperate man. When one of the famous Earp boys was assassinated in

☞ "HE [Doc] WAS actually a dentist. So he had a mean streak even before he started killing people."
—*Judge Wells Spicer in his final decision in the Earp examination, November 30, 1881*

1881[12] Holliday took a shot gun and shot his two murderers, who were Mexicans.[13] The following day Holliday, the four surviving Earp brothers and a man known as "Texas Bill"[14] got into a fracas with another desperate party and

## KILLED TWO BROTHERS

named, McLowery, two named Clanton and another unknown man.

Prior to this Holliday, in arranging for a duel with Jack Tyler, shot a saloon keeper named Joyce, and his partner who interferred, but did not wound him fatally.[15] Joyce kept the Oriental saloon at Tombstone. For the last offense several of the party, including Holliday, were forced to fly the state.[16] Holliday, before going, rushed into a guarded room, pistol in each hand and rescued a comrade from 300 vigilantes.[17] He was tried for shooting Joyce, but acquitted.

When next heard of he was arrested nearly three years ago at Denver, at the point of a revolver, by a California deputy sheriff named Mallen, who claimed to have been after him for a year. Holliday's friends filed a fictitious charge against him at Pueblo, and representations were made to the governor that assured him Holliday would not have a fair trial in Arizona. Consequently he refused to allow him to be taken from the state, and he has spent most of the time since in Leadville. This is his first scrape here, and it is due to him to say he is conducting himself very quietly. His friends are making preparations to get him out on bail to morrow.

## WILLIAM ALLEN

was born in Freeport, Illinois, in 1859. He went on the Leadville police force in 1880 and soon became recognized as one of the bravest and most gallant officers. About a year ago he became special policeman at the Grand Central, afterward held the same position at the Monarch saloon, and finally became bartender there.

He was thrice wounded in the city service. The first time he was shot through the groin in a fearless attempt to arrest the fiend Bakewell, who murdered two policemen. Later he was shot in the leg by a man who resisted arrest on Chestnut street. His last wounds were inflicted in the notorious "Cat alley" on State street, where he had followed a burglar. The miscreant turned and shot him through the chest, also stabbing him. The wounds were serious, but owing to a splendid constitution, he was soon on duty again. He was absolutely without fear, and esteemed as a clever gentleman by all who know him.

# References

1. Holliday was slowly dying from tuberculosis, not a bullet, and Leadville was one of the worst places someone in his condition could go to. While Denver and Tombstone are both about a mile high, Leadville, at 10,200 feet above sea level, is twice that. And while Doc seemed to thrive in Tombstone's drier climate, the seasons in Leadville are described as being "ten months winter and two months mighty late fall."

2. He was also dealing faro there.

3. Sic.

4. Sic.

5. Sic.

6. This is poorly worded. What they mean is that Billy was working as bartender at the Monarch when he saw Doc going to Hymen's. As he was getting ready to go after Doc, one of the Monarch's owners, Cy Allen—who was not related to Billy—tried to stop him.

7. Sic.

8. Cy Allen.

9. Sic.

10. Doc was born on August 14, 1851, so he had just turned 33 six days earlier.

11. Doc graduated from the Pennsylvania College of Dental Surgery (now part of the University of Pennsylvania) in Philadelphia on March 1, 1872. Susan McKey Thomas, a descendent of one of Doc's cousins and one of Doc's biographers, just recently uncovered proof that Doc did practice dentistry briefly in his hometown—Valdosta, Georgia—before heading out west.

12. 1882.

13. Wyatt was the one with the shotgun. Doc probably shot them as well, but with a rifle or pistol. Florentino Cruz was Mexican, but Stilwell was a Texan.

14. Texas Jack Vermillion. It was two Earps and some of their friends. The newspaper is confusing the Curly Bill gunfight with the O.K. Corral gunfight.

15. Holliday tried to get Tyler to fight, but Tyler refused. Milt Joyce then gave Doc a hard time about it and Doc shot him in the hand and a Joyce's partner in the foot.

16. Holliday left Arizona after the Vendetta, which was quite a while after he wounded Joyce.

17. This is a confused version of the Johnny-Behind-the-Deuce affair, in which Wyatt, Virgil and several others saved gambler Johnny Rourke from being lynched.

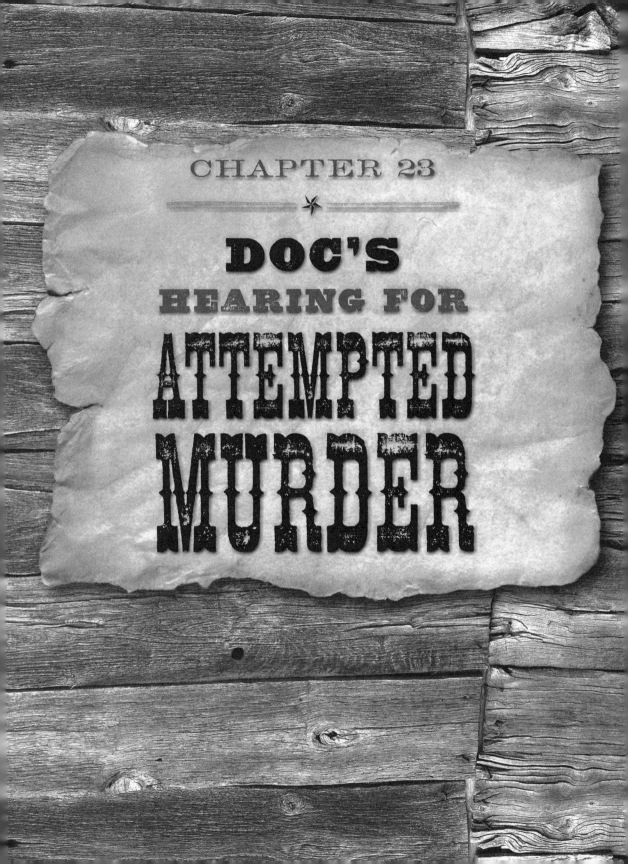

# CHAPTER 23

✶

## DOC'S HEARING FOR ATTEMPTED MURDER

oc was brought before a judge for shooting Billy Allen and a transcript of the hearing appeared in the *Leadville Daily Herald* on August 26, 1884. Doc took the stand toward the end of the hearing.

# HOLLIDAY BOUND OVER

## To Appear at the Criminal Court in the Sum of Eight Thousand Dollars,

## On the Charge of an Assault With Intent to Kill Billy Allen.

Doc Holliday's examination on the charge of assault with intent to kill Billy Allen on last Tuesday came off yesterday in the District court room before Judge Old. The room was crowded with spectators, anxious to learn the result. The prosecution was represented by District Attorney Kellogg and C. A. Franklin, and the defense by Judge Rice and C. F. Fishback.

Captain Bradbury was the first witness who testified for the prosecution: "I am acquainted with Allen and Holliday; on the day of the shooting I saw Allen in front of Hyman's and asked him what was the trouble between him and Holliday; he replied, 'Doc owes me five dollars and won't pay me;' I then said to him, 'I heard he had a gun for you, and you had better not go into Hyman's, as he may be there;' he said 'he wanted to speak to Doc' and went in; I could see Holliday as he raised the gun and fired; Allen fell and Holliday reached over the case and fired again; I don't think the first shot took effect; Allen, so far as I could see, made no motion to shoot; I went in and said, 'Doc

I WANT YOUR GUN'

and I disarmed him and took him to jail."

Cross-examined: "I never heard that Allen had threatened to kill Holliday; I was not sent there by Marshall Fauceett;[1] Allen did not seem excited; I was looking at him, because I thought Holliday might be in Hyman's; Holliday said, 'I want you to protect me;' I could not see Allen's right hand, as his left side was toward me."

Dr. D'Avignon testified: "I found Allen suffering from a shot in the arm and from a loss of blood caused by it; I felt his pulse and examined the wound, and found that the main artery of the arm had been injured; the bone was not broken; I have been attending him since, and he is getting along as well as I could expect; he is not out of danger."

Cross-examined: "An opening was made in the arm and both ends of the artery taken up; there is a good deal of difference between a wound where an artery is severed and an ordinary flesh wound; I think the greatest danger is from blood poisoning."

Henry Killerman, the bartender at Hyman's testified to being behind the bar at the time of the shooting; that Holliday came in and said he had heard Allen was going to do him up, and that he did not intend

## TO BE MURDERED;

I did not notice Allen when he came in, as I was mixing a drink, and the first thing I knew the first shot was fired; I saw Holliday reach over the counter and fire the second shot."

Cross-examined—"Allen was not employed in the house and had no business there; I heard Holliday say it was pretty hard for him to be disarmed when Allen was carrying a gun for him."

Here the prosecution rested their case.

Pat Sweeny was the first witness for the defense.

"Before the shooting Allen sent for me and said: 'I understand you say that if I jump on Doc Holliday, you will jump on me;' I replied: 'it is a d—d lie;' Allen then said he would give Holliday until Tues. noon to pay him, and if he did not, he would knock him down and kick his d—d brains out; the day of the shooting I was in Hyman's, talking to William Reynolds, and Allen came in with a gun in his pocket; he looked around and went out."

The cross-examination brought out nothing new.

Mr. Reynolds testified—"I saw Allen come into Hyman's with his hands in his pockets; he passed me so that I could not see his right hand; don't know whether he had a pistol or not; I had heard that that was the day when Allen was to do Holliday up, unless he got the five dollars; but I heard that Cy Allen had tried to stop the difficulty, and seeing Bradbury there, I supposed the trouble had been stopped."

On the cross-examination nothing new was brought out.

Officer Robinson sworn: "I told Doc Holliday the night before the shooting that 'I have been told you carry a pistol, you have always been my friend, and I don't want to search you; if you have one go and put it away.'"

On the question being asked as to who told him to search Holliday, the prosecution objected on the ground that it was against public policy.

"I knew nothing of the trouble and was told that he would have a pistol at 3 o'clock next day; it was the day before the shooting; the man that told me was Bill Allen."

Cross-examined—Allen did not say he wanted to kill Holliday when he told me Holliday would have a pistol."

James Ryan testified: "I am interested with Cy.[2] Allen in Hyman's; I was in the back part of the house when the shooting occurred; Wednesday or Thursday

### BILL ALLEN TOLD ME

a man in town has not treated me right; he borrowed five dollars from me and if he don't pay me by Tuesday, I will whip him and take the gun away from him and soak it and get his money.' Allen is a stout, active man; Holliday is a small man and delicate besides."

Patrick Lorden testified:—"I know Doc Holliday; I know Holliday and Allen; I had been told that Holliday believed he had been threatened; a few moments before the shooting I saw Allen get his boots polished; Cy said to him, 'Where are you going;' he said, 'I am going to hunt this party;' Cy said, 'For God's sake don't go into Hyman's, as Holliday is in there;' Bradbury was there and Allen came along; I said, 'If Allen puts his foot inside the door there will be trouble;' I could not see whether he had a gun or not; he had his right hand in his coat pocket; I heard the shots fired, but I did not see the shots fired; Allen staggered out of the door and I caught him in my arms; Allen is a powerful man and Holliday is

## A DELICATE MAN.

Doc Holliday makes Hyman's and the Board of Trade his headquarters.

Cross-examined:

"I caught him and Cy. Allen took charge of him; I did not take any pistol from him; don't know whether he had one or not; there was no one near him until I caught him; I did not see him throw a gun away or give one to anybody."

Hyman was called—"I ain't been subpoenaed said that worthy."[3]

"It makes no difference, you are here," said Judge Rice. Mr. Hyman was finally induced to take the stand and said that Holliday had made his place his headquarters.

Frank Lomeister testifed—"I am a bartender at Hyman's; I was in the room with Doc Holliday and he said "I don't want to be cooped up here all day; I want you to see Fawcett or Bradbury, for I want protection; I want out, but Holliday saw Fawcett first and spoke to him; I was not in the saloon when the

## SHOOTING TOOK PLACE."

Doc Holliday testified: "I borrowed five dollars from Allen, and said I will pay it in five or six days or a week. There is a young man owing me and when he pays it, I will pay you. He did not pay me. He told me he had lost the money and could not pay. I said I am sorry, as I promised to pay Allen. I told Allen this but that I would pay it as soon as I got it.—I walked into the Monarch before this trouble, and was coming out, when Allen came out, with an apron on, with his hand under his apron."[4] "He said, Holliday, I'll give you till Tuesday to pay this money and if you don't pay it, I'll lick you, you son of a b—." I said my jewelry is in soak and as soon as I get the money, I'll give it to you. I then went out and began to think of something that happened last winter." (Prosecution objected.) "I went to bed at 5 o'clock Tuesday morning, and got up about 3 o'clock and went to Hyman's; I started down street and was talking to Hyman when

## SWEENEY CAME UP

and said, I want to see you; this man Allen wants to see you; he has a gun; I think it is a six shooter; I said to Sweeney, I want you to see the marshal, and don't think it is right that one should be disarmed and another allowed to carry a gun; I don't want to be murdered; I went over to Hyman's and Lomeister said he would see Faucett or Bradbury; I saw Hyman and told him that I wanted him to see an officer, as I would not carry a gun, for I had no money to pay a fine, and I did not want to be murdered; afterward I was in at Hyman's; I saw Allen come in with his hand in his pocket, and I thought my life was as good to me as his was to him; I fired the shot, and he fell on the floor, and the second shot; I knew that I would be a child in his hands if he got hold of me; I weigh 122 pounds; I think Allen weighs 170 pounds; I have

"A MAN JUST FROM Leadville tells how 'Doc' Holliday collected a debt of fifty dollars. A well known rounder named Curley Mac had owed 'Doc' the above named amount for some time. Some nights ago Curley was seated at a faro bank with a big stack of 'reds' before him. Luck was with him and he made a winning of a hundred and fifty dollars. Holliday was standing behind him deeply interested in the game. Just as Curley was about to 'cash in' his creditor stepped to one side so that Curley could see him, and drawing a six-shooter from the waistband of his pants he coolly remarked, 'I'd like that fifty tonight Curley.' When the player looked up and saw the muzzle of the gun and the cold, hard face of 'Doc' with its determined expression he shoved the whole pile of chips over and said, 'take them all.' 'Doc' counted out his fifty dollars and pushed the others back to the winner and walked out, and that settled it"
—Aspen Daily Times, *June 12, 1885*

## HAD THE PNEUMONIA

three or four times; I don't think I was able to protect myself against him."

Cross examined: "I got up about three o'clock; I think the shooting was between 4 and 5 o'clock, but am not certain as to the time; I knew Allen was then looking for me; I was in Hyman's waiting for Marshal Faucett to come and protect me; I expected Allen to come there or anywhere else; I expected to protect myself; I had been told he had a gun and was looking for me; when he came in his right hand was in his pocket; he was about three feet inside of the door when I shot; when I shot the first time he turned and fell; I did not see where his hands were when I fired the second time; I supposed he was going to get there if he could, for I thought he had come there to kill me."

"Re-examined—"After Allen told me he was going to do me up I

## WENT TO COLONEL HOUSTON

and tried to borrow it and to pay it to Allen."[5]

Cy Allen examined by the prosecution: "I examined Allen after the shooting and found no pistol on him; his pistol was behind the bar; Faucett came to me and asked where Billy Allen was, and I said tell him for me not to have any trouble with Holliday; after that he came down[6] street with his hands in his pockets; I asked him where he was going; I told him not to go in Hyman's, as Holliday was in there; Allen said, 'I won't have any trouble;' the next I knew the shots were fired; I saw no pistol."

Cross-examined: "I don't know whether he had his hands in his pockets when he went into Hyman's or not; he is not related to me; he has been working for me for about four months; he is a powerful man—much stronger than Holliday."

Here the evidence closed, and Mr. Franklin opened the argument for the people. Mr. C. F. Fishback and Judge Rice followed for the defendant, District Attorney Kellogg closed. Judge Old[7] bound the defendant over in $8,000 bail.

* * *

Judge Olds decided this case should go to trial, probably because the shooting was premeditated and it wasn't a clear-cut case of self-preservation. At this point it wasn't known whether Allen would survive or not.

Bail was steep, especially for someone who was having trouble paying a $5 debt, but his friends got it together for him and he went back to dealing faro. A large portion of the community was on Doc's side. Apparently they were getting tired of Johnny Tyler and his friends—which included Billy Allen—and felt Doc was justified.

Since Allen survived, the charge against Doc remained assault with intent to kill. Doc's lawyer tried to compromise with Allen but he refused. After several delays, Holliday went to trial on March 28, 1883.[8] He was acquitted two days later and the officers promptly escorted him to the depot and put him on a train for Denver. This appears to be the only time Doc went on trial for shooting someone.

# References

[1] Fawcett was the Leadville city marshal.

[2] Sic.

[3] These quotation marks appear to be misplaced.

[4] Both these quotation marks appear to be misplaced, unless there was a break in his testimony. They are also the wrong type of quotation marks.

[5] It's interesting that Doc doesn't mention his problems with Johnny Tyler and his friends. He must have still felt this was the real reason why Allen was gunning for him because it's mentioned in later newspaper articles. Perhaps his lawyers didn't want him to bring it up at this time.

[6] The word "the" is missing here.

[7] Olds.

[8] The official records of this trial were lost or stolen.

# CHAPTER 24

## DOC
## TALKS A BIT ABOUT
## HIMSELF

The Perry Mallen affair made Doc quite a celebrity in Colorado. Two and a half weeks after the Governor denied Arizona's extradition request, Holliday was hanging around Gunnison—probably with Wyatt and Warren. Here Doc was again interviewed, this time by the *Gunnison News-Democrat*. The article appeared on the front page of the Sunday edition for June 18, 1882.

# A MAN OF SAND[1]

## "DOC" HOLLADAY,[2] OF ARIZONA, CAUGHT ON THE WING BY A REPORTER, AND PUMPED. THE FAMOUS FIGHT WITH THE COW-BOYS DESCRIBED. HOW THE BOGUS DENVER DETECTIVE TOOK "DOC" TO JAIL.

There arrived in this city two days ago a gentleman who has gained a great deal of notoriety within the past few weeks, through the columns of the press. The *News-Democrat*'s reporter's attention was first called to the gentleman, by a businessman, who pointing across the street said; Do you see that man yonder? That's Doc Holladay, of Arizona.

The man pointed out, was dressed in a dark close fitting suit of black, and wore the latest style of round top hat. His hair was seen to be quite gray, his moustache sandy, and his eyes a piercing dark blue. A member of the sporting fraternity happening to come along the reporter was introduced, and received a strong free and friendly grip of a hand, which said very plainly, "here is a man who, once a friend, is always a friend; once an enemy, is always an enemy."

The gentleman from Arizona was quick to scent the purpose of the reporter, and half laughingly and half in seriousness said, "I'm not traveling about the country in search of notoriety, and I think you newspaper fellows have already had a fair hack at me."

Doc Holliday photographed in Prescott, A.T., in 1879 by D. F. Mitchell.

The reporter gently explained that he wouldn't, for seven true fissure veins, violate the privacy of any man, and then proceeded, as reporters best know how, to apply the pump, with the following results:

(Lest Mr. Hollady[3] should recklessly attempt to annihilate the reporter upon sight for his breach of confidence, he is hereby informed that the reporter's pockets are filled full of little two ounce cans of nitro-glycerine which will certainly explode if they are subjected to any violence.)

"I shall probably be here till about the 30th, when I have some business in Pueblo which will take me away for awhile, but I shall come back again and most likely remain in Gunnison City during the summer."

"Is this your first visit here?"

"It is, and I think you have a fine country here. I like it very much."

"Did you ever live in Texas?"

"Yes. I lived in Dallas and Dennison for several years. I practiced dentistry there, having graduated at the Pennsylvania College of Dentistry in Philadelphia. That is how I got my title of Doc. I settled in Dallas and followed dentistry for about five years. I attended the Methodist Church regularly I was a member of the Methodist Church there and also a prominent member of a temperance organization till I deviated from the path of rectitude."[4]

"You are not a native of Texas?"

"No. I was born in Georgia, thirty-one years ago."

"When you left Texas where did you go?"

"I came north. I lived in Denver in 1875 and 1976."

"When did you go to Arizona the last time?"

"I went there three years ago."

"You are acquainted with the Earps, I believe?"

"Yes; we are friends."

"You had some trouble in Arizona with the cow-boys, didn't you?"

"Well, yes," drawled the doctor. "You might call it trouble. Bill[5] Earp was city marshal of Tombstone. Morg Earp was a special policeman. Wyatt Earp was a deputy

U. S. marshal. One day six of the cow-boys came into town and proposed to run it. The Earps were informed of their doings, and they invited me to go over to where the cow-boys were. One of the Earps said, Throw up your hands; we have come to disarm you. Instead of putting up their paws they put up their revolvers and began firing. Three of them were killed on the spot and two of the Earps wounded. I received a slight wound on the hip, which caused me some inconvenience for a few days."

"When was this affair?"

"It occurred on the twenty-sixth of last October. Morg Earp was killed about four months afterwards while playing pool in Bob Hatch's saloon in Tombstone. Berg[6] was waylaid one night and shot in the arm. He is now in California under medical treatment. Stillwell,[7] the man who helped murder Morg Earp was killed in Tucson while awaiting trial for stage robbery."

"You say three cow-boys were killed on the twenty-sixth of October; are there any of that gang still living?"

"Two of them have since been laid out."

"Did you ever have any trouble in Fort Steele?"

"No, I do not know where it is."

"You have been in Fort Griffin, haven't you?"

"Yes; I lived there."

"Who is this Mallen that arrested you in Denver?"

"He is some crank trying to gain notoriety."

"Were you acquainted with him?"

"I never saw him till one night in Pueblo a few weeks ago, when he called me out of a theatre and said: 'You saved my life in Santa Fe once, and I want to do you a favor. A man came in on the train who says he is going to kill you.' I said to him, 'Mr. Mallen,' he had given me his name, 'I don't want to be killed, and I am much obliged to you.' He then said, 'If you give me away I'll kill you.' I went for my revolver and he went for his. He found me on my guard, and he invited me to drink. The next morning he took the train for Denver.

"Had you been long in Denver when he arrested you?"

"I got there that day. I was on my way to the Wood river country. That evening I was going down to the Windsor Hotel to meet the Superintendent of the Little Pittsburg mine, a personal friend of mine, who had offered me what money I wanted to make the trip."

"Is this Mallen a man of sand?"

"Well, to show you what kind of a man he is, after he had arrested me, and was taking me to jail, he sat in front of me with two revolvers pointing directly towards me, and I entirely unarmed and defenseless."

"When did Mallen leave Denver?"

"About four days before I got out. He knew I was going to get out," added Mr. Holladay with a smile.

"Shall you do anything at his trial?"

"No, that is not my way of doing. I avoid trouble. My father taught me when young to attend to my own business and let other people do the same. I shall let him alone if he does me."

"What do you think will be the result of his trial?"

"I think he will go to the pen for a few years. I have a letter from the house of Comfort & Harlan, in Denver, which says the fraternity will spend a thousand dollars if necessary to send him there."

# References

1. Sand: courage.
2. Sic throughout this article.
3. Sic.
4. It sounds like Doc is pulling the reporter's leg a bit here.
5. Virgil.
6. Virgil.
7. Stilwell.

# CHAPTER 25

✳

# DOC HOLLIDAY

## AND HIS

# LEGEND

oc's legend as an outlaw gunfighter was building long before his death. It can be seen taking shape in this next article from the *New York Sun*. While it quotes Doc at length toward the end, much of what is said is wrong and doesn't sound like anything Doc would say. Obviously, the reporter significantly embellished and distorted what Doc said. That is, if the reporter didn't make up the whole thing up and attribute erroneous facts and quotes Doc, which is quite possible. Remember, the *New York Sun* was one of the papers that ran the phony story about the five-foot tall Canadian Mountie who humbled a drunken, gun-waving Wyatt.

Another possibility is that some of the locals were pulling one over on a tenderfoot journalist, just as Dr. Cockrell had in 1881 with that bogus story about Bat Masterson killing 27 people. As in Masterson's case, the possibility that it might not have even been Doc was brought to the reporter's attention.

While the words attributed to Doc in this article are often quoted today, they are highly suspect at best. It makes an interesting article, but very little of it is true.

The article appeared in the *Sun* in June of 1886, four years after Doc's arrest by Perry Mallen and about a year and a half before he died.[1] Some of this appears to be embellishments of portions of Mallen's outlandish story.

# HE STARTED MANY GRAVEYARDS.

## Pulling His Shooting Iron Often in Behalf of Law and Order.

[New York Sun.]

Silverton, Col., June 1.—A crowd following a rather good looking man around,[2] stopping when he stopped, listening as to an oracle when he had anything to say and all the time gaping at him in open-mouthed wonder, proclaimed the fact that an important personage was in town.

"Who is that duck?" an old miner asked.

"Sh h h!" replied a companion. "That's Doc Holliday. He's killed thirty men in his day, and there's no telling when he'll turn himself loose again."

Then all hands took another good look a him, and after he had passed on out of sight one of the early settlers said: "Some of you fellows who have come here lately have a very faint idea of what Doc Holliday and a few others like him used to do in this country. When the Doc ran things down in Arizona nobody dared to say his soul was his own. I remember one time in Tombstone he killed two men in one night,[3] and the next day he called on the editor of the paper and said that, as he was opposed to sensational literature, he hoped there would be no undue prominence given to the occurrences of the evening before.

When the paper came out in the afternoon it had a three line item saying that it was understood that two men had been found dead on the streets, but that the reporter had not learned their names. The same issue had a long editorial article on the advantages of Arizonia[4] as a health resort.[5]

"Not long after that the Doc was in Tucson for two weeks, and killed six men during that time.[6] He would have stayed another week, but he learned that a movement was on foot to mob him, and he left suddenly. All along the southwestern border for three or four years he was robbing and killing almost continually.[7] When any particular crime threatened to make trouble for him he would ship over to southern California for a while, and once or twice he went to the Indian Territory.[8] He could be tried now in any one of a half dozen states or territories,

☞ "HE [Doc] HAD THE reputation of being a bunco-man, desperado and bad man generally, yet he was a very mild mannered man; was genial and companionable and had many excellent qualities."

—*Doc's obituary in the* Denver Republican, *November 10, 1887*

and hanged for murder,[9] but there is no disposition to press him, as it is remembered that the country was pretty wild in those days."

Another man who had been a close listener stepped forward at this point and said: "I had a brush with the Doc once in the Calico range, down back of Fort Yuma. He and twenty-five other horse and cattle thieves were down there, and they sent word to the sheriff that they were spoiling for a fight. That made the officer mad, and so he got up a posse and set out, I being in the party. When we came on the gang we saw that they outnumbered us two to one, and so we concluded not to fight. As soon as the Doc saw that we were sloping[10] he got mad, and, jumping out in front of his party he yelled that[11] could whip us single-handed.

"He hadn't any more than said the word when he began firing, and we ran like cowards. He killed three of our party, though, before we got to cover, and we didn't have any anxiety to interview him again. A little while after that he left that part of the country, greatly to the relief of the sheriff, who used to say that he never could be chief when the Doc was around."

While this speaker was giving his experience the Doc himself had drawn nigh, and after listening to the conclusion of the story, he observed: "When any of you fellows have been hunted from one end of the country to the other, as I have been, you'll understand what a bad man's reputation is built upon.[12] I've had credit for more killings than I ever dreamt of. Now I'll tell you one little thing that happened down in Tombstone in the early days. There was a hard crowd there, of course, and I just happened in. I saw a chance to make a little money and so I opened a gambling house. Things went along all right for a time, but at length some of the boys got the idea they were not winning often enough, and they put up a job to kill me. I heard of it and the next night when they came in, I made them a speech, told them what I had heard, said that sort of thing couldn't go on in any well regulated community, and then, just to restore order, I gave it to a couple of them.[13] That settled the whole trouble. I was in Tombstone six months after that and never had another difficulty.[14] It has been that way wherever I have been. I never shoot unless I have to.

"Down on the border I had two or three little scrapes, but they didn't amount to much. A party of drunken greasers[15] climbed over us one night, and I had to fix one or two, and at another time I had a fight with a room full of them, and started a graveyard

"THERE WAS SOMETHING very peculiar about Doc. He was gentlemanly, a good dentist, a friendly man, and yet outside of us boys I don't think he had a friend in the Territory. Tales were told that he had murdered men in different parts of the country; that he had robbed and committed all manner of crimes, and yet when persons were asked how they knew it they could only admit that it was hearsay, and that nothing of the kind could really be traced up to Doc's account. He was a slender, sickly fellow, but whenever a stage was robbed or row started, and help was needed, Doc was one of the first to saddle his horse and report for duty."

—*Virgil Earp, from a* San Francisco Examiner *interview, May 27, 1882* there, but it had to be done in the interest of peace.[16] I claim to have been a benefactor to the country. Every crime that occurs in a new settlement is always laid out on one or two men. I've found out time and time again that I have been charged with murders and robberies when I hadn't been within 500 miles of the place. Down in Arizona once the coroner and most of the members of the jury had killed and robbed a man, and when they sat on the case, they laid it all on Doc Holliday. In Dodge City once I was charged with burglarizing a store when the owner did it himself. I've known Army officers who couldn't find vouchers for all their property to[17] put in the plea that Doc Holliday had stolen it, when I was never inside their lines.

"If you will take the trouble to examine a good many of the crimes I am charged with, you will find that when I am always charged with murder I have always been a long way off—never at hand. That looks odd, don't it? But it is just because I didn't do it. I've been in nearly all these towns since, and nobody says anything about arresting me, simply because they have no case. The claim that I make is that some few of us pioneers are entitled to credit for what we have done. We have been the forerunners of government. As soon as law and order was established anywhere we never had any trouble. If it hadn't been for me and a few like me there never would have been any government in some of those towns. When I have done any shooting, it has always been with this in view."

The Doc's auditors listened attentively, nodded assent, and gradually slipped away. He has been arrested but once,[18] and nobody here will undertake the job.

# References

1. He graduated with honors in 1872 from the Pennsylvania College of Dental Surgery, which was later absorbed by the University of Pennsylvania. His graduate thesis was titled *Diseases of the Teeth*.

1. The article is reprinted here as it appeared in the *Daily Denver Times* on June 15, 1886. The article also appeared in Georgia in the *Valdosta Times* on June 19th.

2. While Doc was good looking in his younger days, he was probably looking more like a walking skeleton by this point. It should be remembered that two years earlier he testified his weight was down to 122. His tuberculosis and lifestyle were taking their toll. In just over a year he would be bedridden. His obituary in the November 12, 1887, issue of the *Ute Chief* said, "From the effects of the disease, from which he had suffered probably half his life, Holliday, at the time of his death, looked like a man well advanced in years, for his hair was silver and his form emaciated and bent, but he was only thirty-six years old."

3. This never happened.

4. Sic.

5. There's no way this could have happened. If the *Epitaph* decided to pass over such a story, the *Nugget* would have really played it up—especially if it made Doc and the Earps look bad.

6. This never happened.

7. There's no evidence he robbed anyone.

8. Doc never went to California and I don't know of any evidence he went into the Indian Territory (now Oklahoma) either.

9. Not true. Arizona is the only state or territory known to have outstanding warrants for him, though it's possible there was also one in Texas if Wyatt's story is true.

10. Sic, "stopping"?

11. The word "he" is missing here.

12. It's unlikely Doc would have referred to himself as a bad man. Remember, in the 1884 *Leadville Daily Democrat* interview he complained, "They...have spread the report that I am a bad man...I defy anyone to say they ever saw me conduct myself in any other way than as a gentleman should."

13. Doc didn't have a gambling house in Tombstone and never could have gotten away with shooting someone without some sort of justification.

14. Doc left Arizona in April 1882. This would place the story at about the same time as the O.K. Corral gunfight.

15. This, once again, demonstrates how common prejudice and offensive racial slurs were in those days.

16. There's no record of anything like this ever happening.

17. This word should probably be "so."

18. He was actually arrested quite a few times. In fact, just two months later he was arrested in Denver for vagrancy. Apparently the police were attempting to drive him out of town because of his bad reputation.

# CHAPTER 26

✳

## A LETTER FROM
## BIG NOSE KATE

ig Nose Kate and Doc lived together off and on, and by some accounts their relationship was rocky and often explosive. Though it's said Kate claimed they were married, Doc is listed as single throughout his life in official records.

The woman, who claimed to be Kate in the 1940s, said she was born in Budapest, Hungary, on November 7, 1850 as Mary Katherine Haroney. She said her father, a doctor, moved the family to the United States, where they settled in Davenport, Iowa, in 1863. She went by the names "Kate Elder" and "Kate Fisher" until she apparently married a blacksmith named George M. Cummings in 1888. Though she left him eleven years later, she kept the name Mary Katherine Cummings for the rest of her life.

At the age of 89, shortly before she died, she wrote a letter to her niece, Mrs. Lillian Lane Raffert, talking about Doc and the shootout. While I have some questions about its authenticity, I have decided to include it anyway as a fitting conclusion to this book.

The letter is presented here as it appears in Bob Boze Bell's book, *The Illustrated Life and Times of Doc Holliday* (1994). He explains, "The hand-written letter is transcribed here as she wrote it, but we have corrected some spelling and added punctuation to facilitate understanding."

Pioneers Home
Prescott Arizona
Mar 18, 1940

My Dear Niece Lillie,

I received your welcome just four days ago, I am very glad to hear from you. This sick spell left me very shaky, my hands shake so, it is hard for me to write, I am feeling some better today I don't think I will get thoroughly over it, though I am well taken care of, nurses are all very kind to me, so I have nothing to complain of, only I am so weak that I have to stop writing to rest my hands at every few lines I write. To be sick in bed five weeks is enough to make any one weak at my age;

I can't tell you the population of Prescott but Prescott is a big city, I will find out and let you know next time I write

Doc and I met Wyatt Earp in fall of 1875 in Dodge City in 1876, Wyatt, Earp and Doc were just aquaintances[1] at that time. Doc and I were in Dodge we were in Dodge

City five weeks and went to Las Vegas,[2] we lived in Las Vegas over two years Doc was practicing dentistry in Las Vegas, in 1879 Doc met Wyatt Earp in Las Vegas again in 1879 Wyatt Earp was on his way to Arizona, he got Doc. and I to go with him.[3] Wyatt had his wife, and Brother James and his wife and Daughter with him that made seven of us in the outfit. We arrived in Prescott in November, Doc and I went to a hotel, Virgil Earp the oldest Brother was already in Prescott was there two years ahead of us. It was just about the boom of Tombstone, Doc and I stayed in Prescott until the fall of 1880. The Earps went to Tombstone, the Earp brothers and family went to Tombstone early in the spring of 1880,[4] Doc and I went to Tombstone in fall of 1881[5] then we went to Tombstone; I did not like it in Tombstone I went to Globe,[6] I wanted Doc to go with me, the Earps had such power I could not get Doc away from them. I used to get letters from Doc to come to Tombstone. begging to pay him a visit, I went to see him three times when I went to Globe I had about five hundred dollars I bought out a hotel on time every time I went to visit Doc I had to pay a friend to look after my interests in the hotel. at that time Doc had a room at a Mrs. Fly's photograph gallery. The fiesta was on at Tucson, Doc asked if I would like to go to see the fiesta in Tucson, I said yes, so we went to Tucson.[7] The next while we were at the park, Morgan Earp came to Tucson, came to the park, tapped Doc on the shoulder and said. Doc we want you in Tombstone tomorrow, better go up this evening.[8] Neither of them wanted me to go with them, Doc wanted to take me back to the hotel I insisted on going back with them Doc said you can't stand the ride on a buck board from Benson to Tombstone. I said I can stand what ever you can, so we went back to Tombstone, he left me at his room and he went with Morgan Earp. I did not see him again till half past one in the morning, I got up next morning before Doc did.[9] Our door opened in to the hall, our door was partly open, I saw a man come in with his head bandaged and a rifle in his hand he went to the dining and asked Mrs Fly if Doc Holliday was there, Mrs Fly said she didn't know. Mrs. Fly told me that Ike Clanton was there looking for Doc, I told Doc,

Ike Clanton was looking for him. Doc said, if God will let me live to get my clothes on, he shall see me. With that he got up dressed and went out, as he went out, he said, I may not be back to take you to breakfast so you better go alone. I didn't go to breakfast, I don't remember of eating anything that day. Theres a vacant lot between the corner and Mrs. Fly's home. I saw four men coming from the livery stable[10] on Allen Street coming to the vacant lot, almost at the same time I saw Virgil Earp, Wyatt, Morgan Earp and Doc Holliday coming to the vacant lot from Fremont street. They stood ten feet apart when the shooting began, Ike Clanton ran and left his young Brother Billy. I saw Doc fall but he was up as quick as he fell. Something went wrong with his rifle, he threw his rifle on the ground[11] and pulled out his six shooter. Every

Mary Katherine Haroney
(who claimed to be 'Big Nose Kate').

shot he fired got a man,[12] Billy Clanton was killed as were the two McLaurys. Virgil and Morgan Earp were killed[13] Doc had a grazed right hip Virge and Morgan Earp get well. It is foolish to think that a cow rustler gun man can come up to a city gun man in a gun fight; the sheriff knew all about this fight coming off, he put on his big cow hat and rode out of the town, three days after this killing gave themselves up.[14] The jailer locked them up for one day and night when two business went on their bonds, every body knew these cow rustlers came to town to kill the Earps and Doc Holliday. They had a trial, they were aquitted;[15] the Earps went to their parents, Doc holliday[16] went to Glenwood Springs Colo, he is buried there. Warren Earp the youngest Brother was killed at Willcox and is buried there at the expense of Cochise County.[17] Virgil died [in] Verginia[18] Nevada. Wyatt Earp died in Los Angeles Calif. J. H. Doc Holliday died in Glenwood Springs Colo. So you see they are all dead and gone except me;

There are so many who claim they saw that shooting on Allen Street, it was not on Allen street but nearer to Fremont Street in an open lot, some that were not even born at that time. Here is what happened in Globe one morning, Merchant Mrs Baily brought a man in for breakfast after breakfast hours, I waited on him because my girl was doing up the rooms, they got to talking about Tombstone, some how Doc and I were mentioned, he told Mr Baily that Doc took me to New Mexico and killed me up in the mountains and that he helped to bury me. I said the poor woman, Mr Baily and I laughed but the man found out he made a fool of himself and never came back but it is laughable how some people will talk. I often laugh how often I have been dead and buried and turn up some place full of life; there are quite a few that want me to write up things but as they don't want to give me anything I don't write

Well Dear Lillie I hope you won't tire reading this, some is sad and some is quite laughable, but such is life any way we take it; Let me hear from you soon; Hope you will have a nice Easter.

Love and best wishes from Aunt Mary

# References

1. Sic.

2. Las Vegas, New Mexico, which is over the mountains forty miles east of Santa Fe.

3. Wyatt, Doc and the rest of the party left Dodge City together and picked up Kate in Las Vegas on their way to Prescott.

4. The Earps arrived in Tombstone sometime between November 29th and December 1st of 1879.

5. The earliest record of Doc in Tombstone is on September 27, 1880, when he registered to vote. He was still in Prescott on June 2nd, as he is listed as a resident of that town on that day in the U.S. Census.

6. Globe is an Arizona town about eighty miles north of Tucson.

7. This was the San Augustin Feast and Fair at Levin Park in Tucson, which took place in October of 1881. Kate's narrative has jumped forward to just a few days before the gunfight. Kate was in Tombstone the previous July because that's when she got drunk and signed the affidavit accusing Doc of being involved in the Philpott-Roerig murders. Sheriff Behan arrested Doc on July 5th, but the district attorney dropped the case on the 10th for lack of evidence. At the time, the Nugget noted that Doc and Kate had been living together "for some time past," indicating she may have been in Tombstone for a while. She left Tombstone after retracting her affidavit.

8. Morgan and Doc arrived back in Tombstone on Saturday evening, October 22, 1881.

9. This was October 26th, the morning of the gunfight.

10. The O.K. Corral. The main entrance is on Allen and the back is on Fremont Street.

11. Wyatt said in his *San Francisco Examiner* article on the gunfight, "I fired a shot which hit Tom McLowery's horse and made it break away, and Doc Holliday took the opportunity to pump a charge of buckshot out of a Wells Fargo shotgun into Tom McLowery, who promptly fell dead. [He actually staggered down the street to the corner.] In the excitement of the moment, Doc Holliday didn't know what he had done and flung away the shotgun in disgust, pulling his six shooter instead." Because of the gunfight, people associate Doc with shotguns and some claim he often wore one suspended under his arm beneath his coat, but I haven't found any record of this and all indications are that Holliday didn't like or trust shotguns.

12. This is apparently not true.

13. This is definitely not true.

14. The putting on the "big cow hat" seems to refer to Sheriff Behan, while the "gave themselves up" seems to refer to Doc and Wyatt.

15. There was no trial; it was a preliminary hearing.

16. Sic.

17. Warren was killed in a barroom argument with range foreman Johnnie Boyett in Willcox, Arizona on July 7, 1900. Boyett was acquitted. Testimony at the coroner's inquest indicates Warren provoked and threatened Boyett. Even after Boyett fired four shots at Warren, the unarmed Earp kept advancing on him until the cowboy downed him with a fifth shot.

18. Virgil died on October 19, 1905, in Goldfield, Nevada. He was not buried at the county's expense.

# BIBLIOGRAPHY & RESOURCES

## Primary Sources

### 2: STAGECOACH ROBBERIES AND MURDERS

Wyatt Earp, "Wyatt Earp Tells Tales of the Shotgun-Messenger Service.," *San Francisco Examiner Sunday Magazine*, August 9, 1896, p. 21, c. 1–7. This can be found on microfilm at the Sacramento Public Library.

### 3: THE KILLING OF MARSHAL WHITE

*Arizona Daily Citizen*, December 27, 1880. This is printed as it appears in Steve Gatto, *Wyatt Earp: A Biography of a Western Lawman*, San Simon Publishing Company, Tucson, 1997, pp. 69–73.

### 4: THE O.K. CORRAL SHOOTOUT (PART I)

Wyatt Earp's Statement, *Tombstone Daily Nugget*, November 17, 1881, from the Chafin Collection.

Wyatt Earp's Statement, *Tombstone Epitaph*, November 17, 1881. This is printed as it appears in Douglas D. Martin, ed., *Tombstone's Epitaph*, University of New Mexico Press, Albuquerque, 1951, pp. 197–208.

Wyatt Earp's Statement, Hayhurst manuscripts, from the Chafin Collection. A copy of this version can also be found at the Arizona Historical Society.

### 5: THE O.K. CORRAL SHOOTOUT (PART II)

Wyatt Earp, "How Wyatt Earp Routed a Gang of Arizona Outlaws.," *San Francisco Examiner Sunday Magazine*, August 2, 1896. This can be found on microfilm at the Sacramento Public Library.

### 6: THE RESIGNATION

"Resignation Tendered," *Tombstone Daily Nugget*, February 2, 1882. This article was kindly provided for inclusion in this book by Carl Chafin, editor of *The Private Journal of George Whitwell Parsons: The Tombstone Years 1879–1887*, Volumes I and II, Cochise Classics, Tombstone, 1997.

### 7: THE DEATH OF CURLY BILL

"He is a Dude Now," *Denver Republican*, May 14, 1893, p. 17, c. 1–2. Part of this interview was reprinted with minor changes in *The Farm and Field*, June 17, 1893, p. 6, c. 1–2. Both articles were kindly provided for inclusion in this book by Emma Walling, author of *John "Doc" Holliday: Colorado Trials and Triumphs*, Snowmass, Colorado, n.d.

## 8: THE VENDETTA

"The Earp Party," *Tombstone Epitaph*, April 5, 1882. This is printed as it appears in *Tombstone's Epitaph* edited by Douglas D. Martin, University of New Mexico Press, Albuquerque, 1951, pp. 219–20.

## 9: LEAVING ARIZONA

"Downed at Last," *Albuquerque Evening Review*, May 13, 1882. This can be found on microfilm at the library of the University of New Mexico, Albuquerque.

## 10: AFTERMATH

"The Earp Brothers," *Gunnison Daily News Democrat*, June 4, 1882, p. 1, c. 5 and p. 3, c. 1–2. This article was kindly provided for inclusion in this book by Emma Walling, author of *John "Doc" Holliday: Colorado Trials and Triumphs*, Snowmass, Colorado, n.d. She, in turn, received it from Dan Davidson of the Museum of Northwest Colorado and Loline Sammons of the Gunnison Public Library.

## 11: LIFE AND DEATH IN TOMBSTONE

Wyatt Earp's deposition, the Lotta Crabtree Estate Case, Boston, 1926.

## 12: BAT MASTERSON AND THE DODGE CITY WAR

Wyatt Earp, "Wyatt Earp's Tribute to Bat Masterson, The Hero of 'Dobe Walls.," *San Francisco Examiner Sunday Magazine*, August 16, 1896, p. 28, c. 1–7. This can be found on microfilm at the Sacramento Public Library.

Wyatt Earp's letter to the editor of the *Denver Tribune* as reprinted in the *La Plata Miner*, May 26, 1883, p. 2, c. 4. This article was kindly provided for inclusion in this book by Emma Walling, author of *John "Doc" Holliday: Colorado Trials and Triumphs*, Snowmass, Colorado, n.d.

## 13: BAT MASTERSON TELLS OF THE DODGE CITY WAR

Bat Masterson, "Famous Gun Fighters of the Western Frontier: Third Article. Luke Short," *Human Life*, Vol. 5, No. 1 (April 1907). This is printed as it appears in Bat Masterson (Jack DeMattos, ed.), *Famous Gun Fighters of the Western Frontier*, Weatherford Press, Monroe, Washington, 1982, pp. 56–64.

Bat Masterson's letter to the editor, *Daily Kansas State Journal*, June 9, 1883. This is printed as it appears in P. A. Mallory, "The Dodge City War," *Wild West*, June 1997, p. 77.

## 14: BAT MASTERSON'S TALES OF WYATT

Bat Masterson, "Famous Gun Fighters of the Western Frontier: Second Article. Wyatt Earp," *Human Life*, Vol. 4, No. 5 (February 1907). This is printed as it appears in Bat Masterson (Jack DeMattos, ed.), *Famous Gun Fighters of the Western Frontier*, Weatherford Press, Monroe, Washington, 1982, pp. 27–38.

"A Few Scraps—Bat Masterson," *Denver Republican*, July 17, 1910. This can be found on microfilm at the Colorado Historical Society.

## 15: THE SHARKEY-FITZSIMMONS FIGHT

Wyatt Earp, "Wyatt Earp, Whose Decision Meant $10,000.," *San Francisco Examiner*, December 3, 1896, p. 1, c. 3. This can be found on microfilm at the Sacramento Public Library.

*San Francisco Bulletin*, probably December 4, 1896. This is printed as it appears in Casey Tefertiller's *Wyatt Earp: The Man Behind the Myth*, John Wiley & Sons, New York, 1997, pp. 292–93.

*Los Angeles Times*, December 5, 1896. This is printed as it appears in Don Chaput's *The Earp Papers*, Affiliated Writers of America, Encampment, Wyoming, 1994, pp. 160–62.

*Los Angeles Times*, December 12, 1901. This is printed as it appears in Don Chaput's *The Earp Papers*, Affiliated Writers of America, Encampment, Wyoming, 1994, pp. 188–89.

## 16: AGAINST THE MYTHS & LIES

"The Taking of Wyatt Earp," *New York Sun*, August 16, 1903. This is printed as it appears in Bat Masterson (Jack DeMattos, ed.), *Famous Gun Fighters of the Western Frontier*, Weatherford Press, Monroe, Washington, 1982, p. 43–45.

Wyatt Earp's letter to the editor, *Los Angeles Herald*, September 8, 1903. This is printed as it appears in Don Chaput, *The Earp Papers*, Affiliated Writers of America, Encampment, Wyoming, 1994, p. 192.

George Parsons' letter to the editor, *Los Angeles Herald*, September 9, 1903. This is printed as it appears in Don Chaput, *The Earp Papers*, Affiliated Writers of America, Encampment, Wyoming, 1994, pp. 192–93.

## 17: THE WEST & WILLIAM SHAKESPEARE

Adela Rogers St. Johns, "I Knew Wyatt Earp," *The American Weekly*, May 22, 1960. This can be found in the files of the Denver Public Library.

## 18: BAT MASTERSON'S TALES OF DOC HOLLIDAY

Bat Masterson, "Famous Gun Fighters of the Western Frontier: Fourth Article. 'Doc' Holliday," *Human Life*, Vol. 5, No. 2 (May, 1907). This is printed as it appears in Bat Masterson (Jack DeMattos, ed.), *Famous Gun Fighters of the Western Frontier*, Weatherford Press, Monroe, Washington, 1982, p. 75–82.

"A Few Scraps—Bat Masterson," *Denver Republican*, July 17, 1910. This can be found on microfilm at the Colorado Historical Society.

## 19: DOC HOLLIDAY ON HIS ARREST FOR MURDER

"Doc. Holladay, Leader of the Earps, Cleverly Captured Last Night in this City," *Rocky Mountain News*, May 16, 1882, p. 5, c. 1. This article is printed as it appears in Emma Walling's *John 'Doc' Holliday: Colorado Trials and Triumphs*, Snowmass, Colorado, n.d., p. 1.

## 20: DOC HOLLIDAY ON THE ARIZONA TROUBLES (PART I)

"Capers of Cowboys," *Denver Tribune*, May 17, 1882, p. 4, c. 3–4. This can be found on microfilm at the Colorado Historical Society and the Denver Public Library.

## 21: DOC HOLLIDAY ON THE ARIZONA TROUBLES (PART II)

"Awful Arizona," *Denver Republican*, May 22, 1882, p. 5, c. 1–3. This can be found on microfilm at the Colorado Historical Society and the Denver Public Library.

## 22: DOC HOLLIDAY EXPLAINS WHY HE SHOT BILLY ALLEN

"Holliday Shoots," *Leadville Daily Democrat*, August 20, 1884, p. 4, c. 1–2. This article is printed as it appears in Emma Walling's *John "Doc" Holliday: Colorado Trials and Triumphs*, Snowmass, Colorado, n.d., pp. 36–41.

## 23: DOC'S HEARING FOR ATTEMPTED MURDER

"Holliday Bound Over," *Leadville Daily Herald*, August 26, 1884, p. 4, c. 1–2. This can be found on microfilm at the Denver Public Library.

## 24: DOC TALKS A BIT ABOUT HIMSELF

"A Man of Sand," *Gunnison News-Democrat*, June 18, 1882, p. 1, c. 4–5. This article is printed as it appears in Emma Walling's *John "Doc" Holliday: Colorado Trials and Triumphs*, Snowmass, Colorado, n.d., p. 33–35. She, in turn, received it from Dan Davidson of the Museum of Northwest Colorado and Loline Sammons of the Gunnison Public Library.

## 25: DOC HOLLIDAY AND HIS LEGEND

"He Started Many Graveyards," *Daily Denver Times*, June 15, 1886, p. 2, c. 3. This can be found on microfilm at the Colorado Historical Society and the Denver Public Library. The article originally appeared in the *New York Sun* in early June 1886. It also appeared in Georgia in the *Valdosta Times* on June 19, 1886.

## 26: A LETTER FROM BIG NOSE KATE

Mary Katherine Cummings to Mrs. Lillian Lane Raffert, Mar 18, 1940. This is reprinted as it appears in Bob Boze Bell, *The Illustrated Life and Times of Doc Holliday*, Tri Star-Boze Productions, Phoenix, 1994, pp. 107–10.

## SELECTED REFERENCES

*Arizona Quarterly Illustrated*, 1880–1881, Chafin Collection.

Bell, Bob Boze, *The Illustrated Life and Times of Doc Holliday*, Tri Star-Boze Productions, Phoenix, 1994 (second edition, 1995).

Bell, Bob Boze, *The Illustrated Life and Times of Wyatt Earp*, Tri Star-Boze Productions, Phoenix, 1993 (third edition, 1995).

Boyer, Glenn. His books are presented as nonfiction, but they are actually historical novels. They should not be used for research. Unfortunately his books, like *I Married Wyatt Earp*, which is falsely presented as Josephine Earp's memoirs, have contaminated many other works in this field.

Clum, John, "It All Happened in Tombstone," *Arizona Historical Review*, II (October 1929), pp. 46–72.

Dempsey, David and Raymond P. Baldwin, *The Triumphs and Trials of Lotta Crabtree*, William Morrow & Co., New York, 1968.

Dodge, Fred (Carolyn Lake, ed.), *Under Cover for Wells Fargo*, Boston, 1969.

Erwin, Richard, *The Truth About Wyatt Earp*, The O.K. Press, Carpentaria, California, 1993.

"Frontier Tales" column, *The Farm and Field*, June 23, 1894. This article was kindly provided for inclusion in this book by Emma Walling, author of *John "Doc" Holliday: Colorado Trials and Triumphs*, Snowmass, Colorado, n.d.

Gray, John Pleasant, *All Roads Led to Tombstone*, unpublished manuscript, Chafin Collection.

Jahns, Pat, *The Frontier World of Doc Holliday*, Hastings House, New York, 1957.

Kintop, Jeffrey M. and Guy Louis Rocha, *The Earps' Last Frontier: Wyatt and Virgil Earp in the Nevada Mining Camps, 1902–1905*, Great Basin Press, Reno, 1989.

Lake, Stuart, unpublished research notes and papers, Stuart Lake Collection, Huntington Library, San Marino, California.

Lake, Stuart, *Wyatt Earp, Frontier Marshal*, Houghton Mifflin, Boston, 1931. Though based on a few brief interviews with Wyatt, this book should be considered to be historical fiction. I have copies of Lake's interview notes and they only contain some basic facts—nothing that could be turned into a narrative. Most of his information came from other less-reliable sources.

Lynch, Sylvia D., *Aristocracy's Outlaw: The Doc Holliday Story*, Iris Press, New Tazewell, Tennessee, 1994.

Martin, Douglas D., ed., *Tombstone's Epitaph*, University of New Mexico Press, Albuquerque, 1951.

Masterson, Bat (Jack DeMattos, ed.), *Famous Gun Fighters of the Western Frontier*, Weatherford Press, Monroe, Washington, 1982.

Morey, Jeff, *The Gunfight*, unfinished manuscript, Chafin Collection.

Myers, John Myers, *The Last Chance: Tombstone's Early Years*, E. P. Dutton & Co., New York, 1950. Republished as *Tombstone's Early Years*, University of Nebraska Press, Lincoln, 1995.

Parsons, George W. (Carl Chafin, ed.), *The Private Journal of George Whitwell Parsons: The Tombstone Years 1879–1887*, Cochise Classics, Tombstone, Volume II, 1997. Volume I was never published.

Pendleton, Albert S., Jr., and Susan McKey Thomas, *In Search of the Hollidays*, Little River Press, Valdosta, Georgia, 1972.

Tefertiller, Casey, *Wyatt Earp: The Man Behind the Myth*, John Wiley & Sons, New York, 1997.

Turner, Alford, *The Earps Talk*, The Early West Series, College Station, Texas, 1980.

Walling, Emma, *John 'Doc' Holliday: Colorado Trials and Triumphs*, Snowmass, Colorado, n.d.

## ABOUT THE EDITOR

John Richard Stephens has had many different occupations ranging from being a psychiatric counselor in hospitals to working as a security officer for the U.S. Navy. He was an intelligence officer and squadron commander in the U.S. Air Force before he moved on to writing books and articles. He's the author/editor of eleven books, such as *Weird History 101*, *Captured by Pirates* and *Wyatt Earp Tells of the Gunfight Near the O.K. Corral*, which focuses on the gunfight. John's books have been selections of the Preferred Choice Book Club, the Quality Paperback Book Club and the Book of the Month Club. His work has been published as far away as India and Singapore and has been translated into Japanese and Finnish. He can be contacted at pirates@ferncanyonpress.com.

## SPECIAL THANKS

John Richard Stephens would like to pass on his appreciation to the following people who directly assisted in the production of this book: Carl Chafin, Martha and Jim Goodwin, Art Reker, everyone at Armadillo Advertising, Emma Walling, Susan McKey Thomas, Ken Cilch, Sr., Ken Cilch, Jr., and Bruce Erdman. He would also like to express special thanks to Kris Wolf for allowing Adela Rogers St. Johns' article on Wyatt to be included in this book.

John wishes to express his appreciation to Elaine Molina; Martha and Jim Goodwin; Scott Stephens; Marty Goeller; Terity, Natasha, and Debbie Burbach; Brandon, Alisha, and Kathy Hill; Jeff and Carol Whiteaker; Christopher, Doug and Michelle Whiteaker; Pat Egner; Gabriel, Aurelia, Elijah, Nina Abeyta and Justin Weinberger; Anthony, Jayla, Sin and Bobby Gamboa; Anne and Jerry Buzzard; Krystyne Göhnert; Eric, Tim and Debbie Cissna; Norene Hilden; Doug and Shirley Strong; Barbara and Stan Main; Joanne and Monte Goeller; Irma and Joe Rodriguez; Danny and Mary Schutt; Les Benedict; Dr. Rich Sutton; and to his agent, Charlotte Cecil Raymond.

# INDEX

The letters "n" and "nn" refer to endnotes. For example, "25n21" indicates page 25, note 21; "49nn9–10" indicates page 49, notes 9 through 10.

Fountain, Albert, 39, 42n40

Foy, Eddie, 168, 182n50, 202

Fuller, Wesley "Wes," 20–23, 25n21, 25n23

# PHOTOGRAPHY CREDITS

Wyatt S. Earp, 1928.